FAST TRACK
TO *Fine Dining*

A Step-by-Step Guide to Planning a Dinner Party

Linda Mutschler

FAST TRACK
TO *Fine Dining*

A STEP-BY-STEP GUIDE TO PLANNING A DINNER PARTY

FRP.

Favorite Recipes® Press

Copyright © 2009 by Linda Mutschler
Box 135
4230 North Oakland Avenue
Shorewood, Wisconsin 53211-2042
www.fasttracktofinedining.com

Photography © by Steve Lalich
Food Styling by Susan Lalich
Photo Styling by Julee Rauch

Library of Congress Control Number: 2008935698
ISBN: 978-0-9815867-0-0

Favorite Recipes Press is an imprint of FRP, Inc.,
a wholly owned subsidiary of Southwestern/Great American, Inc.
P.O. Box 305142
Nashville, Tennessee 37230
800-358-0560

Art Direction and Book Design: Starletta Polster
Project Manager: Tanis Westbrook

Manufactured in the United States of America
First Printing 2009
5,000 copies

Acknowledgments

There are so many people who helped me to make this book a reality. To the people I worked with at FRP, thank you for your publishing help and expertise. To the people at Lalich Photography, thank you for the beautiful pictures.

To the employees of Downer Avenue Wine & Spirits, Nehring's Sendik's on Oakland, Sabor Brazilian Churrascaria, and Sendik's on Downer, thank you for your advice and willingness to answer my seemingly endless questions.

To everyone who shared recipes with me, thank you. I could not have written this book without your input. My sincere thanks to Loralie Barker, Sue Bisbee, Donna Butz, Dora Ching, Jill Heindl, Sharon Heiple, Barbara Henderson, Judy Hogan, Ruth Ann Jordan, Allison Knox, Lisa Lipovsek, Beth Milem, Lora Moon, Barbara Mutschler, Jody Mutschler, Gail Runyon Perry, Christina Plzak, Mark Robers, Georgia Sledge, Margie Sung, Ina Voloshin, and Brian Yunker.

In addition to those above, thank you to all of you who came to dinner. There are too many of you to list but know that you made this whole journey worthwhile. To the regulars, including the DePoys, the Dolgovs, the Fitzsimmons, the Glusmans, the Hinkes, the Jochmanns, the Primacks, the Rocklins, the Sellars, the Smiths, the Whitneys, and the Zieberts, thank you for being willing to try menu after menu.

To Rachel Schulz, thank you for suggesting the title for this book. I'll never forget the day you walked in and asked, "What do you think about *Fast Track to Fine Dining*?"

To Lori Cummings, thank you for all your hours of proofreading, patience, and encouragement.

And, to my husband, Jock, and my children, Jordan and Brodie, thank you. Because of you, everything is possible.

Preface

You're busy, you're tired, but you want to entertain.

Sound familiar?

It does to me. I spent my career working on Wall Street, and as a result, I was rarely home and hardly knew any of my neighbors. That said, all my life I always wanted to have a home where people came and had a great time. As part of this, I envisioned food, conversation, and lots of laughter.

But there was one small problem. I didn't cook.

When I was single, dinner was often spaghetti, pizza, microwave popcorn, or cereal. To be honest, I ate a lot of cereal.

When I got married, things didn't improve much. I was still working, and I still didn't cook. Fortunately, my husband didn't seem to mind. When I had children, things improved only marginally. I was still working, and I still didn't cook, but I added frozen fish and frozen chicken to my repertoire of dinner alternatives.

Then one day I decided enough was enough. I needed to learn how to cook. I wanted to have people to dinner, but I had absolutely no idea how to go about it.

At the time, we were living in London, where we had moved with our two small children for my job at Merrill Lynch. Because my responsibilities were in the U.S. and Europe, I ended up being at work or traveling virtually all of the time and being at home virtually none of the time.

While I often thought that it would be great to have people over, I would leave invitations until too late. On the rare occasion people didn't have plans and accepted my invitation, I would race around like a crazy woman trying to get everything done. As a result, I hardly ever had a chance to talk to my guests because I was constantly running in and out of the kitchen.

I quickly decided that this strategy was not going to work. I wanted to host dinner parties and lots of them, but I wanted to be able to prepare many of the items ahead so that it would work with my schedule. I also wanted to be able to spend time with my guests instead of in the kitchen.

So one Saturday, I walked up the road to the local bookstore to see if there was a book explaining how to do this. I looked, but I couldn't find the book I had in mind. Don't get me wrong—there were lots of dinner party books. They had wonderful photographs and recipes, but how, exactly, were you supposed to go about it?

Basically, I was looking for an instruction manual on how to throw a dinner party. I wanted to know that if I followed certain steps, I would get to the end result. I figured that if I had such a book, I would be able to entertain, despite the fact that I wasn't home much and didn't have a lot of experience cooking. I knew that I could follow directions. I just needed the directions.

It turns out that not too long after my trip to the bookstore, I retired from Merrill Lynch—not because I wanted to learn how to cook, but because I had promised myself many years earlier that I would walk away from Wall Street when I turned forty and do something entirely different.

At that point, I had no idea what something different was going to be. In fact, I made a list of things that I wanted to do, and one of the top five was learn to cook.

Almost immediately, I started cooking. Since then, I have been cooking constantly, often making four or five things in a given day. In fact, one year, we hosted thirty dinner parties so that I could try out different recipes and menus.

That's approximately one dinner party every twelve days. Can you imagine doing that to your spouse or partner?

You may wonder where I found people to come to thirty dinner parties. Well, I would ask anyone and everyone. I would ask people I met on airplanes. I would ask people I met at yoga. I would ask people I met at my kids' soccer practices. I would ask people I met knocking on doors. Literally. I would sometimes take my daughter and our dog along for moral support. I would walk up to the door of one of the neighbors I didn't know, I would ring the bell, and I would say:

"Hi. I'm Linda. I live _____ (fill in the blank: next door, across the street, down the block, etc.), and I was wondering if you'd like to come to dinner? You see, I'm writing a cookbook about dinner parties, and as a result, I am always looking for people to feed. Would you be interested?"

You'd be amazed how many of these people actually said yes. In the early days, more often than not, we would have a dinner party where none of the couples knew each other (or us for that matter).

When people came, I would often hand out memo pads and pencils for feedback—about the decorations, the food, the wine, anything. Sometimes I would make three different versions of a dish and ask people which one they preferred. Other times, I would make three different desserts and ask people which one they liked best. The feedback was often really helpful, with people making some great suggestions about alternative dishes, ingredients, and seasonings.

In the end, it was a great way to learn, and it was a tremendous amount of fun. You see, in the process of having all these dinner parties, my husband and I met some truly wonderful people and made some fantastic new friends—all simply as a result of having people to dinner.

Although I wasn't aware of it when I started, friendship is ultimately what this journey has really been about: cooking food for friends, sharing laughs, enjoying others, and becoming true neighbors.

Throwing a multicourse dinner party takes work, but it's not rocket science, especially if you're organized and you plan ahead. Furthermore, the object of this book is to provide you with all the tools necessary to be able to cook fabulous meals, many of which can be prepared ahead, so that you can get out of the kitchen and enjoy your guests.

If you didn't grow up cooking, don't worry. I didn't either. I've tried to make the recipes as straightforward as possible. If I can make them, which I have done over and over again, so can you.

Trust me, people like going to a dinner party, and in the process, you'll meet some incredible people.

So, go on. Start knocking and get cooking.

How to Use FAST TRACK TO *Fine Dining*

The goal of this book is to provide you with all the tools necessary to plan and prepare fabulous dinner parties. The timeline, which is included with each menu, is the key to success. The timeline indicates how and when to prepare each food item, as well as reminds you to focus on what I like to call Creating the Ambience, or the checklist for decorating the home and table.

In total, there are sixteen menus, four in each season. The seasons are a guideline but feel free to make any menu at any time. Each menu includes a listing of the courses and wine pairings for that menu. Of the sixteen menus, fourteen include a Champagne aperitif, appetizers, a starter, a salad, a palate cleanser, a main course, a dessert, and an after-dinner sweet. The two exceptions, Thanksgiving and Christmas, are served buffet style.

Following each menu are the recipes for that menu. You will see that almost all of the recipes have information on how to prepare a particular item ahead. Where applicable, I have included some handy tips and substitutions that I have found helpful. In addition, many of the recipes also include a presentation tip, providing advice about how to serve a particular item.

The timeline for each menu follows the recipes. I use the timeline as my indispensable guide, as it outlines the steps you need to accomplish in order to complete, garnish, and serve a particular course at the right temperature and at the right time. If the timeline says, "Prepare ahead" a particular item, go to the recipe for that item and read the "TO PREPARE AHEAD" instructions. If the timeline says, "Finish" a particular item, go to the recipe for that item and read the "TO FINISH" instructions. If the timeline says, "Plate according to the Presentation Tip," go to the recipe for that item and read the "PRESENTATION TIP." Follow the timeline, and you shouldn't have any surprises on the day of your party.

The grocery list for each menu follows the timeline. The grocery list is broken down by day and is tied to the order of the timeline. If it says to buy something a week ahead on the grocery list, generally you need that item for something you are preparing a week ahead. In addition, I have broken the grocery list down into pantry items, alcohol and drinks, produce, dairy, freezer, meat, fish and deli, and bakery. Hopefully, this will help to streamline your trip to the store.

So, How Do You Proceed?

Look over the menus and find one that appeals to you. At the start of each season, there is a summary of the four menus in that season. You can look at the summaries, or you can look at the complete menu, including wine pairings, at the start of each set of recipes. Once you have picked a menu, look over the timeline for that menu and make sure it works with your schedule.

If you have time, try a few of the different recipes in the menu for practice. For example, try making the main course or the soup or the dessert. Although I've tried to make the recipes as clear as possible, there is nothing better than firsthand experience. You don't have to try all the recipes (once you've made one sorbet, you can pretty much make them all), but see if you can try some of them.

Remember—if you follow the timeline, you'll get everything done. If you make all the recipes in a menu, it will take about five to six hours of total preparation time. However, because you are making several items ahead, you will be dividing this up into much smaller and more manageable segments. The timeline indicates how much time you will need on a given day excluding grocery shopping and creating the ambience.

Note that I use a 7:30 p.m. start time for all of the dinners except Thanksgiving and Christmas. Obviously, you may want to start your dinner at a different time. If so, adjust the times accordingly. And be flexible! The different times are a guideline. If you serve the soup fifteen minutes late, don't worry. I've tried to organize the timeline so that you put things in the oven and take things out at natural breaks. If the timing does change, make sure that you look over the timeline to see how you will have to adjust various items. And if the courses are taking longer than expected, don't worry. It probably means that your guests are having a great time.

Contents

Creating the Ambience

I am sure that you have heard it before, but I'm going to repeat it. The mood, the lighting, the music, and the decoration of your home and table are just as important as the food—if not more important.

If you can get the ambience right, the food may even taste better—or at least seem that way.

In my view, there are five components to creating the right atmosphere. These include preliminary organization, exterior home decoration, interior home decoration, table setting, and music.

PRELIMINARY ORGANIZATION

Four weeks before—Send out invitations, either by regular mail or e-mail. Figure out how many people you want to have. In my view, a total of six to eight is ideal, although ten can work as well. I find that more than ten makes things pretty hectic, especially if you don't have outside help. In our house, we like to do everything ourselves. Our objective is to have parties that are formal in the sense of elegant but informal in the sense that it's just us working to make a nice evening for our friends.

Three weeks before—Decide on a menu and familiarize yourself with the timeline for that menu.

Two weeks before—Start chasing up guests. If a guest hasn't responded, follow up with a phone call or an e-mail to see if he or she is coming.

One week before—Buy groceries and start cooking the items you can prepare ahead. Make sure your table linens are clean and pressed. Think about the table decorations you are going to use. If you are using silver, make sure it's clean and polished. If a guest still hasn't responded, follow up again.

EXTERIOR HOME DECORATION

There are a number of things you can do to get the exterior of your home ready. Remember, unless it is pitch-dark outside, it's the first thing your guests are going to see.

From the moment your guests start to walk up to your door, you want to get them into the mood of the evening. In the summer, we like to put pots of flowers on the steps and porch leading to the door. In the fall and winter, we like to arrange luminaries on either side of the path leading to the door.

Although we now use lanterns, we used paper lunch bags when we first started entertaining. We would fill the bottom of each bag with about two cups of sand and place a tea light securely in the middle. If you're not comfortable using candles, you can always use small battery-operated tea lights instead.

We would line both sides of the path leading to our door with these paper bag luminaries, and it was lovely. Not only did it create atmosphere, but it also let guests know which house it was, and for us, that was a good thing, especially in the beginning when we didn't know many of the people who were coming! All I had to tell people was to look for the house with the luminaries out front.

INTERIOR HOME DECORATION

With candles, flowers, and music, you can create a wonderful atmosphere inside your home. We like to use lots of flowers and candles. For flowers, you can use fresh or a combination of fresh and dried. During the holidays, we hang a garland on our stair banister. Not only does it look nice, but it also smells great.

For candles, you can use a combination of standard candles and tea lights. We tend to have candles everywhere and have found that a good resale shop is a great resource. For example, we have purchased lots of inexpensive cut glass dessert bowls. We place these on mantels, window ledges, and tables, and put a tea light in each one. It's an incredibly simple way to achieve a warm glow in a room.

In the entrance hall, we have a decorative easel on which we place an old theatrical frame displaying the evening's menu. It's often a topic of conversation, and it lets people know what they will be having.

There are also some basic decisions to make—such as where to put coats when guests arrive. What bathroom are guests going to use? Is it clean? Is there a clean hand towel out for guests? Frankly, a scented candle and a small vase of flowers are a wonderful addition to a guest bathroom.

TABLE SETTING

There's no question that your table setting is key to creating your ambience. Make sure to choose a nice tablecloth and coordinating napkins. Make sure your silverware is polished.

If you can, set out the silverware for each course. The general rule of thumb is that you should have no more than three pieces of silverware on each side of the plate—which usually represents the starter, the salad, and the main course. If we have enough matching silverware, we'll put a dessert spoon and fork above the plate, and if we don't have enough, we'll bring them out later when we arrive at that part of the meal. We serve the sorbet palate cleanser with small teaspoons.

Make sure that your glasses are clean and spotless. Put out or aside as many of the dishes you will need as possible and set the table as far ahead as you can. It's one less thing to do on the day.

In addition, make sure your candlesticks are clean and polished, and replace any candles that need replacing. Make sure your salt and pepper shakers are clean and full. Create a centerpiece for the table. Put out some seasonal decorations. Most importantly, have fun!

MUSIC

There's no question that music is one of the most important aspects of an evening, and yet for us, music was one of the things we would often leave until last, and by last I mean five minutes before our guests arrived. We would then run around trying to find some appropriate music. This is clearly not the way to go about it, and it resulted in some truly disastrous musical moments!

Prepare your music well in advance and have it ready to go. You can do compilations or themes. You can mix and match. Just make sure you have thought about it and know what you're going to do—well before your guests arrive.

Creating the Ambience Checklist

These are just a few of the things you should consider when thinking about creating the ambience for your party. I've put these and others into this checklist. I'd recommend that you keep it handy.

Before we had this checklist, we had numerous little mishaps, forgetting one thing or another and discovering it during the meal. The checklist eliminates this problem because it's all right there in black and white.

So, if you can, use the list or make one of your own. It will help you avoid the unexpected, and trust me, avoiding the unexpected during a dinner party is a good thing.

ONE WEEK BEFORE PARTY:

Perform any larger lawn care jobs (mowing, raking, etc.)
Hang season-appropriate wreath on front door (if using)
Lay the fire in the fireplace (if using)
Check tablecloth and napkins are clean and pressed
Check you have enough standard candles and tea lights and replace where necessary
Check you have appropriate replacement lightbulbs in case one should burn out
Check you have a scented candle and place it in the guest bathroom
Polish all silver props that you are going to use, if needed
Buy party favors for guests, if applicable

TWO DAYS BEFORE PARTY:

Buy flowers for home decoration
Arrange flowers (dining room, living room, guest bathroom, etc.)
Check Champagne, water, wine, and dessert wine glasses are clean and spotless
Set aside coffee cups, saucers, and spoons
Set aside tea selection (individual tea bags), if offering tea
Set out napkins for aperitifs and appetizers
Set out coasters for aperitifs, if needed
Clear space for guests' coats
Make sure you have plenty of ice for ice water

ONE DAY BEFORE PARTY:

Sweep path to the door
Perform last-minute maintenance on lawn and shrubs
Vacuum and dust dining room, living room, and other appropriate rooms
Water houseplants
If dining table is not used for daily dining, put out tablecloth
Create centerpiece and place on table
Arrange candlesticks and/or candleholders that you are going to use on the table
Put any other table decorations on the table
Put out silverware, glasses, service plates (if using), and napkins
Put out bread plates and bread knives
Put out place cards and menu cards (if using)
Fill and put out salt and pepper shakers
Set aside dessert forks and spoons (if not part of the place setting)
Select music for the evening and load
If you have a pet, groom it!
Lay out the clothes you are going to wear

DAY OF PARTY:

Clean guest bathroom and put out a clean hand towel

A Few Words About Teamwork

To wrap up, I think that it's important to talk about teamwork because it can make a huge difference to the success of a dinner party.

In our household, I take care of the cooking and the grocery shopping, while my husband takes care of the decorating and the table setting. If you have a husband, partner, or friend who can help, that's great. Put him or her to work! That said, you can do it all on your own. It will just take a bit more time.

If you do have someone to work with, there are a few things you should think about in advance. For example, during a dinner party, my husband prepares the cocktails. He passes the appetizers. He pours the wine and water. We both clear dishes (remember, serve from the left and clear from the right). In the kitchen, he consolidates dishes and silverware, while I prepare the next course. Sometimes, he even has a chance to put dishes in the dishwasher, saving on cleanup later. While I plate the food, he'll add the garnish and start carrying the plates to the table.

After you do this a few times, you'll figure out how to work together most effectively. I would recommend deciding a few things in advance. Which one of you is going to light the candles? Turn on the music? Answer the door and collect coats? Pour the aperitif? Pass the appetizers? Put out the rolls and butter? Pour the wine and water? Clear the butter plates, salt, and pepper? Serve the coffee and tea?

This is only a partial list, but it provides an idea of a few things you might want to consider. If you know in advance who is going to do what, it makes things go that much more smoothly.

So figure out who is going to do what, work together, follow the timeline, and start having fun!

Spring

Chicken Stuffed with Spinach and Ricotta

SERVES 6

Saronno Kir Imperial • Mozzarella, Pepperoni, Tomato and Basil Sticks • Marinated Mushrooms • Herbed Asparagus with Parmesan Cheese • Mixed Greens with Roasted Red Pepper and Goat Cheese • Raspberry Lime Sorbet • Chicken Stuffed with Spinach and Ricotta • Crispy Roast Potatoes • Carrots with Butter and Dill • Orange Cake with Blackberries and Mascarpone Cream • White Chocolate Macadamia Nut Cookies

Veal with Sage and Wine

SERVES 8

Apricot and Orange Champagne • Cucumber Rounds with Smoked Salmon • Eggplant, Mozzarella and Tomato Stacks • Arugula with Parmesan • Grapefruit Sorbet • Veal with Sage and Wine • Risotto with Spring Vegetables • Tiramisu • Orange Chocolate Cookies

Sole Florentine

SERVES 8

Ritz Fizz • Warm Crab Meat Dip with Crackers and Vegetables • Cream of Asparagus Soup • Mixed Greens with Truffle Oil Dressing • Pineapple Orange Sorbet • Sole Florentine • Seasoned Long Grain and Wild Rice • Shredded Zucchini • Chocolate Mousse • Almond Crisps

Lamb Tagine

SERVES 8

Melon-Infused Champagne • Hummus with Pita and Vegetables • Phyllo Cheese Bites • Carrot, Fennel and Orange Soup • Mixed Greens with Grapes and Feta • Mango Sorbet • Lamb Tagine • Couscous with Cilantro and Parsley • Crème Brûlée • Cinnamon Cookies

Chicken Stuffed with Spinach and Ricotta

menu

SERVES 6

Cocktail & Hors d'Oeuvres

Saronno Kir Imperial

Mozzarella, Pepperoni, Tomato and Basil Sticks

Marinated Mushrooms

Olives, Breadsticks and Mixed Nuts

Starter

Herbed Asparagus with Parmesan Cheese

Rolls and Butter

 Gruner Veltliner or Sancerre

Salad

Mixed Greens with Roasted Red Pepper and Goat Cheese

Palate Cleanser

Raspberry Lime Sorbet

Main Coruse

Chicken Stuffed with Spinach and Ricotta

Crispy Roast Potatoes

Carrots with Butter and Dill

 Barbera

Dessert

Orange Cake with Blackberries and Mascarpone Cream

White Chocolate Macadamia Nut Cookies

 Muscat

Coffee & Tea

Saronno Kir Imperial

1 1/2 tablespoons amaretto

1/2 cup plus 2 tablespoons Champagne or dry sparkling wine

Lemon tie for garnish

Pour the amaretto into a Champagne glass. Fill the glass with the Champagne. Garnish with a lemon tie.

PRESENTATION TIP: To make a lemon tie, pull a zester along the lemon to create strips. Tie 2 strips together by looping 1 over the other and tying as you would start to tie shoelaces. You can then prop the tied twist on the edge of the Champagne glass. This takes a bit of practice. If you want to save time, you can just make a lemon twist. To help your ties or twists maintain their shapes, put them in the freezer until just before serving.

TO PREPARE AHEAD: Pour the amaretto into the bottom of each Champagne glass, and place the glasses near where you are going to serve the apéritif. Have a few empty glasses available in case some guests prefer water. Make the lemon ties, cover, and freeze.

TO FINISH: Pour the Champagne, garnish with the lemon tie, and serve.

HANDY TIP: I like Disaronno Amaretto, although other brands will do. I often use dry sparkling wine instead of Champagne when making Champagne cocktails. One bottle of Champagne will make enough to serve 6.

Mozzarella, Pepperoni, Tomato and Basil Sticks

9 cherry tomatoes

18 fresh basil leaves

18 small fresh mozzarella balls

9 slices pepperoni

1/4 cup balsamic vinegar for dipping

Thin Italian breadsticks

Wash the cherry tomatoes and remove the stems. Let dry. Wash the basil leaves and pat dry.

Stick a cocktail pick through a mozzarella ball. Next, add a basil leaf (folding the leaf in half if it's too big). Place a cherry tomato stem side down on the end of the cocktail pick. Repeat with the remaining cherry tomatoes, 8 of the basil leaves and 8 of the mozzarella balls.

Stick a cocktail pick through a folded pepperoni slice. Add a basil leaf (folding the leaf in half if it's too big). Place a mozzarella ball onto the end of the cocktail pick. Repeat the procedure with the remaining pepperoni slices, basil leaves and mozzarella balls.

On a platter, place a bowl with the balsamic vinegar for dipping. Arrange the prepared cocktail picks around the bowl. Serve with thin Italian breadsticks.

TO PREPARE AHEAD: On the day of the party, assemble the cocktail picks ahead of time. Arrange the cocktail picks on a platter with the balsamic vinegar in a bowl for dipping, cover, and refrigerate until needed. Place the breadsticks in a decorative container. Make sure to put out napkins.

Marinated Mushrooms

1/3 cup extra-virgin olive oil
2 tablespoons balsamic vinegar or red wine vinegar
1/4 cup finely chopped onion
1 clove garlic, minced
1/2 teaspoon oregano
1/4 teaspoon kosher salt
1/4 teaspoon freshly ground black pepper
1/4 teaspoon sugar
8 ounces small fresh button mushrooms

Preparation Time:
10 min. plus 24 hours marinating time

In a medium bowl, mix together the extra-virgin olive oil, balsamic vinegar, onion, garlic, oregano, salt, pepper and sugar. Wipe any remaining dirt off of the mushrooms and trim the base of the stems. Add the mushrooms to the marinade and toss until well coated.

Cover and refrigerate for 24 hours, stirring occasionally.

To Prepare Ahead: You can marinate the mushrooms up to 5 days ahead. Store, covered, in the refrigerator. On the day of the party, place the mushrooms in a serving bowl. Chill, covered, until ready to serve.

Handy Tip: If you are pressed for time, you can always purchase marinated mushrooms.

Herbed Asparagus with Parmesan Cheese

SERVES 6

1/4 cup butter, softened
1 tablespoon chopped fresh chives
1 tablespoon chopped fresh dill
1 tablespoon chopped fresh rosemary
1 tablespoon chopped fresh flat-leaf parsley
1 teaspoon freshly ground black pepper
1 teaspoon kosher salt
2 pounds fresh asparagus
4 ounces Parmesan cheese, shaved

Preparation Time: 15 min.
Cooking Time: 5 min.
Total Time: 20 min.

Presentation Tip: Place the asparagus spears in the middle of each plate with the stems pointing in the same direction. Sprinkle with the Parmesan cheese and serve immediately.

Bring a large pot of water to a boil. Combine the butter, chives, dill, rosemary, parsley and pepper in a small bowl. Blend thoroughly. Set aside.

Rinse the asparagus and trim off the tough ends. When the water comes to a boil, add the salt and then the asparagus. Simmer until tender-crisp, about 1 1/2 to 2 minutes if the spears are pencil thin or 3 to 4 minutes if the spears are thick. Drain and pat dry.

Melt the butter mixture over medium heat in a large frying pan. Add the asparagus and cook for 2 to 3 minutes or until heated through, stirring gently.

To Prepare Ahead: Prepare the herb butter ahead and store, covered, in the refrigerator for up to a week. On the day of the party, trim the tough ends off the asparagus and chill until ready to cook. Shave the Parmesan cheese, and chill, covered, until ready to use.

To Finish: Bring a large pot of water to a boil. Add salt, cook, and finish the asparagus as directed above.

To Freeze: You may freeze the herb butter for up to 3 months. Wrap the herb butter in plastic wrap, seal in a plastic bag, and freeze.

Mixed Greens with Roasted Red Pepper and Goat Cheese

Preparation Time: 15 min.
Cooking Time: 6 to 8 min.
Total Time: 21 to 23 min.

SALAD
1	red bell pepper
1/3	cup pine nuts
8	ounces mixed baby greens

DRESSING AND ASSEMBLY
2	tablespoons balsamic vinegar
1/4	teaspoon kosher salt
1/8	teaspoon freshly ground black pepper
1/3	cup extra-virgin olive oil
4	ounces crumbled goat cheese

For the salad: Preheat the oven broiler. Line a baking sheet with aluminum foil. Cut the red pepper in half from stem to stem. Seed and core the red pepper and place skin side up on the foil-lined baking sheet. Broil the red pepper until the skin blisters, about 3 to 5 minutes. Remove from the oven and place in a bowl. Cover with plastic wrap and let sit for 5 minutes.

While the red pepper is cooling, place the pine nuts in a small nonstick frying pan. Heat over medium heat, tossing occasionally, until the pine nuts start to turn golden brown, about 3 minutes. Watch them closely because when they go, they go quickly! Set aside.

When the red pepper is cool enough to handle, remove and discard the skin and chop into 1/2-inch pieces. Rinse and spin dry the mixed greens. Place in a large bowl.

For the dressing: In a small bowl, whisk together the balsamic vinegar, salt and pepper. While continuing to whisk, add the extra-virgin olive oil in a steady stream. Continue whisking until the dressing thickens and emulsifies. Set aside

To serve family style, toss the mixed greens with enough dressing to coat. Sprinkle the dressed greens with the red pepper, pine nuts and goat cheese.

TO PREPARE AHEAD: On the day of the party, make the salad dressing, cover, and refrigerate. Roast, peel, and chop the red pepper as directed; cover and refrigerate. Toast the pine nuts and set aside. Rinse and spin dry the mixed greens. Place in a large bowl, cover with a damp towel, and refrigerate. An hour before serving, remove the salad dressing from the refrigerator and return to room temperature.

TO FINISH: Whisk the dressing. Toss the mixed greens with enough dressing to coat and place on individual plates. Sprinkle with the red pepper, pine nuts, and goat cheese.

HANDY TIP: If you're in a rush and want to cut down on preparation and cooking time, buy a jar of roasted red peppers. You'll only need a few, but you can store the rest in the refrigerator for later use.

Raspberry Lime Sorbet

1	cup sugar	Juice of 2 limes	
1	cup water	2	tablespoons raspberry liqueur
16	ounces fresh raspberries	Mint sprigs for garnish	

Preparation Time: 10 min.
Cooking Time: 5 min.
Ice Cream Maker: 20 min.
Total Time: 35 min. plus cooling time

In a medium saucepan, heat the sugar and water until the sugar melts and the mixture starts to boil. Boil for 2 minutes. Remove from the heat and cool completely.

Rinse and pat dry the raspberries. Place the raspberries in the bowl of a blender. Add the sugar syrup, lime juice and raspberry liqueur. Process until smooth.

Pour the raspberry mixture through a fine sieve. Using the back of a spoon, push the mixture through the sieve.

Pour the strained mixture into an ice cream maker and process according to the manufacturer's directions. When finished, pour into an airtight container and freeze until ready to serve.

PRESENTATION TIP: Because sorbet is a palate cleanser, servings should be small—about 1/4 to 1/3 cup. Using a small ice cream scoop or spoon, place 1 or 2 scoops of sorbet in a sorbet bowl or a small, preferably stemmed, glass dessert bowl. Garnish with the top few leaves of a sprig of mint.

TO PREPARE AHEAD: Prepare the sorbet up to a month ahead, place in an airtight container, and freeze.

TO FINISH: Remove the sorbet 15 minutes before serving to allow it to soften slightly. When ready, scoop into bowls, garnish with the mint, and serve.

HANDY TIP: If you don't have an ice cream maker, you can still prepare the sorbet. That said, I strongly recommend that you get an ice cream maker. Sorbet made in an ice cream maker will be creamier and smoother than sorbet made without one. If you don't have an ice cream maker, pour the puréed and strained mixture into a 9×13-inch metal pan. Spread out the sorbet mixture so that it freezes quicker. Cover and place in the freezer. Stir every half hour. In about 2 to 3 hours, your sorbet should be ready to serve.

Spring

Chicken Stuffed with Spinach and Ricotta

SERVES 6

Preparation Time: 25 min.
Cooking Time: 20 to 27 min.
Total Time: 45 to 52 min.

1	(10-ounce) package frozen chopped spinach		6	(6- to 8-ounce) skinless, boneless chicken breasts, trimmed
8	ounces ricotta cheese		12	to 15 slices good-quality imported prosciutto
1/2	teaspoon ground nutmeg		1/4	cup extra-virgin olive oil, divided
	Kosher salt and freshly ground black pepper to taste		6	lemon spirals for garnish
				Flat-leaf parsley for garnish

PRESENTATION TIP:
Cut each chicken parcel at a slight angle into thick slices and arrange on a plate. Garnish with the lemon spirals and parsley and serve with Crispy Roast Potatoes and Carrots with Butter and Dill. To make the lemon spiral, slice a lemon into 1/4-inch slices. Make a slit from 1 edge to the center of the slice. Holding the lemon on either side of the cut, twist and place the ends of the slice on the plate.

Preheat the oven to 400°F/200°C.

Thaw the frozen spinach in the microwave. The easiest way is to put the spinach in a bowl, cover with plastic wrap, make a few slits with a knife and microwave for about 3 minutes. Then, let sit for a minute. If it's not yet thawed, microwave for another minute. When the spinach has thawed, squeeze out the excess liquid; a cheesecloth works best, but your hands will do in a pinch.

In a small bowl, mix together the spinach and ricotta. Add the nutmeg. Season with salt and pepper.

Cut a horizontal slit through the thickest part of each chicken breast, creating a pocket. Be careful not to cut all the way through the breast.

Spoon equal amounts of the spinach mixture into the slits in the chicken breasts. You may have a little spinach mixture left over. Wrap each breast in 2 pieces of prosciutto, winding it around the chicken to cover it completely. Use extra prosciutto if necessary.

If you have 2 large frying pans, you can sear all 6 chicken parcels at 1 time. Heat 2 tablespoons extra-virgin olive oil in each frying pan. Add 3 of the chicken parcels to each pan and sauté over medium heat for 5 to 7 minutes, making sure to brown the prosciutto on all sides. Place the chicken parcels on an ungreased rimmed baking sheet. Bake for 15 to 20 minutes or until cooked through (165°F/74°C on a meat thermometer). Remove to a cutting board and let rest for 5 minutes.

TO PREPARE AHEAD: You can make the chicken parcels, stopping before baking, early on the day of your party. Thaw the spinach and cool completely. When the spinach is cold, make the filling and stuff, wrap, and brown the chicken parcels as instructed. Place the parcels on a baking sheet and let cool. Chill, covered, in the refrigerator. Prepare the parsley and the lemon spirals for garnish, and chill, covered, in the refrigerator until ready to serve.

TO FINISH: When ready to serve, bake the chicken parcels, uncovered, at 400°F/200°C for 20 minutes. Continue as directed above.

HANDY TIP: Use a good-quality imported prosciutto for this recipe. I usually buy a few extra slices just in case. Ask for your prosciutto at the deli counter. You want it thin but not so thin it tears when you wrap the chicken.

Crispy Roast Potatoes

3	pounds Yukon Gold potatoes, peeled and cut into 1 1/2-inch pieces		Kosher salt to taste
		9	tablespoons vegetable oil

Preparation Time: 5 min.
Cooking Time: 65 to 75 min.
Total Time: 70 to 80 min.

Preheat the oven to 400°F/200°C. Place the potatoes in a large pot and add enough water to cover. Bring to a boil and boil for 5 minutes. Drain the potatoes, cover and shake the saucepan 5 to 10 times to roughen the edges of the potatoes. Season with salt.

Meanwhile, heat the oil in the oven in a large roasting pan or on a rimmed baking sheet for 5 minutes. Arrange the potatoes in a single layer in the pan. Bake for 30 minutes. Turn the potatoes with a spatula and return to the oven for another 20 to 30 minutes. Season with salt. Drain on paper towels.

TO PREPARE AHEAD: On the day of the party, prepare the potatoes as directed. Let cool to room temperature.

TO FINISH: Place the potatoes in a roasting pan or on a rimmed baking sheet and heat in a 400-degree oven for 5 to 10 minutes or until heated through. If you are making the Chicken Stuffed with Spinach and Ricotta, return the potatoes to the oven at the same time you remove the chicken from the oven. The chicken and the potatoes will be ready to plate at the same time.

HANDY TIP: If you are feeding more than 6, increase the amount of potatoes by 1/2 pound and vegetable oil by 1 1/2 tablespoons for each additional person.

Carrots with Butter and Dill

2	pounds carrots	2	tablespoons butter
1	teaspoon sugar	2	tablespoons chopped fresh dill
1	teaspoon kosher salt		Kosher salt to taste

Preparation Time: 10 min.
Cooking Time: 4 to 6 min.
Total Time: 14 to 16 min.

Fill a large pot with water and bring to a boil. Peel the carrots, cut off the ends and slice on a diagonal, making each slice about 1/4-inch thick. Add the sugar, 1 teaspoon salt and the carrots to the boiling water. Return to a boil and boil for 4 to 6 minutes or until tender-crisp; drain.

Add the butter. Stir in the chopped dill. Season with salt.

TO PREPARE AHEAD: On the day of the party, prepare and cook the carrots in advance. Drain and plunge the carrots into cold water to stop the cooking process. Drain, pat dry, and store, covered, in a microwave-safe bowl in the refrigerator. Chop the dill and chill, covered, until ready to use.

TO FINISH: Prior to serving, add the butter and microwave for 2 to 4 minutes or until heated through. Stir in the dill and season with salt.

HANDY TIP: If you want to dress up your carrots, you can use a crinkle cutter to create wavy ridges on your slices. Crinkle cutters are available at most kitchen shops.

Orange Cake with Blackberries and Mascarpone Cream

Preparation Time: 30 min.
Cooking Time: 50 min.
Total Time: 80 min.

PRESENTATION TIP:
Place a slice of the cake on a plate and garnish with a few of the remaining blackberries.

ORANGE CAKE
1   cup butter, softened
1^1/3   cups sugar
Grated zest of 1 orange
4   eggs
1^1/3   cups flour
2   teaspoons baking powder
3/4   teaspoon kosher salt
1/2   cup almond meal
3/4   cup orange juice

BLACKBERRY SAUCE
1/3   cup blackberry jam
1   tablespoon Cointreau

MASCARPONE CREAM
2/3   cup whipping cream
8   ounces mascarpone cheese
1/3   cup confectioners' sugar
Grated zest of 1/2 orange
1   tablespoon Cointreau

ASSEMBLY
12   ounces blackberries

For the cake: Preheat the oven to 325°F/160°C. Grease a 9-inch springform pan and line the bottom with parchment paper.

In a large bowl, cream the butter, sugar and orange zest until light and fluffy. Add the eggs 1 at a time, beating after each addition.

In a small bowl, combine the flour, baking powder, salt and almond meal. Blend the dry ingredients into the butter mixture alternately with the orange juice.

Pour the batter into the prepared pan and bake for 50 minutes or until the cake tests done. Let rest for 5 minutes. Invert onto a wire rack, top side up, and cool completely.

For the sauce: In a small bowl, whisk together the blackberry jam and Cointreau. The mixture should be easy to spread. If not, warm briefly in the microwave.

For the cream: In a small bowl, combine the cream, mascarpone cheese and confectioners' sugar. Beat until soft peaks form. Stir in the orange zest and Cointreau. You want the cream to be easy to spread.

For the assembly: Rinse and pat dry 6 ounces of the blackberries. Slice the blackberries into halves lengthwise. Using a bread knife, cut the cake horizontally into 3 layers. Place the bottom layer on a cake plate. Spread with half the blackberry sauce, making sure to let it soak into the cake as much as possible. Then, spread with about 1/3 of the Mascarpone Cream. Place half the sliced blackberries, cut side down, on top of the Mascarpone Cream. Place the next layer of the cake on top. Spread with the rest of the Blackberry Sauce and half the remaining Mascarpone Cream. Place the remaining blackberries, cut side down, on top of the Mascarpone Cream. Top with the last layer of cake. Spread the remaining Mascarpone Cream carefully over the top of the cake. Cover and refrigerate for at least an hour and up to 2 days. Prior to serving, rinse and pat dry the remaining 6 ounces of blackberries.

TO PREPARE AHEAD: You can make and assemble the cake up to 2 days ahead. Cover and refrigerate. Rinse and pat dry the blackberries for the garnish and refrigerate until ready to serve.

HANDY TIP: One tool I use all the time is a microplane zester/grater. It's great not only for zesting but also for grating cheese and nutmeg.

White Chocolate Macadamia Nut Cookies

1 cup butter, softened	1 teaspoon baking soda
3/4 cup packed light brown sugar	1/2 teaspoon kosher salt
1/2 cup sugar	1 cup coarsely chopped
2 eggs	macadamia nuts
1 teaspoon vanilla extract	12 ounces white chocolate bits
2 1/2 cups flour	

Preparation Time: 10 min.
Cooking Time: 10 to 12 min. per batch

Preheat the oven to 350°F/180°C.

In a large bowl, cream together the butter, brown sugar and sugar using an electric mixer. Add the eggs 1 at a time, beating after each addition. Beat in the vanilla.

Blend in the flour, baking soda and salt. Stir in the macadamia nuts and white chocolate bits.

Drop by teaspoonfuls 2 inches apart onto an ungreased cookie sheet. Bake for 10 to 12 minutes or until golden brown. Remove to a wire rack and cool completely.

TO PREPARE AHEAD: You can make the cookies up to 5 days ahead. You'll only need about 12 cookies for your dinner party. Bake the number needed, place the cooled cookies for your party on a small serving platter, and cover securely with plastic wrap. Freeze the extra cookie dough, or bake the cookies and store in an airtight container.

TO FREEZE: Refrigerate unbaked cookie dough for 15 minutes or until firm enough to handle. Place a piece of plastic wrap on your work surface. Separate the dough into 3 equal pieces (4 pieces if you haven't baked a batch). Shape each piece into a log 1 1/2-inch in diameter. Roll each log in plastic wrap, sealing the ends. Place the logs in a sealable freezer bag and freeze for up to 3 months. When ready to bake, thaw at room temperature for 30 minutes (or briefly in the microwave) and bake as directed.

HANDY TIP: Be sure to use the unsalted "raw" macadamia nuts—not the dry-roasted ones!

Timeline

**ONE WEEK BEFORE
(ABOUT 1 HOUR)**

Buy groceries and create the ambience

Prepare the Raspberry Lime Sorbet

**TWO DAYS BEFORE
(ABOUT 3/4 HOUR)**

Buy groceries and create the ambience

Put sparkling water, Champagne, white wine and dessert wine (if using) in refrigerator

Put out red wine

Prepare ahead White Chocolate Macadamia Nut Cookies

Prepare ahead Marinated Mushrooms

**ONE DAY BEFORE
(ABOUT 1 1/2 HOURS)**

Prepare ahead Orange Cake with Blackberries and Mascarpone Cream

DAY OF PARTY (ABOUT 3 HOURS)

Buy groceries and create the ambience

Prepare ahead Herbed Asparagus with Parmesan Cheese

Prepare ahead Mixed Greens with Roasted Red Pepper and Goat Cheese

Prepare ahead Crispy Roast Potatoes

Prepare ahead Carrots with Butter and Dill

Prepare ahead Chicken Stuffed with Spinach and Ricotta

Prepare ahead Mozzarella, Pepperoni, Tomato and Basil Sticks

5:00 PM
Shower and dress

6:30 PM
Prepare coffeemaker

Open wines, turn on music, light candles

Put out starter plates, salad plates, sorbet bowls, main course plates, and dessert plates

Prepare sugar and milk for coffee

7:00 PM
Put butter pats and rolls on butter plates

Put a cucumber slice in each water glass

Prepare ahead Saronno Kir Imperial

Put out appetizer platter, olives, mushrooms, and toothpicks

Put out breadsticks and nuts

Put water on to boil for asparagus

Remove salad dressing from refrigerator

7:30 PM (GUESTS ARRIVE)
Open and pour Champagne, garnish with a lemon tie (have water ready for those who prefer water)

8:05 PM
Call people to table

Serve starter wine and water

8:10 PM
Finish Herbed Asparagus and serve

Preheat oven to 400°F/200°C

8:30 PM
Finish salad and serve

Take sorbet out of freezer

8:45 PM
Put uncovered chicken parcels in oven

Serve sorbet, garnished with mint

9:05 PM
Remove chicken parcels from oven and let rest

Put Crispy Roast Potatoes in oven to reheat

Finish Carrots with Butter and Dill

Plate Chicken Stuffed with Spinach and Ricotta according to Presentation Tip

Remove Orange Cake from refrigerator

9:15 PM
Serve main course and wine

Turn on coffeemaker

9:45 PM
Plate Orange Cake and garnish with blackberries

Serve dessert and dessert wine (if using)

10:00 PM
Serve coffee, tea, and after-dinner cookies

Grocery List

ONE WEEK BEFORE PARTY

PANTRY ITEMS

1   cup extra-virgin olive oil
9   tablespoons vegetable oil
1/2 cup good-quality balsamic vinegar
     Kosher salt
     Freshly ground black pepper
1/2 teaspoon dried oregano
1/2 teaspoon ground nutmeg
3 2/3 cups sugar
1/3 cup confectioners' sugar
3/4 cup light brown sugar
4   cups flour
2   teaspoons baking powder
1   teaspoon baking soda
1   teaspoon vanilla extract
1   (12-ounce) package white
     chocolate chips
1   cup coarsely chopped
     macadamia nuts
1/3 cup pine nuts
1/2 cup almond meal
1   package thin Italian breadsticks
1/3 cup blackberry jam
1   (12-ounce) jar mixed nuts
1   package 4-inch wooden cocktail picks
1   package wooden toothpicks

Decaffeinated and regular coffee
Regular and herbal tea bags

ALCOHOL AND DRINKS

1   bottle Champagne or sparkling wine
2   bottles white wine for starter (Gruner
     Veltliner or Sancerre)
2   bottles red wine for main (Barbera)
1   bottle dessert wine, if using (Muscat)
3   bottles sparkling water
9   tablespoons Disaronno Amaretto (or
     other amaretto)
2   tablespoons raspberry liqueur
2   tablespoons Cointreau

PRODUCE

1   clove garlic
1   onion
16   ounces raspberries
2   limes
2   lemons

DAIRY

1   cup whole milk
2 7/8 cups butter
6   eggs

TWO DAYS BEFORE PARTY

PRODUCE

2   oranges
12   ounces blackberries
1   tablespoon chopped fresh chives
3   tablespoons chopped fresh dill
1   tablespoon chopped fresh rosemary
1   tablespoon chopped fresh flat-leaf parsley
1   bunch fresh flat-leaf parsley for main
     garnish
1   bunch fresh mint for sorbet garnish
1   bunch fresh basil
8   ounces baby mixed greens
9   cherry tomatoes
8   ounces small button mushrooms
2   pounds asparagus (preferably pencil thin)
1   red bell pepper
3   pounds Yukon Gold potatoes
2   pounds carrots
1   cucumber (for water)

DAIRY

18   miniature mozzarella balls
4   ounces crumbled goat cheese
8   ounces ricotta cheese
4   ounces Parmesan cheese, shaved
2/3 cup whipping cream
8   ounces mascarpone cheese
3/4 cup orange juice

MEAT AND DELI

6   (6- to 8-ounce) skinless boneless
     chicken breasts
9   slices pepperoni
15   slices good-quality imported prosciutto
8   ounces marinated pitted olives

FREEZER

10   ounces frozen chopped spinach

DAY OF PARTY

BAKERY

6   rolls

Veal with Sage and Wine menu

Serves 8

Cocktail & Hors d'Oeuvres

Apricot and Orange Champagne

Cucumber Rounds with Smoked Salmon

Roasted Almonds

Starter

Eggplant, Mozzarella and Tomato Stacks

Rolls and Butter

🍇 Vernaccia

Salad

Arugula with Parmesan

Palate Cleanser

Grapefruit Sorbet

Main Course

Veal with Sage and Wine

Risotto with Spring Vegetables

🍇 Dolcetto

Dessert

Tiramisu

Orange Chocolate Cookies

🍇 Sauternes or Moscato d'Asti

Coffee & Tea

Apricot and Orange Champagne

2	teaspoons apricot brandy	1/2	cup plus 2 tablespoons Champagne
2	teaspoons orange juice		or dry sparkling wine
1	teaspoon Grand Marnier		Orange twist for garnish

Fill the bottom of a Champagne glass with the apricot brandy, orange juice and Grand Marnier. Fill the glass with Champagne. Garnish with an orange twist.

TO PREPARE AHEAD: Pour the apricot brandy, orange juice, and Grand Marnier into the bottom of each Champagne glass and place the glasses near where you are going to serve the apéritif. Have a few empty glasses available in case some guests prefer water. Make the orange twists and freeze.

TO FINISH: Pour the Champagne, garnish with the orange twist by propping it on the edge of the glass, and serve.

HANDY TIP: A bottle of Champagne will make enough to serve 6.

SUBSTITUTION: If you don't have Grand Marnier, you can use Cointreau instead.

Preparation Time: 10 min.

PRESENTATION TIP: Make an orange twist by using the blade in the middle of a zester/channel knife. Cut a spiral around the orange, starting at the top. Make sure to press hard enough as you twist to get a good piece of the peel. If your twist isn't shaped the way you want, wrap it around a plastic straw and secure it with 2 pins. Place the straw in the freezer. Just before pouring the Champagne, remove the twist from the freezer, cut off a 1 1/2-inch piece and prop on the edge of the Champagne glass.

Cucumber Rounds with Smoked Salmon

4	ounces cream cheese, softened	1	English cucumber
1/4	cup sour cream	4	ounces thinly sliced smoked salmon
2	teaspoons chopped fresh dill		Fresh sprigs of dill for garnish
1	teaspoon grated lemon zest		

In a small bowl, mix together the cream cheese and sour cream until smooth. Stir in the chopped dill and lemon zest. Slice the cucumber into 3/8-inch-thick rounds. You should have about 20 slices. Cut the salmon into 20 pieces. Place a teaspoonful of the herbed cream cheese on each slice of cucumber. Top with a piece of smoked salmon and a small sprig of dill.

TO PREPARE AHEAD: Make the Cucumber Rounds with Smoked Salmon early on the day of the party. Store, covered, in the refrigerator until needed.

HANDY TIP: If you can't find an English cucumber, use a regular cucumber instead. Also, if you're having a crowd, you'll have enough herbed cream cheese left over to make up another cucumber. Just use a smaller piece of salmon on each one, and you can easily increase your rounds from 20 to 40.

Preparation Time: 15 min.

PRESENTATION TIP: Place the Cucumber Rounds on a platter and serve.

Eggplant, Mozzarella and Tomato Stacks

Preparation Time: 20 min.
Cooking Time: 15 min.
Total Time: 35 min.

PRESENTATION TIP:
Remove the stack from the oven. Place the stacks on individual plates and carefully remove the wooden cocktail picks. Drizzle a little pesto around each stack. Top each stack with a spoonful of pesto and a small sprig of basil. Serve immediately.

2	medium eggplant
3	tablespoons extra-virgin olive oil for brushing
6	medium vine-ripened tomatoes
3	(8-ounce) mozzarella balls

PESTO

2	cups loosely packed basil leaves (about 3 ounces)

3	cloves garlic
3	tablespoons pine nuts
1/2	cup extra-virgin olive oil
1/4	cup grated Parmesan cheese

Kosher salt and freshly ground black pepper to taste
Basil sprigs for garnish

Preheat the oven to 375°F/190°C.

Slice the eggplant into 24 (3/8-inch-thick) slices. Brush lightly with the extra-virgin olive oil and arrange on a nonstick preheated grill pan. Cook until browned on both sides. If you don't have a grill pan, place the slices on an ungreased baking sheet under the broiler. Brown and then turn and brown the other side.

Cut off the ends of the tomatoes and slice into 24 (3/8-inch-thick) slices. Set aside.

Slice the mozzarella balls into 8 slices each for a total of 24 slices, trying to keep the thickness similar to the tomatoes and eggplant.

Place 8 of the eggplant slices on a lightly oiled baking sheet. Top each with a tomato and a mozzarella slice. Sprinkle with salt and pepper. Add a second layer of eggplant, tomato and mozzarella. Sprinkle with salt and pepper. Repeat the layers a third time. Skewer each stack with a wooden cocktail pick through the middle. Bake for 10 minutes.

For the pesto: While the mozzarella stacks are baking, make the pesto. In the bowl of a food processor, place the basil, garlic and pine nuts. Pulse until chopped. While continuing to process, slowly add the extra-virgin olive oil in a constant stream. Add the Parmesan cheese and pulse until blended. Season with salt and pepper. Serve according to the Presentation Tip.

TO PREPARE AHEAD: On the day of the party, you can make the eggplant stacks ahead, stopping before baking. Cover and refrigerate. Prepare the basil garnish and refrigerate. Make the pesto and store, covered, in the refrigerator.

TO FINISH: Bake the uncovered stacks in a preheated 375°F/190°C oven for 10 minutes. Remove and serve according to the Presentation Tip.

TO FREEZE: You can freeze pesto for up to a month. Freeze the pesto in small sealable containers or in an ice tray. When the cubes of pesto have frozen, transfer them to a plastic bag. Thaw the amount you need.

HANDY TIP: Try to pick eggplant, tomatoes, and mozzarella balls that have a similar diameter. If you don't want to make homemade pesto, use a good-quality ready-made pesto.

Arugula with Parmesan

8   ounces arugula

DRESSING
2   tablespoons freshly squeezed
     lemon juice

$^1/_4$ teaspoon kosher salt
$^1/_8$ teaspoon freshly ground
     black pepper
$^1/_3$ cup extra-virgin olive oil
4   ounces shaved Parmesan cheese

Rinse and spin dry the arugula. Place in a large bowl.

For the dressing: In a small bowl, whisk together the lemon juice, salt and pepper. While continuing to whisk, add the extra-virgin olive oil in a steady stream. Continue whisking until the dressing thickens and emulsifies. Set aside.

Toss the arugula with enough dressing to coat. To serve family-style, sprinkle the dressed arugula with the shaved Parmesan cheese.

TO PREPARE AHEAD: On the day of the party, make the salad dressing, cover, and refrigerate. Rinse and spin dry the arugula. Place in a large bowl, cover with a damp towel, and refrigerate. Shave the Parmesan cheese and store, covered, in the refrigerator. An hour before serving, remove the salad dressing from the refrigerator and return to room temperature.

TO FINISH: Whisk the dressing. Toss the arugula with enough dressing to coat and place on individual plates. Sprinkle with the shaved Parmesan cheese.

Grapefruit Sorbet

1   cup water
1   cup sugar
2   cups fresh pink grapefruit juice
     (about 2 to 2$^1/_2$ grapefruits)

1   tablespoon vodka
Mint springs for garnish

In a medium saucepan, heat the water and sugar until the sugar melts and the mixture starts to boil. Boil for 2 minutes. Remove from the heat and cool completely.

Stir in the grapefruit juice. Add the vodka. Pour into an ice cream maker and process according to the manufacturer's directions.

When finished, pour into an airtight container and freeze until ready to serve.

TO PREPARE AHEAD: Prepare the sorbet up to a month ahead, place in an airtight container, and freeze.

TO FINISH: Remove the sorbet 15 minutes before serving to allow it to soften slightly. When ready, scoop into bowls, garnish with the mint, and serve.

HANDY TIP: The purpose of the alcohol is to create a creamier texture. You can leave it out if you prefer.

Veal with Sage and Wine

1/4	cup extra-virgin olive oil, divided	1/3	cup chopped fresh sage leaves (about 3/4 ounce)
1/4	cup butter, divided	1 1/4	cups white wine
1	cup flour	1	teaspoon kosher salt
3	pounds lean veal stew meat, cut into 1-inch cubes	1/4	teaspoon freshly ground black pepper
1	medium onion, finely chopped		Fresh sage leaves for garnish
2	cloves garlic, minced		

Preparation Time: 15 min.
Cooking Time: 1 1/2 to 1 3/4 hours
Total Time: 1 3/4 to 2 hours

PRESENTATION TIP:
Place a mound of Risotto in the center of a dinner plate. Spread it slightly, making a circular shape. Top with the veal and garnish with a few sage leaves.

In a large deep skillet with a lid, heat 2 tablespoons extra-virgin olive oil and 2 tablespoons butter. Place the flour on a plate. Dip half the pieces of veal in the flour, coating on all sides. Shake off the excess flour. Add the veal to the skillet and brown on all sides. Remove the browned veal and set aside. Add the remaining 2 tablespoons extra-virgin olive oil and 2 tablespoons butter to the skillet and repeat with the rest of the veal. When browned, remove and set aside with the first batch.

Add the onion and garlic to the skillet and sauté over medium heat until translucent but not browned, about 5 minutes.

Add the chopped sage and stir to coat. Add the wine. Turn up the heat and bring the mixture to a boil. Boil for 1 minute, scraping up any brown bits on the bottom of the pan.

Turn the heat down to low. Return the browned veal to the pan. Add the salt and pepper. Cover and cook over low heat, stirring from time to time, for about 1 1/4 to 1 1/2 hours or until the veal is tender when pricked with a fork.

TO PREPARE AHEAD: You can make Veal with Sage and Wine a day ahead. Cool and then refrigerate in a covered ovenproof casserole dish.

TO FINISH: Preheat the oven to 350°F/180°C. Add 1/3 to 1/2 cup warm water and stir. Cover the veal and place in the oven. Cook for 30 to 35 minutes or until heated through. Serve, garnished with fresh sage leaves.

TO FREEZE: You can freeze the Veal with Sage and Wine for up to 3 months. After you take the veal out of the oven, cool and then freeze in an airtight container. Thaw and reheat as above.

Spring

Risotto with Spring Vegetables

Preparation Time: 10 min.
Cooking Time: 30 min.
Total Time: 40 min.

6	cups vegetable broth	1	pound thin asparagus, trimmed and cut into 1-inch pieces
2	tablespoons extra-virgin olive oil		
2	tablespoons butter	1	cup frozen petite peas
1	medium onion, finely chopped	1/4	cup chopped fresh flat-leaf parsley
1	medium leek, white part only, sliced	2	tablespoons butter
1	clove garlic, minced	1/2	cup grated Parmesan cheese
2	cups arborio rice		Kosher salt and freshly ground black pepper to taste
3/4	cup dry white wine		

In a medium saucepan, heat the vegetable broth. Cover and keep warm.

In a large, deep skillet, heat the extra-virgin olive oil and 2 tablespoons butter over medium-low heat. Add the onion, leek and garlic. Sauté until translucent but not browned, about 5 minutes.

Add the rice and cook for 2 minutes, stirring constantly. Add the wine. Cook, stirring constantly, until the wine has evaporated, about 2 minutes. Add 1 cup of the broth at a time, cooking and stirring until the liquid is absorbed. Continue until the rice is tender but firm to the bite, about 15 to 20 minutes.

Add the asparagus and peas. Cook until the peas are heated through and the asparagus is tender-crisp, about 2 minutes. Remove from the heat. Stir in the chopped parsley. Add 2 tablespoons butter and the grated Parmesan cheese. Season with salt and pepper.

To Prepare Ahead: Although risotto is best served immediately, you can partially cook it up to 2 days ahead. Follow the directions above, using 4 cups vegetable broth instead of 6. When the broth has been absorbed, and prior to adding the asparagus, peas, and parsley, place the rice in a shallow casserole dish, cool, cover, and refrigerate. Trim the asparagus stems, cut the asparagus into 1-inch pieces, and store, covered, in the refrigerator. About an hour before serving, remove the rice from the refrigerator and let sit at room temperature.

To Finish: When ready to serve, place the remaining 2 cups vegetable broth in a large deep skillet and bring to a boil. Reduce the heat to medium-low and stir in the partially cooked rice, the asparagus, and peas. Stir until the liquid is absorbed and the rice is heated through, about 4 to 5 minutes. Stir in the chopped parsley. Add the remaining 2 tablespoons butter and the grated Parmesan cheese and serve immediately.

Tiramisu

Preparation Time: 20 min.
plus 2 hours refrigeration

PRESENTATION TIP:
Place a slice of tiramisu
on a dessert plate and
garnish with a few fresh
raspberries.

4	egg whites
4	egg yolks
2/3	cup sugar
16	ounces mascarpone cheese
3	cups strong coffee, cooled
1/2	cup sweet marsala

1	(14-ounce) package of Savoiardi ladyfingers (48 ladyfingers)
2	tablespoons unsweetened cocoa powder
6	ounces fresh raspberries for garnish

In a small bowl, beat the egg whites until stiff with an electric mixer. Set aside. In a medium bowl, beat the egg yolks and sugar until thick and light in color. Stir in the mascarpone cheese and mix until well combined, working to get the lumps out. Fold in the whipped egg whites.

In a small bowl, combine the coffee and wine. Dip the ladyfingers in the coffee 1 at a time, turning quickly to coat on both sides. Lay the coffee-soaked ladyfingers side by side in a 9×13-inch pan, creating a solid layer. If you need to trim a few ladyfingers, do so just after dipping in the coffee.

Spread half the mascarpone cream on top of the ladyfingers. Place more ladyfingers soaked in coffee on top of the mascarpone cream to complete a second layer of ladyfingers. Top with another layer of mascarpone cream, spreading it evenly over the top with a spatula.

Using a sieve, sprinkle the unsweetened cocoa powder over the top. Refrigerate for at least 2 hours and preferably overnight.

Before serving, rinse and pat dry the raspberries.

TO PREPARE AHEAD: You can prepare the Tiramisu a day ahead and store, covered, in the refrigerator until ready to serve. Rinse and pat dry the raspberries and store in the refrigerator.

TO FINISH: Serve according to the Presentation Tip.

HANDY TIP: The type of ladyfingers you use is critical to the success of this recipe. Make sure you get Savoiardi ladyfingers—available at Italian specialty shops and many gourmet grocery stores.

SUBSTITUTION: If you prefer, you can use pasteurized eggs for the Tiramisu.

Orange Chocolate Cookies

1   cup butter
1/2   cup sugar
1/2   cup packed light brown sugar
Grated zest of 1 orange
2   tablespoons freshly squeezed
     orange juice

1   egg
3   cups flour
1/2   teaspoon baking soda
6   ounces miniature semisweet
     chocolate bits

Preparation Time: 15 min.
plus refrigeration
Cooking Time: 10 to
12 min. per batch

In a large mixing bowl, cream together the butter, sugar and light brown sugar with an electric mixer until light and fluffy.

Add the grated orange zest and the orange juice. Beat in the egg. Blend in the flour and baking soda. Stir in the semisweet chocolate bits.

On a flat surface, shape the dough into 4 logs, each with a diameter of about 1-inch. Make them as evenly round as possible. Wrap the logs in plastic wrap and refrigerate 4 hours or overnight.

Preheat the oven to 375°F/190°C. Cut the logs into 1/4-inch slices. Bake on an ungreased cookie sheet for 10 to 12 minutes or until the edges start to brown. Cool on a wire rack.

TO PREPARE AHEAD: You can make the cookies up to a week ahead. You'll only need about 16 cookies for your dinner party. Place the cooled cookies you need for your party on a small serving platter and cover securely with plastic wrap. Freeze the extra cookie dough or bake the cookies and store in an airtight container.

TO FREEZE: You can freeze the logs for up to 3 months. Wrap each log in plastic wrap and place in a sealable plastic bag. When ready to bake, thaw for 30 minutes (or briefly in the microwave), slice, and bake as directed.

Spring

Timeline

<table>
<tr>
<td>

ONE WEEK BEFORE
(ABOUT 3/4 HOUR)

Buy groceries and create the ambience

Prepare ahead Grapefruit Sorbet

</td>
<td>

TWO DAYS BEFORE
(ABOUT 3/4 HOUR)

Buy groceries and create the ambience

Put sparkling water, Champagne, white wine, and dessert wine (if using) in refrigerator

Put out red wine

Prepare ahead Orange Chocolate Cookies

</td>
<td>

ONE DAY BEFORE
(ABOUT 1 HOUR)

Prepare ahead Tiramisu

Prepare ahead Risotto with Spring Vegetables

</td>
</tr>
</table>

DAY OF PARTY (ABOUT 3 HOURS)

Buy groceries and create the ambience

Prepare ahead Veal with Sage and Wine

Prepare ahead Eggplant, Mozzarella and Tomato Stacks

Prepare ahead Arugula with Parmesan

Prepare ahead Cucumber Rounds with Smoked Salmon

5:00 PM
Shower and dress

6:30 PM
Prepare coffeemaker

Open wines, turn on music, light candles

Put out starter plates, salad plates, sorbet bowls, main course plates, and dessert plates

Prepare sugar and milk for coffee

7:00 PM
Preheat oven to 375°F/190°C

Put butter pats and rolls on butter plates

Put a cucumber slice in each water glass

Prepare ahead Apricot and Orange Champagne

Put out Cucumber Rounds with Smoked Salmon

Remove salad dressing from refrigerator

7:30 PM (GUESTS ARRIVE)
Open and pour Champagne; garnish with an orange twist (have water ready for those who prefer water)

8:00 PM
Finish Eggplant, Mozzarella and Tomato Stacks

Remove Risotto with Spring Vegetables from refrigerator

8:05 PM
Call people to table

Serve starter wine and water

8:10 PM
Serve Eggplant, Mozzarella and Tomato Stacks

Turn down oven to 350°F/180°C

8:30 PM
Finish Veal with Sage and Wine

Finish salad and serve

Take sorbet out of freezer

8:45 PM
Serve sorbet, garnished with mint

9:05 PM
Finish Risotto

Remove Veal with Sage and Wine from oven and plate according to Presentation Tip

9:15 PM
Serve main course and wine

Turn on coffeemaker

9:45 PM
Plate Tiramisu and garnish with raspberries

Serve dessert and dessert wine (if using)

10:00 PM
Serve coffee, tea, and after-dinner cookies

Grocery List

PANTRY ITEMS

1¹/₃ cups extra-virgin olive oil
Kosher salt
Freshly ground black pepper
2²/₃ cups sugar
¹/₂ cup light brown sugar
4 cups flour
¹/₂ teaspoon baking soda
6 cups vegetable broth
2 cups arborio rice
1 (14-ounce) package Savoiardi ladyfingers (about 48)
2 tablespoons unsweetened cocoa powder
6 ounces miniature semisweet chocolate bits
3 tablespoons pine nuts
1 (12-ounce) jar roasted almonds
8 (4-inch) wooden cocktail picks
Decaffeinated and regular coffee
Regular and herbal tea bags

ALCOHOL AND DRINKS

2 bottles Champagne or sparkling wine
2 bottles white wine for starter (Vernaccia)
2 bottles red wine for main (Dolcetto)
1 bottle dessert wine, if using (Sauternes or Moscato d'Asti)
4 bottles sparkling water
¹/₃ cup apricot brandy
3 tablespoons Grand Marnier
1 tablespoon vodka
2 cups dry white wine (for veal and risotto)
¹/₂ cup sweet marsala

PRODUCE

3 pink grapefruits

TWO DAYS BEFORE PARTY

PRODUCE

2 lemons
2 oranges
6 ounces raspberries
3 ounces fresh basil leaves
1 bunch fresh basil for starter garnish
1 bunch fresh dill
2 bunches fresh sage
¹/₄ cup chopped fresh flat-leaf parsley
1 bunch fresh mint for sorbet garnish
8 ounces arugula
2 medium eggplant
6 medium vine-ripened tomatoes
6 cloves garlic
2 medium onions
1 medium leek
1 pound asparagus
1 English cucumber
1 cucumber

DAIRY

1 cup whole milk
2 cups butter
5 eggs
4 ounces cream cheese
¹/₄ cup sour cream
3 (8-ounce) fresh mozzarella balls
³/₄ cup grated Parmesan cheese
4 ounces shaved Parmesan cheese
16 ounces mascarpone cheese
¹/₃ cup orange juice

MEAT, FISH AND DELI

4 ounces thinly sliced smoked salmon
3 pounds boned lean veal stew meat, cut into 1-inch pieces

FREEZER

1 cup frozen petite peas

DAY OF PARTY

BAKERY

8 rolls

Sole Florentine
menu

SERVES 8

Cocktail & Hors d'Oeuvres

Ritz Fizz

Warm Crab Meat Dip with Crackers and Vegetables

Cashews and Party Mix

Starter

Cream of Asparagus Soup

Rolls and Butter

 Gruner Veltliner or Verdejo

Salad

Mixed Greens with Truffle Oil Dressing

Palate Cleanser

Pineapple Orange Sorbet

Main Course

Sole Florentine

Seasoned Long Grain and Wild Rice

Shredded Zucchini

 White Bordeaux

Dessert

Chocolate Mousse

Almond Crisps

 Tawny Port or Banyuls

Coffee & Tea

Ritz Fizz

1	tablespoon amaretto	1/2	cup plus 2 tablespoons Champagne or dry sparkling wine	
1	tablespoon blue curaçao		Rose petal for garnish	
1	tablespoon lemon juice			

Fill the bottom of a Champagne glass with the amaretto, blue curaçao and lemon juice. Fill the glass with Champagne or dry sparkling wine. Garnish with a rose petal.

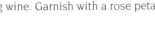

TO PREPARE AHEAD: Pour the amaretto, blue curaçao, and lemon juice into the bottom of each Champagne glass and place the glasses near where you are going to serve the apéritif. Have a few empty glasses available in case some guests prefer water. Place the rose petals in a bowl.

TO FINISH: Pour the Champagne, garnish with a rose petal, and serve.

HANDY TIP: One bottle of Champagne will make enough to serve 6.

Warm Crab Meat Dip

DIP

1	medium onion, chopped	8	ounces crab meat or flake-style crab meat substitute	
3/4	cup mayonnaise			
3/4	cup grated sharp white Cheddar cheese	1	package crackers	
1	clove garlic, minced	1/2	pound carrots, peeled and sliced	
1	teaspoon Beau Monde seasoning	1/2	pound celery, sliced	
1/4	teaspoon freshly ground black pepper			

Preparation Time: 10 min.
Cooking Time: 20 to 25 min.
Total Time: 30 to 35 min.

PRESENTATION TIP: Place the warm dip on a platter with the sliced carrots and celery and make sure to put out a spoon for the dip. Serve the crackers in a small basket.

Preheat the oven to 350°F/180°C. In a medium bowl, stir together the onion, mayonnaise, Cheddar cheese, garlic, Beau Monde seasoning, pepper and crab meat until well combined. Place in an ovenproof bowl. Bake for 20 to 25 minutes or until heated through.

TO PREPARE AHEAD: You can prepare the dip a day ahead, stopping before baking. Cover and store in the refrigerator. Prepare the carrots and celery and arrange on a platter. Cover with plastic wrap and refrigerate.

TO FINISH: Bake as directed above and serve according to the Presentation Tip.

HANDY TIP: This dip tastes great on Triscuit crackers.

Cream of Asparagus Soup

Preparation Time: 10 min.
Cooking Time: 25 min.
Total Time: 35 min.

PRESENTATION TIP:
To serve, ladle the soup into bowls. Garnish with a small dollop of sour cream and top with a small sprig of fresh dill.

1/2	cup butter
2	cups chopped onions
2	pounds asparagus, trimmed and cut into 1-inch pieces
1 1/2	teaspoons kosher salt, divided
1/2	cup flour

3	cups vegetable broth
3	cups milk
2	teaspoons chopped fresh dill
1/4	teaspoon white pepper, or to taste
1/4	cup sour cream for garnish
	Fresh dill sprigs for garnish

In a large soup pot, melt the butter. Add the chopped onions, asparagus and 1/2 teaspoon salt. Cook for 8 minutes over medium heat, stirring frequently.

Sprinkle the asparagus and onions with the flour. Cook over very low heat for 5 minutes, stirring constantly. Add the vegetable broth. Turn up the heat to medium and cook for 8 minutes, stirring frequently, until thickened. Remove from the heat and stir in the milk.

In the bowl of a blender, purée the asparagus mixture in batches until smooth. Return the purée to the cleaned-out soup pot. Add the chopped dill and the remaining 1 teaspoon salt. Season with the white pepper. Heat the soup gently, being careful not to let it boil.

TO PREPARE AHEAD: You can make the soup up to 2 days ahead, stopping before reheating. Cool, cover, and refrigerate.

TO FINISH: Reheat gently and serve according to the Presentation Tip.

HANDY TIP: If you prefer a thinner soup, feel free to add 1/4 cup milk a little at a time, until you reach the desired consistency.

SUBSTITUTION: If you don't have fresh dill, you can always use dried instead. If using dried herbs, use about 1/3 of the amount. For example, in this case you'd use just under 3/4 teaspoon dried dill.

Mixed Greens with Truffle Oil Dressing

4 ounces mixed baby greens

4 ounces baby spinach

DRESSING

2 tablespoons Champagne vinegar

1 teaspoon fresh lemon juice

$1/2$ teaspoon kosher salt

$1/4$ teaspoon freshly ground black pepper

3 tablespoons white truffle oil

2 tablespoons extra-virgin olive oil

Preparation Time: 10 min.

Rinse and spin dry the mixed greens and spinach. Place in a large bowl.

For the dressing: In a small bowl, whisk together the Champagne vinegar, lemon juice, salt and pepper. While continuing to whisk, add the truffle oil and extra-virgin olive oil in a steady stream. Continue whisking until the dressing thickens and emulsifies. Set aside.

To serve family-style, toss the mixed greens and spinach with enough dressing to coat.

TO PREPARE AHEAD: On the day of the party, make the salad dressing, cover, and refrigerate. Rinse and spin dry the mixed greens and spinach. Place in a large bowl, cover with a damp towel, and refrigerate. An hour before serving, remove the salad dressing from the refrigerator and return to room temperature.

TO FINISH: Whisk the dressing. Toss the mixed greens and spinach with enough dressing to coat and place on individual plates.

Spring

Pineapple Orange Sorbet

Preparation Time: 10 min.
Cooking Time: 5 min.
Ice Cream Maker: 20 min.
Total Time: 35 min. plus cooling time

2/3	cup sugar	1	cup orange juice
2/3	cup water	1	tablespoon Grand Marnier
1	(20-ounce) can sliced pineapple in own juice, drained		Mint sprigs for garnish

In a medium saucepan, heat the sugar and water until the sugar melts and the mixture starts to boil. Boil for 2 minutes. Remove from the heat and cool completely.

Place the sugar syrup, drained pineapple slices, orange juice and Grand Marnier in the bowl of a blender. Purée until smooth. Pour into an ice cream maker and process according to the manufacturer's directions. When finished, pour into an airtight container and freeze until ready to serve.

To Freeze: Prepare the sorbet up to a month ahead, place in an airtight container, and freeze.

To Finish: Remove the sorbet 15 minutes before serving to allow it to soften slightly. When ready, scoop into bowls, garnish with the mint, and serve.

Substitution: If you don't have Grand Marnier, try using Cointreau or Triple Sec instead.

Sole Florentine

1	(10-ounce) package frozen chopped spinach	8	skinless sole fillets
1	tablespoon butter	1	cup whipping cream
1	medium onion, finely chopped	3	tablespoons grated Parmesan cheese
1/2	teaspoon dried thyme		Paprika
	Kosher salt and freshly ground black pepper to taste		Flat-leaf parsley for garnish
			Lemon wedges for garnish

Preparation Time: 20 min.
Cooking Time: 30 min.
Total Time: 50 min.

Preheat the oven to 400°F/200°C. Butter a 9×13-inch ovenproof dish (or one that is big enough to just hold the fish).

Thaw the frozen spinach in the microwave. The easiest way is to put the spinach in a bowl, cover with plastic wrap, making a few slits with a knife, and microwave for about 3 minutes. Then let sit for a minute. If it's not yet thawed, microwave for another minute. When the spinach has thawed, squeeze out the excess liquid; a cheesecloth works best, but your hands will do.

Meanwhile, melt the butter in a large frying pan. Add the onion and cook over medium heat for about 5 to 8 minutes or until translucent. Stir in the thyme.

Add the thawed spinach to the onion. Season with salt and pepper. Cook over medium heat until the excess water has evaporated. Remove from the heat.

Place a fillet on your work surface, skinned side up. Season with salt and pepper. Place a mound of the spinach mixture in the middle of the fillet. Fold over the narrow end and then fold over the wider end, creating a tidy parcel. Repeat with the other fillets. Arrange the fillets seam side down in the prepared ovenproof dish. Make sure to leave a little space between the parcels. Season again with salt and pepper.

Pour the cream over the fillets. Sprinkle with the Parmesan cheese and paprika.

Bake for about 25 minutes or until the fish is white and cooked through. Remove from the oven and serve immediately.

PRESENTATION TIP:
To serve, place a mound of the Shredded Zucchini in the middle of a plate. Spread outwards, creating a ring of Shredded Zucchini with a hole in the middle. Fill the hole with a serving of the Seasoned Long Grain and Wild Rice. Top the rice with the fish and pour over a little of the cream from the pan. Garnish with the flat-leaf parsley and lemon wedges.

TO PREPARE AHEAD: If your fish is fresh, you can make up the parcels a day ahead. Make sure that the spinach mixture has cooled completely before you make up the parcels. Assemble the fish as directed above, stopping before the addition of the cream. Place the parcels in the ovenproof dish, cover with plastic wrap, and refrigerate. Prepare the flat-leaf parsley garnish and the lemon wedges, cover separately, and refrigerate.

TO FINISH: When ready to bake, add the cream, sprinkle with the Parmesan cheese and paprika, and bake as directed above. Serve according to the Presentation Tip.

Seasoned Long Grain and Wild Rice

Preparation Time: 10 min.
Cooking Time: 50 min.
Total Time: 60 min.

3	cups chicken broth	1	tablespoon butter
1	cup water	1	cup wild rice
3/4	teaspoon dried thyme	1	cup long grain white rice
3/4	teaspoon dried oregano		Kosher salt and freshly ground black
1	teaspoon garlic powder		pepper to taste
1/2	teaspoon onion powder		

In a large saucepan, combine the broth, water, thyme, oregano, garlic powder, onion powder and butter. Bring to a boil.

Add the wild rice and return to a boil. Reduce the heat to low; cover and simmer for 30 minutes.

After 30 minutes, add the long grain rice. Recover and simmer for an additional 20 minutes or until the liquid has evaporated. Let rest for 5 minutes and fluff with a fork. Season with salt and pepper.

TO PREPARE AHEAD: You can make the rice a day ahead. Place in a microwave-safe bowl, cool, cover, and refrigerate.

TO FINISH: Reheat in the microwave, fluff with a fork, and serve.

Shredded Zucchini

Preparation Time: 5 min.
Cooking Time: 5 min.
Total Time: 10 min.

2	pounds zucchini	Kosher salt and freshly ground black
2	tablespoons butter	pepper to taste

Rinse the zucchini and cut off the ends. Grate the zucchini either in a food processor or on the large holes of a box grater.

Melt the butter in a large sauté pan over medium heat. Toss the zucchini in the butter and sauté until just tender, about 2 to 3 minutes. Season with salt and pepper. Remove from the heat and serve.

TO PREPARE AHEAD: You can sauté the zucchini early on the day of the party. Place in a microwave-safe bowl, cool, cover, and refrigerate.

TO FINISH: Microwave to heat through.

Chocolate Mousse

MOUSSE

8	ounces semisweet chocolate bits
4	ounces dark chocolate
2	eggs, at room temperature
4	egg yolks, at room temperature
2	tablespoons Grand Marnier
4	egg whites
2	tablespoons sugar
1 1/4	cups whipping cream

WHIPPED CREAM

1	cup whipping cream
2	tablespoons sugar
1	ounce semisweet chocolate bits, grated

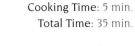

Preparation Time: 30 min.
Cooking Time: 5 min.
Total Time: 35 min.

PRESENTATION TIP:
Serve the Chocolate Mousse in stemmed glass dessert bowls. Top each Chocolate Mousse with a dollop of whipped cream. Using a microplane, grate a chocolate bit over the top and garnish with an Almond Crisp. This makes for a lovely presentation, and the crispness of the cookie is a nice complement to the smoothness of the mousse. Make sure to serve the extra Almond Crisps on a platter. They are always a hit!

For the mousse: Melt the semisweet chocolate and dark chocolate in the top of a double boiler over simmering water. Remove from the heat and cool slightly.

Beat the whole eggs and 4 egg yolks in a large bowl until blended. Beat in the Grand Marnier. Add the melted chocolate to the egg yolk mixture, beating constantly to prevent the eggs from cooking.

In a small bowl, beat the egg whites until frothy. Add 2 tablespoons sugar to the egg whites and beat until soft peaks form.

In another bowl, beat the whipping cream until soft peaks form. Fold a large spoonful of the egg whites into the chocolate mixture to loosen. Fold in the remaining egg whites and then the whipped cream.

Spoon the mousse into 8 serving dishes. Refrigerate for 6 hours or overnight.

For the whipped cream: When ready to serve, beat the whipping cream with the sugar in a small bowl with an electric mixer until firm peaks form.

TO PREPARE AHEAD: You can make the mousse up to 2 days ahead. Cover and refrigerate until ready to serve. On the day of the party, make the whipped cream and store, covered, in the refrigerator.

TO FINISH: Re-whip the cream if needed and serve according to the Presentation Tip.

HANDY TIP: An easy way to separate eggs is to open an egg onto your fingers. Let the white run between your fingers into a bowl; the yolk should stay intact in your hand. Make sure that your hands are completely clean and dry and free of any soap residue. Furthermore, make sure your bowl and beaters are clean, too. If you have any grease or soap residue in your bowl or on your beaters, your whites will not form stiff peaks when beaten.

SUBSTITUTIONS: If you prefer, you can use 2 tablespoons cold coffee in place of 2 tablespoons Grand Marnier. You can use pasteurized eggs for the mousse.

Almond Crisps

1/2	cup almond meal	1/2	cup sugar
1 1/2	tablespoons flour		A few drops almond extract
1/4	cup butter, softened		1 to 2 tablespoons milk

Preparation Time: 10 min.
Cooking Time: 5 min.
per batch

Preheat the oven to 400°F/200°C. Grease an airbake cookie sheet and line with parchment paper. If you don't have an airbake cookie sheet, grease and line a regular cookie sheet with parchment paper.

In a medium bowl, combine the almond meal, flour, butter, sugar and almond extract. With an electric mixer, blend until combined. Stir in the milk a little at a time, until the mixture is the consistency of a soft putty.

You can either drop the batter by small teaspoonfuls at least 2 inches apart on the prepared cookie sheet or use an icing pipe.

Bake until the cookies are set and a rich golden brown, about 6 to 8 minutes. You have to watch these closely because they burn relatively quickly. Remove the cookie sheet from the oven and let cool until set before removing to a wire rack.

TO PREPARE AHEAD: You can make the Almond Crisps a day ahead. Set aside 8 Almond Crisps in an airtight container for the garnish for Chocolate Mousse. Make up a small serving platter with a number of the remaining Almond Crisps, cover securely with plastic wrap, and put aside to serve after dinner with coffee.

TO FREEZE: You can freeze the unbaked dough for up to 3 months. Place in an airtight container and freeze. Thaw before using and bake as directed above.

HANDY TIP: If you want perfectly round Almond Crisps, use a pastry cutter to cut out rounds when the Almond Crisps are cooling on the baking sheet. Let cool until set before removing to a wire rack. Or, if you want to make curved Almond Crisps, try wrapping a warm Almond Crisp around a greased rolling pin. Let cool until set before removing to a wire rack to cool completely.

SUBSTITUTION: If you can't find almond meal, you can make your own by grinding 1/2 cup blanched almonds and 1 1/2 teaspoons sugar in a coffee grinder or food processor. If you prefer, you may also substitute 1/2 cup ground pecans for the almond meal.

Spring

Timeline

ONE WEEK BEFORE
(ABOUT 3/4 HOUR)

Buy groceries and create the ambience

Prepare ahead Pineapple Orange Sorbet

TWO DAYS BEFORE
(ABOUT 1/4 HOUR)

Buy groceries and create the ambience

Put sparkling water, Champagne, and white wines in refrigerator

Put out dessert wine (if using)

ONE DAY BEFORE
(ABOUT 1 3/4 HOURS)

Prepare ahead Chocolate Mousse

Prepare ahead Almond Crisps

Prepare ahead Warm Crab Meat Dip

DAY OF PARTY (ABOUT 2 HOURS)

Buy groceries and create the ambience

Prepare ahead Cream of Asparagus Soup

Prepare ahead Mixed Greens with Truffle Oil Dressing

Prepare Ahead Seasoned Long Grain and Wild Rice

Prepare ahead Shredded Zucchini

Prepare ahead Sole Florentine

5:00 PM
Shower and dress

6:30 PM
Prepare coffeemaker

Open wines, turn on music, light candles

Put out starter bowls, salad plates, sorbet bowls, main course plates, and dessert plates

Prepare sugar and milk for coffee

7:00 PM
Preheat oven to 350°F/180°C

Put butter pats and rolls on butter plates

Put a cucumber slice in each water glass

Prepare ahead Ritz Fizz

Put out cashews, party mix and crackers for dip

7:10 PM
Put Warm Crab Meat Dip in oven to heat

Remove salad dressing from refrigerator

7:30 PM (GUESTS ARRIVE)
Open and pour Champagne; garnish with a rose petal (have water ready for those who prefer water)

7:35 PM
Remove Warm Crab Meat Dip from oven and serve with vegetable platter

Turn up oven to 400°F/200°C

Start to reheat soup over medium-low heat; stir and check occasionally

8:00 PM
Check soup is hot

8:05 PM
Call people to table

Serve starter wine and water

8:10 PM
Serve Cream of Asparagus Soup according to Presentation Tip

8:30 PM
Finish salad and serve

Take sorbet out of freezer

8:45 PM
Finish Sole Florentine

Serve sorbet, garnished with mint

9:05 PM
Reheat Seasoned Long Grain and Wild Rice in microwave

Reheat Shredded Zucchini in microwave

Remove Sole Florentine from oven

Plate Sole Florentine according to Presentation Tip

9:15 PM
Serve main course and wine

Turn on coffeemaker

9:45 PM
Finish Chocolate Mousse and plate according to Presentation Tip

Serve dessert and dessert wine (if using)

10:00 PM
Serve coffee, tea, and after-dinner cookies

Grocery List

ONE WEEK BEFORE PARTY

PANTRY ITEMS
2 tablespoons extra-virgin olive oil
3 tablespoons white truffle oil
2 tablespoons Champagne vinegar
3/4 cup mayonnaise
Kosher salt
Freshly ground black pepper
1/4 teaspoon white pepper
1 teaspoon Beau Monde seasoning
1 1/4 teaspoons dried thyme
3/4 teaspoon dried oregano
1 teaspoon garlic powder
1/2 teaspoon onion powder
1 teaspoon paprika
2 cups sugar
2/3 cup flour
Few drops almond extract
3 cups vegetable broth
3 cups chicken broth
9 ounces semisweet chocolate bits
4 ounces dark chocolate
1/2 cup almond meal or blanched
    whole almonds
1 cup wild rice
1 cup long grain white rice

1 (20-ounce) can sliced pineapple in
    own juice
1 box crackers (Triscuits work well)
1 (12-ounce) jar cashews
1 (8.75-ounce) package party mix
Decaffeinated and regular coffee
Regular and herbal tea bags

ALCOHOL AND DRINKS
2 bottles Champagne or sparkling wine
2 bottles white wine for starter
    (Gruner Veltliner or Verdejo)
2 bottles white wine for main
    (White Bordeaux)
1 bottle dessert wine, if using
    (Tawny Port or Banyuls)
4 bottles sparkling water
1/2 cup Disaronno amaretto
    (or other amaretto)
1/2 cup blue curaçao
2 tablespoons Grand Marnier

DAIRY
1 1/2 cups butter
1 cup orange juice

TWO DAYS BEFORE PARTY

PRODUCE
6 lemons
8 rose petals for drink garnish
1 bunch fresh dill
1 bunch fresh mint for sorbet
    garnish
1 bunch fresh flat-leaf parsley for
    main garnish
4 ounces mixed baby greens
4 ounces baby spinach
4 onions
1 clove garlic
1/2 pound carrots
1/2 pound celery
2 pounds asparagus
2 pounds zucchini
1 cucumber

DAIRY
4 1/8 cups whole milk
6 eggs
3/4 cup grated sharp white Cheddar cheese
1/4 cup sour cream
3 1/4 cups whipping cream
3 tablespoons grated Parmesan cheese

MEAT, FISH AND DELI
8 skinless sole fillets
8 ounces crab meat or flake-style
    crab meat substitute

FREEZER
10 ounces frozen chopped spinach

DAY OF PARTY

BAKERY
8 rolls

Lamb Tagine
menu
SERVES 8

Cocktail & Hors d'Oeuvres
Melon-Infused Champagne

Hummus with Pita and Vegetables

Phyllo Cheese Bites

Mixed Nuts

Starter
Carrot, Fennel and Orange Soup

Rolls and Butter

 Spätlese Riesling

Salad
Mixed Greens with Grapes and Feta

Palate Cleanser
Mango Sorbet

Main Course
Lamb Tagine

Couscous with Cilantro and Parsley

 Rioja

Dessert
Crème Brûlée

Cinnamon Cookies

 Late Harvest Riesling or Cream Sherry

Coffee & Tea

Melon-Infused Champagne

MELON MIXER FOR 8
1/2 cantaloupe melon, seeded and diced
2/3 cup vodka
1/3 cup blue curaçao

FOR EACH COCKTAIL
2 tablespoons Melon Mixer
1/2 cup plus 2 tablespoons Champagne
or dry sparkling wine

Preparation Time: 10 min.
plus refrigeration

For the mixer: Place the melon in a small pitcher with the vodka and blue curaçao. Cover and let steep in the refrigerator for at least 2 hours. Before serving, strain the mixture through a sieve.

For each cocktail: Fill the bottom of a Champagne glass with 2 tablespoons of the Melon Mixer. Fill the glass with Champagne or dry sparkling wine.

TO PREPARE AHEAD MELON MIXER: A day before your party, mix together the melon, vodka, and blue curaçao. Cover and refrigerate overnight.

TO PREPARE AHEAD MELON-INFUSED CHAMPAGNE: Strain the melon mixture, pour 2 tablespoons into the bottom of each Champagne glass, and place the glasses near where you are going to serve the apéritif. Have a few empty glasses available in case some guests prefer water.

TO FINISH: Pour the Champagne and serve.

HANDY TIP: One bottle of Champagne makes enough to serve 6.

Hummus with Pita and Vegetables

1 (15-ounce) can chickpeas, drained
and rinsed
2 tablespoons extra-virgin olive oil
1/4 cup water
1/3 cup lemon juice
2 cloves garlic, minced
1/2 teaspoon kosher salt

1/3 cup tahini
Curly parsley for garnish
1 package pita bread, cut into
triangles
1 red bell pepper, cored,
seeded and sliced
1/2 pound carrots, peeled and sliced

Preparation Time: 25 min.

Combine the chickpeas, extra-virgin olive oil, water, lemon juice, garlic, salt and tahini in the bowl of a food processor. Blend until smooth.

Place in a serving bowl. Garnish with curly parsley. Serve with pita bread triangles, red pepper strips and carrot sticks.

TO PREPARE AHEAD: You can make the hummus up to 3 days ahead. Cover with plastic wrap and store in the refrigerator. Up to a day before the party, prepare the red pepper and carrots, place in plastic bags, and refrigerate. Cut up the pita bread and store in a plastic bag.

TO FINISH: Arrange an appetizer platter with the hummus, vegetables, and pita. Garnish the hummus with the curly parsley just before serving.

Phyllo Cheese Bites

8	ounces cream cheese, softened	2	tablespoons chopped fresh dill
6	ounces feta cheese, crumbled	1	egg
1/4	cup grated Parmesan cheese	1	pound frozen phyllo sheets, thawed
1	cup flat-leaf parsley, chopped	3/4	cup butter, melted

Preparation Time: 60 min.
Cooking Time: 20 to 25 min.
Total Time: 80 to 85 min.

Preheat the oven to 350°F/180°C.

In a medium bowl, combine the cream cheese, feta cheese, Parmesan cheese, parsley, dill and egg. Mix until well combined.

Place 1 phyllo sheet on the work surface with the long side facing you. Brush with butter. Cover with another phyllo sheet. Brush with butter. Cover with a third phyllo sheet and brush with butter. Cover the remaining phyllo sheets with a damp towel to prevent them from drying out. Cut the buttered phyllo sheets into 4 strips, starting from the long side.

Spoon about 1 1/2 teaspoons of the cheese mixture about 1 inch in from the short end of each of the 4 phyllo strips, leaving about 1/2 inch on each side. Start to roll in a cigar shape. After about 1 1/2 turns, fold in the sides and keep rolling, making an enclosed package. Place the phyllo rolls seam side down on an ungreased baking sheet. Brush with melted butter. Repeat the same procedure with the remaining phyllo sheets.

Bake until the phyllo bites are golden, about 20 to 25 minutes.

TO PREPARE AHEAD: Place the unbaked Phyllo Cheese Bites in the freezer. When frozen, transfer the Phyllo Cheese Bites to a sealable plastic bag and freeze for up to 3 months.

TO FINISH: Just before your guests arrive, place as many Phyllo Cheese Bites as you'll need on an ungreased baking sheet with the buttered side facing up. Bake as directed above and serve.

Carrot, Fennel and Orange Soup

Preparation Time: 15 min.
Cooking Time: 35 min.
Total Time: 50 min.

PRESENTATION TIP: To serve, ladle the soup into bowls. Garnish with a small dollop or swirl of crème fraîche and top with a pinch of reserved fennel greens.

2	tablespoons butter
1	fennel bulb, trimmed and chopped (set aside greens)
2	pounds carrots, peeled and cut into 1/4-inch slices
1	clove garlic, minced
5	cups vegetable stock

Grated zest of 1/2 orange
1/2	cup orange juice
1/2	teaspoon kosher salt, or to taste
1/4	teaspoon white pepper, or to taste
1	cup crème fraîche, divided

Reserved fennel greens for garnish

Melt the butter in a large soup pot. Add the chopped fennel and cook over medium heat, stirring occasionally, until softened, about 5 minutes.

Turn the heat to low and add the carrots and minced garlic. Cover and cook, stirring occasionally, for 10 minutes.

Add the stock, turn up the heat and bring to a boil. Cover and simmer for 20 minutes or until the carrots are soft.

Purée the soup in batches in the bowl of a food processor or blender until smooth. Return the soup to the cleaned-out soup pot. Add the orange zest and orange juice. Season with salt and pepper to taste.

Stir in 1/2 cup crème fraiche and then gently reheat until heated through.

TO PREPARE AHEAD: You can prepare the soup up to 2 days ahead. Cool, cover, and refrigerate. Remember to refrigerate the fennel greens for the garnish.

TO FINISH: Reheat the soup gently and serve according to the Presentation Tip.

TO FREEZE: This soup freezes well. Stop before adding the crème fraîche. Cool and freeze in an airtight container for up to 3 months. Thaw the soup and place in a large soup pot. Reheat gently, whisking often to make smooth. Once smooth, add the crème fraîche and heat through. Garnish with a dollop of crème fraîche.

HANDY TIP: For garnishes, you have several options. You can use a dollop of crème fraîche or a swirl of crème fraîche. To make a swirl, place the crème fraîche in a small plastic bag. Cut a very small hole in the corner. Dip the corner slightly into the soup and squeeze out a little crème fraîche as you make the shape of a swirl. With regard to greens, if you make the soup ahead and don't have any leftover fennel, you can always substitute chopped chives instead.

SUBSTITUTION: If you can't find crème fraîche at your local store, you can make your own. Stir together 1/2 cup whipping cream at room temperature with 1/4 cup sour cream at room temperature. Cover and let rest at room temperature for 24 hours, stirring once or twice. At the end of 24 hours, stir the thickened crème fraîche and refrigerate, covered, for at least 6 hours.

Mixed Greens with Grapes and Feta

DRESSING

2	tablespoons balsamic vinegar
1/4	teaspoon kosher salt
1/8	teaspoon freshly ground black pepper
1/3	cup extra-virgin olive oil

SALAD

8	ounces mixed baby greens
1	head radicchio
1/2	pound red grapes, halved
1/2	pound green grapes, halved
4	ounces crumbled feta cheese

For the dressing: In a small bowl, whisk together the balsamic vinegar, salt and pepper. While continuing to whisk, add the extra-virgin olive oil in a steady stream. Continue whisking until the dressing thickens and emulsifies. Set aside.

For the salad: Rinse and spin dry the mixed greens. Rinse and thinly slice the radicchio. Place the mixed greens and radicchio in a large bowl. Toss the mixed greens and radicchio with enough dressing to coat.

To serve family style, sprinkle the dressed mixed greens with the grape halves and the crumbled feta cheese.

TO PREPARE AHEAD: On the day of the party, make the salad dressing, cover, and refrigerate. Place the rinsed mixed greens and sliced radicchio in a large bowl, cover with a damp towel, and refrigerate. Slice the grapes and store in the refrigerator.

TO FINISH: Whisk the dressing. Toss the mixed greens and radicchio with enough dressing to coat and place on individual plates. Sprinkle with the grape halves and the crumbled feta cheese.

SUBSTITUTION: If you don't have feta, try using Roquefort or Gorgonzola.

Mango Sorbet

1	cup sugar
1	cup water
	Zest of 1 lime
2	pounds mangoes (about 3)

1/2	cup fresh lime juice (3 to 4 limes)
1	tablespoon vodka
	Mint sprigs for garnish

In a medium saucepan over medium heat, combine the sugar, water and lime zest. Heat until the sugar melts and the mixture starts to boil. Boil for 2 minutes. Remove from the heat and cool.

Cut the flesh from the mangoes and place in the bowl of a blender. Add the cooled sugar syrup, lime juice and vodka. Purée until smooth.

Pour into an ice cream maker and process according to the manufacturer's directions. When finished, pour into an airtight container and freeze until ready to serve.

TO FREEZE: Prepare the sorbet up to a month ahead, place in an airtight container, and freeze.

TO FINISH: Remove the sorbet 15 minutes before serving to allow it to soften slightly. When ready, scoop into bowls, garnish with the mint, and serve.

Lamb Tagine

1	large pinch of saffron stamens		$1^1/2$	teaspoons ground ginger
3	tablespoons hot water		$1^1/2$	teaspoons ground cinnamon
3	tablespoons extra-virgin olive oil, divided		1	teaspoon kosher salt
3	pounds stewing lamb, cut into 1-inch pieces		1	teaspoon ground cumin
3	onions, coarsely chopped		$1/2$	teaspoon cayenne
4	cloves garlic, minced		$1/2$	teaspoon turmeric
6	ounces dried apricots, halved		3	tablespoons honey
$2/3$	cup golden raisins		3	(14.5-ounce) cans diced tomatoes
1	tablespoon paprika			Freshly ground black pepper to taste
				Kosher salt to taste
				Curly parsley for garnish

Preparation Time: 15 min.
Cooking Time: $2^1/4$ to $2^3/4$ hours
Total Time: $2^1/2$ to 3 hours

PRESENTATION TIP:
Place a spoonful of Couscous with Cilantro and Parsley in the middle of each plate. Top with a spoonful of Lamb Tagine. Garnish with the curly parsley and serve.

Preheat the oven to 325°F/160°C. In a small bowl, combine the saffron and hot water. Set aside.

Heat 1 tablespoon of the extra-virgin olive oil in a large Dutch oven with a lid. Add $1/3$ of the lamb and cook until brown. When browned, remove with a slotted spoon and set aside. Add another tablespoon of olive oil to the Dutch oven and repeat with another $1/3$ of the lamb. Repeat with the remaining olive oil and lamb.

Once the lamb has been removed, add the chopped onions and minced garlic to the Dutch oven. Cook, stirring occasionally, over medium heat for 5 to 8 minutes or until translucent.

Stir in the saffron and hot water, apricots, golden raisins, paprika, ginger, cinnamon, 1 teaspoon salt, cumin, cayenne, turmeric, honey and tomatoes. Add the browned lamb. Stir to combine. Bring to a boil. Season with pepper and place, covered, in the oven. Cook for 2 to $2^1/2$ hours or until the meat is very tender. Remove from the oven and season with salt and pepper to taste.

TO PREPARE AHEAD: You can make the Lamb Tagine up to 2 days ahead. After you take the Lamb Tagine out of the oven, cool, cover, and refrigerate.

TO FINISH: When ready to serve, preheat the oven to 350°F/180°C. Add $1/3$ to $1/2$ cup water to the Lamb Tagine and place in the oven, covered, for 30 to 40 minutes, or until heated through. Serve according to the Presentation Tip.

TO FREEZE: You can freeze the Lamb Tagine for up to 3 months. After you take the Lamb Tagine out of the oven, cool and freeze in an airtight container. Thaw and reheat as above.

Couscous with Cilantro and Parsley

4	cups water		¼	cup chopped flat-leaf parsley
2	tablespoons extra-virgin olive oil		2	(10-ounce) boxes couscous
¼	cup chopped fresh cilantro			

In a large saucepan, bring the water, extra-virgin olive oil, cilantro and flat-leaf parsley to a boil. Stir in the couscous. Remove from the heat, cover and let stand for 5 minutes.
Just before serving, fluff the couscous with a fork.

TO PREPARE AHEAD: You can make the couscous ahead on the day of the party. Place in a microwave-safe bowl, cool, cover and refrigerate.

TO FINISH: Reheat in the microwave. Fluff with a fork before serving.

SUBSTITUTION: For a slightly different flavor, you could always substitute chopped mint for the cilantro.

Cinnamon Cookies

COOKIE DOUGH

1	cup butter		2	teaspoons cream of tartar
1½	cups sugar		¼	teaspoon salt
2	eggs			
2	teaspoons vanilla extract		**SUGAR COATING AND ASSEMBLY**	
2¾	cups flour		¼	cup sugar
1	teaspoon baking soda		2	teaspoons ground cinnamon

For the dough: In a large mixing bowl, cream together the butter and sugar with an electric mixer. Beat in the eggs and vanilla.
In a medium bowl, sift together the flour, baking soda, cream of tartar and salt. Beat the flour mixture into the butter mixture until thoroughly combined. Cover and chill for an hour.
For the coating: In a small bowl, mix together the sugar and cinnamon. Remove the dough from the refrigerator and roll the dough into 1-inch balls. Roll each ball in the sugar coating to coat.
If baking immediately, place two inches apart on an ungreased cookie sheet. Bake at 375°F/190°C for 10 to 12 minutes or until the edges of the cookies are golden brown.
Cool cookies on a wire rack. Store the cookies in an airtight container for up to a week.

TO PREPARE AHEAD: Make the dough balls and roll in the sugar coating. Place the balls on an ungreased cookie sheet and freeze. When frozen, transfer the dough balls to a plastic bag and freeze for up to 3 months.

TO FINISH: Preheat the oven to 375°F/190°C and bake as many cookies as you'll need for your party according to the directions above. When cool, place on a small serving platter and cover securely with plastic wrap.

Crème Brûlée

1	quart whipping cream	1 1/2	tablespoons vanilla extract
10	egg yolks	1/3	cup sugar for caramelized topping
3/4	cup sugar		

Preparation Time: 15 min.
Cooking Time: 40 to 50 min.
Total Time: 55 to 65 min.

Preheat the oven to 300°F/140°C. Put on a kettle of water to boil.

In a large heavy saucepan, heat the cream until it simmers. While you are heating the cream, beat the egg yolks with an electric mixer in a medium bowl until smooth. Beat in the sugar gradually, blending until the eggs are a light lemon yellow in color.

When the cream starts to simmer, remove it from the heat. While beating on very low speed, pour the cream slowly into the egg mixture. Make sure to keep beating in order to prevent the eggs from cooking. Add the vanilla. Strain the mixture through a fine sieve.

Divide the mixture among 8 ramekins. Place the ramekins in a large roasting pan. Pour enough boiling water into the pan to come halfway up the sides of the ramekins. If using 1 1/2-inch-tall ramekins, bake, uncovered, for 40 to 50 minutes or until the custard is set.

Using tongs, remove the custards from the boiling water and let cool to room temperature. Cover and refrigerate for at least 3 hours and up to 2 days.

For the caramelized topping: Sprinkle about 1 1/2 to 2 teaspoons of sugar over the top of each custard. Use a kitchen torch to caramelize the tops. If you don't have a kitchen torch, place the sugar-topped custards in a shallow flameproof dish filled with ice cubes and place under a preheated broiler until the sugar melts and caramelizes. This won't take long, so watch them closely!

TO PREPARE AHEAD: You can make the Crème Brûlée up to 2 days ahead, stopping after baking. Cool, cover, and refrigerate. Make sure your kitchen torch is in working order if you are using one to make the caramelized topping.

TO FINISH: Follow the Caramelized Topping directions above. Place each ramekin on a dessert plate and serve.

HANDY TIP: Ramekins can vary in size. I use 6-ounce ramekins, but there are some that are smaller and some that are larger. If you end up having leftover custard, don't worry! It may have to do with the size of your ramekins. If you use 3/4-inch-tall ramekins, reduce the cooking time to 35 to 45 minutes.

Timeline

ONE WEEK BEFORE
(ABOUT 2 HOURS)

Buy groceries and create the ambience

Prepare ahead Mango Sorbet

Prepare ahead Phyllo Cheese Bites

Prepare ahead Cinnamon Cookies

TWO DAYS BEFORE
(ABOUT 1/4 HOUR)

Buy groceries and create the ambience

Put sparkling water, Champagne, white wine, and dessert wine (if using) in refrigerator

Put out red wine

ONE DAY BEFORE
(ABOUT 1 HOUR)

Prepare ahead Crème Brûlée

Prepare ahead Hummus

Prepare ahead Melon Mixer

DAY OF PARTY (ABOUT 3 HOURS)

Buy groceries and create the ambience

Finish Cinnamon Cookies

Prepare ahead Lamb Tagine

Prepare ahead Carrot, Fennel and Orange Soup

Prepare ahead Mixed Greens with Grapes and Feta

Prepare ahead Couscous with Cilantro and Parsley

5:00 PM
Shower and dress

6:30 PM
Prepare coffeemaker

Open wines, turn on music, light candles

Put out starter bowls, salad plates, sorbet bowls, main course plates, and dessert plates

Prepare sugar and milk for coffee

7:00 PM
Preheat oven to 350°F/180°C

Put butter pats and rolls on butter plates

Put a cucumber slice in each water glass

Prepare ahead Melon-Infused Champagne

Finish Hummus with Pita and Vegetables and put out

Put out mixed nuts

7:15 PM
Finish Phyllo Cheese Bites

Remove salad dressing from refrigerator

7:30 PM (GUESTS ARRIVE)
Open and pour Champagne (have water ready for those who prefer water)

7:35 PM
Remove Phyllo Cheese Bites from oven and serve

Keep oven at 350°F/180°C

Start to reheat soup over medium-low heat; stir and check occasionally

8:00 PM
Check soup is hot

8:05 PM
Call people to table

Serve starter wine and water

8:10 PM
Serve soup according to Presentation Tip

8:30 PM
Finish Lamb Tagine

Finish salad and serve

Take sorbet out of freezer

8:45 PM
Serve sorbet, garnished with mint

9:05 PM
Reheat Couscous with Cilantro and Parsley in microwave

Remove Lamb Tagine from oven

Plate Lamb Tagine according to Presentation Tip

9:15 PM
Serve main course and wine

Turn on coffeemaker

9:45 PM
Finish Crème Brûlée

Serve dessert and dessert wine (if using)

10:00 PM
Serve coffee, tea, and after-dinner cookies

Grocery List

Pantry Items

3/4 cup extra-virgin olive oil
2 tablespoons good-quality balsamic vinegar
Kosher salt
Freshly ground black pepper
1/4 teaspoon white pepper
1 pinch saffron stamens
1 tablespoon paprika
1 1/2 teaspoons ground ginger
3 1/2 teaspoons ground cinnamon
1 teaspoon ground cumin
1/2 teaspoon cayenne
1/2 teaspoon turmeric
4 cups sugar
2 3/4 cups flour
1 teaspoon baking soda
2 teaspoons cream of tartar
2 1/4 tablespoons vanilla extract
5 cups vegetable broth
2 (10-ounce) boxes couscous
1 (15-ounce) can chickpeas
3 (14.5-ounce) cans diced tomatoes
3 tablespoons honey
1/3 cup tahini
6 ounces dried apricots
2/3 cup golden raisins
1 (12-ounce) jar mixed nuts
1 small kitchen torch for caramelizing the Crème Brûlée (optional)

8 ramekins for Crème Brûlée
Decaffeinated and regular coffee
Regular and herbal tea bags

Alcohol and Drinks

2 bottles Champagne or sparkling wine
2 bottles white wine for starter (Spätlese Riesling)
2 bottles red wine for main (Rioja)
1 bottle dessert wine, if using (Late Harvest Riesling or Cream Sherry)
4 bottles sparkling water
3/4 cup vodka
1/3 cup blue curaçao

Produce

3 mangoes
4 limes
1 cup flat-leaf parsley
1/8 cup chopped fresh dill

Dairy

2 3/8 cups butter
13 eggs
8 ounces cream cheese
6 ounces feta cheese
1/4 cup grated Parmesan cheese

Freezer

1 (1-pound) package frozen phyllo sheets

Produce

1/2 cantaloupe
2 lemons
1 orange
1/2 pound seedless red grapes
1/2 pound seedless green grapes
1/4 cup chopped flat-leaf parsley
1 bunch curly parsley for appetizer and main garnish
1/4 cup chopped fresh cilantro
1 bunch fresh mint for sorbet garnish
8 ounces mixed baby greens
1 head radicchio
7 cloves garlic
2 1/2 pounds carrots
1 red bell pepper

1 fennel bulb
3 onions
1 cucumber

Dairy

1 cup whole milk
1 cup crème fraîche
4 ounces crumbled feta cheese
1 quart whipping cream
1/2 cup orange juice

Meat, Fish and Deli

3 pounds stewing lamb, cut into 1-inch pieces

Bakery

1 package pita bread

Bakery

8 rolls

Summer

Fish Milanese

SERVES 6

Sparkling Raspberry • Pepperoni Pinwheels • Basil Parmesan Spread with Crostini • Spaghetti with Tomato Sauce • Caesar Salad • Strawberry Mint Sorbet • Fish Milanese with Parsley Garlic Sauce • Sautéed Red and Yellow Peppers • Mixed Berries with Moscato and Vanilla Ice Cream • Walnut Biscotti

Marinated Flank Steak

SERVES 8

Amaretto and Peach Champagne • Shrimp Cocktail • Herbed Goat Cheese and Grape Crostini • Potato Leek Soup • Baby Spinach with Pine Nuts and Goat Cheese • Melon Sorbet • Marinated Flank Steak • Wild Rice Salad • Summer Corn Salad • Strawberry-Glazed Cheesecake • Shortbread

Lemon Chicken with Rosemary

SERVES 8

Peach Champagne • Tzatziki with Pita and Vegetables • Stuffed Mushrooms with Provolone • Shells with Garlic, Tomato and Basil • Mixed Greens with Goat Cheese Rounds • Blackberry Sorbet • Lemon Chicken with Rosemary • Tabbouleh • Roasted Asparagus • Panna Cotta with Fresh Berries • Lemon Wafers

Mahi Mahi with Mango Salsa

SERVES 8

Margarita Champagne • Guacamole, Tomato Salsa and Chips • Zucchini Soup • Mixed Greens with Citrus Vinaigrette • Pineapple Sorbet • Mahi Mahi with Mango Salsa • Sugar Snap Peas • Baby New Potatoes • Lime Pie • Sugar Cookies

Fish Milanese

menu

SERVES 6

Cocktail & Hors d'Oeuvres

Sparkling Raspberry

Pepperoni Pinwheels

Basil Parmesan Spread with Crostini

Roasted Almonds

Starter

Spaghetti with Tomato Sauce

Rolls and Butter

Dolcetto

Salad

Caesar Salad

Palate Cleanser

Strawberry Mint Sorbet

Main Course

Fish Milanese with Parsley Garlic Sauce

Sautéed Red and Yellow Peppers

Soave

Dessert

Mixed Berries with Moscato and Vanilla Ice Cream

Walnut Biscotti

Moscato d'Asti

Coffee & Tea

Sparkling Raspberry

1 1/2 tablespoons raspberry liqueur
1/2 cup plus 2 tablespoons Champagne
or dry sparkling wine

Raspberry for garnish

Fill the bottom of a Champagne glass with the raspberry liqueur. Fill the glass with Champagne or dry sparkling wine. Garnish with a raspberry.

TO PREPARE AHEAD: Pour the raspberry liqueur into the bottom of each Champagne glass and place the glasses near where you are going to serve the apéritif. Have a few empty glasses available in case some guests prefer water. Set aside the raspberries in a bowl.

TO FINISH: Pour the Champagne, stir, garnish with a raspberry, and serve.

HANDY TIP: One bottle of Champagne makes enough to serve 6.

Pepperoni Pinwheels

1 sheet frozen puff pastry, thawed
4 teaspoons Dijon mustard
2 teaspoons honey
24 slices pepperoni
1/3 cup grated Parmesan cheese

1/2 teaspoon dried thyme
1/2 teaspoon dried oregano
1/4 teaspoon freshly ground
black pepper
1 egg, beaten

Preparation Time: 20 min.
Cooking Time: 10 to
15 min.
Total Time: 30 to 35 min.
plus freezing time

Cut the sheet of puff pastry in half, beginning in the middle of the longer side.

In a small bowl, mix together the Dijon mustard and honey. Spread half the mustard mixture on 1 of the pieces of pastry, leaving a 1-inch plain border along 1 of the long edges.

Place 1/2 of the pepperoni in a single layer on top of the mustard, making sure to maintain the plain edge. You may have to cut some of the pieces. Sprinkle 1/2 of the Parmesan cheese on top, again maintaining the plain edge. Sprinkle with 1/4 teaspoon thyme, 1/4 teaspoon oregano and 1/8 teaspoon pepper. Brush the plain edge with the beaten egg.

Starting from the side opposite the plain edge, roll up the pastry, sealing at the plain edge. Repeat with the remaining ingredients. Wrap the rolls in plastic. Freeze until firm, about 30 minutes.

Preheat the oven to 400°F/200°C. Slice each roll into approximately twenty-five 1/4-inch rounds. Place the rounds on 2 ungreased baking sheets and bake for 10 to 15 minutes, or until golden brown. Remove to a tray and serve.

TO PREPARE AHEAD: Make the Pepperoni Pinwheels as directed above, stopping before baking. Place the trays of unbaked Pepperoni Pinwheels in the freezer. Once frozen, transfer the Pepperoni Pinwheels to a sealable plastic bag and store in the freezer for up to 3 months.

TO FINISH: Place the number of Pepperoni Pinwheels you need on an ungreased baking sheet and bake as directed above.

Basil Parmesan Spread with Crostini

Preparation Time: 30 min.
Cooking Time: 20 min.
Total Time: 50 min. plus refrigeration

PRESENTATION TIP:
Invert the bowl of spread on a platter and peel off the plastic wrap. Garnish the top with a few leaves of basil. Serve with the crostini. Don't forget to put out a knife!

SPREAD
1   cup packed baby spinach leaves
1   cup packed fresh basil leaves
1   clove garlic
1/4 cup extra-virgin olive oil
1   cup grated Parmesan cheese
8   ounces cream cheese, softened
4   ounces goat cheese, softened
1/3 cup chopped walnuts

1/3 cup sun-dried tomatoes in oil, drained and chopped
Basil leaves for garnish

CROSTINI
French baguette
2   tablespoons extra-virgin olive oil for brushing

For the spread: Combine the spinach, basil and garlic in the bowl of a food processor. Process until chopped. While continuing to process, gradually add the extra-virgin olive oil and Parmesan cheese.

In a small bowl, mix together the cream cheese and goat cheese until smooth.

Line a 3-cup bowl with plastic wrap. Carefully spread 1/3 of the cream cheese mixture over the bottom. Then top with 1/2 of the spinach mixture, 1/2 of the walnuts and 1/2 of the sun-dried tomatoes. Repeat the layers, ending with the remaining 1/3 of the cream cheese mixture. Cover and refrigerate for at least 8 hours and preferably overnight.

For the crostini: Preheat the oven to 350°F/180°C. Cut the baguette into 3/8-inch slices. Brush both sides of each slice with the extra-virgin olive oil and place on an ungreased baking sheet. Bake for 10 minutes, turn the slices over and bake for another 10 minutes, or until lightly toasted. Remove to a wire rack to cool completely.

TO PREPARE AHEAD: You can make the Basil Parmesan Spread up to 3 days ahead. Store, covered, in the refrigerator. You can toast the crostini up to 2 days ahead. When cool, store the crostini in a plastic bag at room temperature.

TO FINISH: Arrange an appetizer platter according to the Presentation Tip.

HANDY TIP: If you prefer, you can also use a 3-cup springform pan for the spread. Grease the pan and line the bottom with parchment paper. Proceed as above. When chilled, release the edge and invert on a plate. You can then peel off the parchment paper.

HANDY TIP #2: Leftover spread tastes great on sandwiches, chicken, or mixed with a little extra-virgin olive oil and tossed with spaghetti.

SUBSTITUTION: If you don't have sun-dried tomatoes in oil, substitute sun-dried tomatoes from the deli. For a change, try serving the spread with crackers or baguette slices instead of the crostini.

Spaghetti with Tomato Sauce

1/4 cup extra-virgin olive oil
1 medium onion, chopped
1 clove garlic, minced
1 carrot, chopped
1 celery stalk, chopped
1 (28-ounce) can diced tomatoes
Kosher salt and freshly ground black
    pepper to taste

1 tablespoon chopped fresh basil
1 pound spaghetti
2/3 cup grated Parmesan cheese
    to serve
Basil sprigs for garnish

Preparation Time: 15 min.
Cooking Time: 30 min.
Total Time: 45 min.

PRESENTATION TIP:
Place a mound of the spaghetti coated in the sauce in each bowl. Sprinkle each bowl with a little grated Parmesan cheese. Top with a dollop of the reserved sauce. Place the top of the basil sprig in the center. Make sure to have extra grated Parmesan cheese on the table.

Place the extra-virgin olive oil, onion, garlic, carrot, celery and tomatoes in a large saucepan. Simmer for 30 minutes. Purée the sauce in a blender or the bowl of a food processor. Return the puréed sauce to the pan. Season with salt and pepper and reheat gently.

Bring a large pot of water to a boil. Cook the spaghetti according to the package directions. Drain. Toss the pasta with enough of the sauce to coat, reserving some sauce for garnish.

TO PREPARE AHEAD: Make the sauce, cool, and place in an airtight container. Freeze for up to 3 months.

TO FINISH: Thaw the sauce overnight or in the microwave. Cook the pasta according to the package directions, reheat the sauce in the microwave, and serve according to the Presentation Tip.

HANDY TIP: I like to double, triple, and sometimes even quadruple this recipe and freeze it in airtight containers. That way, I can always have it on hand, either for a fancy get-together or for a midweek meal with family.

Caesar Salad

Preparation Time: 15 min.
Cooking Time: 12 min.
Total Time: 27 min.

CROUTONS

1½ tablespoons extra-virgin olive oil
1 clove garlic, minced
¼ teaspoon dried thyme
¼ teaspoon dried rosemary
3 slices bread, crusts removed and
   bread cut into ¾-inch cubes
   (about 3 cups)

DRESSING

1 egg yolk
1 teaspoon Dijon mustard
1 clove garlic, minced
1 teaspoon anchovy paste
1 teaspoon lemon juice
1 teaspoon Worcestershire sauce
⅛ teaspoon kosher salt
Freshly ground black pepper to taste
⅓ cup extra-virgin olive oil
2 tablespoons grated
   Parmesan cheese
1 large head romaine
   (about 10 ounces)
⅓ cup shredded Parmesan cheese

Preheat the oven to 375°F/190°C.

For the croutons: Heat the extra-virgin olive oil in a large frying pan. Add the garlic, thyme and rosemary and sauté until fragrant, about 1 minute. Add the bread cubes and toss to coat. Place the cubes on an ungreased baking sheet in a single layer and bake for 10 minutes or until golden. Let cool.

For the dressing: While the croutons are baking, place the egg yolk, Dijon mustard, garlic, anchovy paste, lemon juice, Worcestershire sauce, salt and pepper in a bowl. Mix together with a whisk. While continuing to whisk, add the extra-virgin olive oil in a stream, whisking until the mixture thickens. Stir in the grated Parmesan cheese.

Wash the romaine and spin dry. Cut crosswise into 1½-inch pieces. Place in a large bowl. Toss the romaine with enough dressing to coat.

To serve family style, sprinkle the romaine with the shredded Parmesan cheese and top with the croutons.

TO PREPARE AHEAD: You can make the croutons up to a week ahead, cool, and store in a plastic bag. You can make the dressing early on the day, cover, and refrigerate. Wash the romaine, spin dry, cut crosswise into 1½-inch pieces, place in a large bowl, cover with a damp towel, and refrigerate.

TO FINISH: Whisk the dressing. Toss the romaine with enough dressing to coat and place on individual plates. Sprinkle with the shredded Parmesan cheese and top with the croutons.

SUBSTITUTION: If you're uncomfortable using a raw egg, use 1 tablespoon of mayonnaise instead.

Strawberry Mint Sorbet

1	cup sugar		16	ounces fresh strawberries
1	cup water			Juice of 1 lemon
1/3	cup chopped fresh mint leaves		1	tablespoon vodka
	(about 3/4 ounce)			Mint sprigs for garnish

Preparation Time: 10 min.
Cooking Time: 5 min.
Ice Cream Maker: 20 min.
Total Time: 35 min. plus
cooling time

In a medium saucepan, heat the sugar, water and chopped mint until the sugar melts and the mixture starts to boil. Boil for 2 minutes. Remove from the heat and cool completely.

Pour the mint mixture through a fine sieve. Use the back of a spoon to push the mixture through the sieve. Cover and refrigerate until cold, about an hour.

Rinse, dry and hull the strawberries. Place the strawberries in the bowl of a blender. Add the minted sugar syrup, lemon juice and vodka. Purée until smooth.

Pour into an ice cream maker and process according to the manufacturer's directions. When finished, pour into an airtight container and freeze until ready to serve.

TO PREPARE AHEAD: Prepare the sorbet up to a month ahead, place in an airtight container, and freeze.

TO FINISH: Remove the sorbet 15 minutes before serving to allow it to soften slightly. When ready, scoop into bowls, garnish with the mint, and serve.

Summer

Fish Milanese with Parsley Garlic Sauce

SERVES 6

Preparation Time: 20 min.
Cooking Time: 10 min.
Total Time: 30 min. plus
1 hour marinating time

PRESENTATION TIP:
Place a small mound of the dressed arugula on a plate. Place the tilapia overlapping some of the arugula. Spoon some Parsley Garlic Sauce over the top of the tilapia and add a spoonful of Sautéed Red and Yellow Peppers. Garnish with lemon wedges and flat-leaf parsley.

MARINADE
1	medium onion, chopped
3	tablespoons lemon juice
1/2	cup extra-virgin olive oil
6	skinless tilapia fillets
1	cup flour
3	eggs
2	tablespoons milk
1 1/2	cups plain bread crumbs
1/4	cup extra-virgin olive oil, divided
1/4	cup butter, divided

PARSLEY GARLIC SAUCE
1/2	cup butter
2	cloves garlic, minced

2	tablespoons finely chopped fresh flat-leaf parsley

ARUGULA WITH LEMON OIL DRESSING
4	ounces arugula
1 1/2	tablespoons fresh lemon juice
1/4	teaspoon kosher salt
1/8	teaspoon freshly ground black pepper
3	tablespoons extra-virgin olive oil

Lemon wedges for garnish
Flat-leaf parsley for garnish

For the marinade: Combine the chopped onion, lemon juice and extra-virgin olive oil in a shallow dish. Mix well. Add the fish and coat with the onion mixture. Cover and marinate in the refrigerator for 1 hour, turning the fish after 30 minutes. Remove the fillets from the marinade and discard the marinade.

Place the flour on a dinner plate. In a medium bowl, beat together the eggs and milk. Place the plain bread crumbs on another dinner plate.

Coat the fillets in the flour, shaking off the excess. Dip the fillets in the egg mixture. Dredge both sides of the fillets in the breadcrumbs, making sure to press the breadcrumbs on firmly.

Heat 2 tablespoons extra-virgin olive oil and 2 tablespoons butter in a large frying pan. If you are using more than 1 frying pan, put a similar amount of extra-virgin olive oil and butter in the second frying pan.

Cook the fish over medium heat until golden brown and cooked through, about 2 to 3 minutes per side. Drain on paper towels. Repeat with the rest of the fillets.

For the sauce: While the fish is cooking, melt the butter in a small frying pan over medium heat. Add the garlic and cook until the garlic is fragrant, about 1 minute. Stir in the chopped parsley. Remove from the heat.

For the arugula: Rinse and spin dry the arugula. In a small bowl, whisk together the lemon juice, salt, pepper and extra-virgin olive oil until the mixture thickens and emulsifies. Toss the arugula with enough dressing to coat. Serve according to the Presentation Tip.

TO PREPARE AHEAD: On the day of the party, marinate and bread the fish ahead. Place on a plate, separating the layers with parchment paper. Cover and refrigerate until needed. If using 2 frying pans, place the oil and butter in the pans in preparation. Rinse, spin dry, and place the arugula in a large bowl. Cover with a damp towel and refrigerate. Make the Lemon Oil Dressing and refrigerate. Make the Parsley Garlic Sauce and set aside.

TO FINISH: When ready to cook, heat the oil and butter, add the fish, and cook as directed above. While the fish is cooking, gently reheat the Parsley Garlic Sauce. Whisk the Lemon Oil Dressing and toss the arugula with enough dressing to coat. Serve according to the Presentation Tip.

HANDY TIP: Although cooking the fish during the meal is really pretty easy, if you must, you can cook the fish ahead on the day. Cool to room temperature on paper towels. If possible, leave at room temperature until needed. Preheat the oven to 400°F/200°C. Place the fish on a baking sheet and reheat for 8 to 10 minutes. Serve immediately. Although not exactly the same as cooking it just before serving, it will still be good.

HANDY TIP #2: Pressed for time? Skip marinating the fish. It will still taste great.

SUBSTITUTION: If you prefer, you can make this recipe with chicken cutlets instead of fish. Prepare as directed above. If you want, substitute 1/2 cup grated Parmesan cheese for 1/2 cup of the bread crumbs. Note that seasoned bread crumbs would work well with the chicken, too.

Sautéed Red and Yellow Peppers

Preparation Time: 15 min.
Cooking Time: 5 to 8 min.
Total Time: 20 to 23 min.

2	tablespoons extra-virgin olive oil	1	large onion, sliced
2	red bell peppers, cored and sliced	2	cloves garlic, minced
2	yellow bell peppers, cored and sliced		Kosher salt and freshly ground black pepper

Heat the extra-virgin olive oil in a large frying pan over medium heat. Add the red and yellow peppers, onion and garlic. Sauté until tender-crisp, about 5 to 8 minutes. Season with salt and pepper.

TO PREPARE AHEAD: You can sauté the red and yellow peppers a day ahead. Place in a microwave-safe bowl, cool, cover, and refrigerate.

TO FINISH: Reheat in the microwave. Note that the red bell peppers may lose a bit of their color, but they will still taste great.

HANDY TIP: For a different look, you can chop the peppers and onion into 1/2-inch dice and cook as directed above.

Mixed Berries with Moscato and Vanilla Ice Cream

PRESENTATION TIP:
Place a scoop of vanilla ice cream in a dessert bowl. Add a heaping spoonful of the mixed berries and Moscato d'Asti. Serve with Walnut Biscotti for dipping.

6	ounces blackberries	1/4	cup sugar
6	ounces blueberries	1 1/2	cups Moscato d'Asti
6	ounces raspberries	1	quart vanilla ice cream
12	ounces strawberries		

Rinse the berries and pat dry. Hull and halve the strawberries. Gently combine all the berries in a medium bowl. Add the sugar and toss to coat. Add the Moscato d'Asti. Cover and refrigerate for 30 to 60 minutes.

TO PREPARE AHEAD: You can rinse and pat dry the berries early on the day. Hull and halve the strawberries and place all the berries in a bowl. Cover and refrigerate.

TO FINISH: Thirty to sixty minutes before serving, add the sugar and Moscato D'Asti, cover, and refrigerate. Serve according to the Presentation Tip.

HANDY TIP: The great thing about this dessert is that you will have enough Moscato d'Asti left over to serve as the dessert wine.

Walnut Biscotti

1 1/2 cups coarsely chopped walnuts
1/2 cup butter
1 cup sugar
2 eggs
Zest of 1 orange
Zest of 1 lemon

1 1/2 teaspoons vanilla extract
1/4 teaspoon almond extract
2 1/2 cups flour
1/2 teaspoon baking soda
1/2 teaspoon baking powder
1/4 teaspoon kosher salt

Preparation Time: 20 min.
Cooking Time: 40 to 45 min.
Total Time: 60 to 65 min. plus 20 min. cooling

Preheat the oven to 350°F/180°C. Grease a large cookie sheet with butter.

In a nonstick frying pan over medium heat, toast the walnuts for 3 to 5 minutes. Stir occasionally and watch them closely. Set aside and chop when cool.

In a large bowl, cream together the butter and sugar with an electric mixer until light and fluffy.

Add the eggs 1 at a time, beating after each addition. Add the orange zest, lemon zest, vanilla and almond extract.

In a medium bowl, sift together the flour, baking soda, baking powder and salt. Add to the butter mixture and stir until combined. Stir in the nuts.

Shape the dough into 2 flattish logs that are approximately 2 inches wide and 14 inches long. They will rise and spread, so make sure you have plenty of room between the logs when you place them on the greased cookie sheet. Bake for 25 minutes.

Remove and let cool for 20 minutes. Using a bread knife, cut the logs into 3/4-inch-thick slices.

Return the biscotti cut side down to the cookie sheet and bake 15 to 20 minutes or until golden brown. Remove the biscotti to a wire rack and cool completely.

TO PREPARE AHEAD: Biscotti store very well. You can make the biscotti up to a week ahead, cool completely, and store in an airtight container. On the day of the party, make sure to arrange a platter of Walnut Biscotti and cover securely with plastic wrap.

Summer

Timeline

ONE WEEK BEFORE
(ABOUT 1 1/2 HOURS)

Buy groceries and create the ambience

Prepare ahead Spaghetti with
Tomato Sauce

Prepare ahead Strawberry Mint Sorbet

Prepare ahead Pepperoni Pinwheels

TWO DAYS BEFORE
(ABOUT 1/4 HOUR)

Buy groceries and create the ambience

Put sparkling water, Champagne, white
wine, and dessert wine in refrigerator

Put out red wine

ONE DAY BEFORE
(ABOUT 1 1/2 HOURS)

Prepare ahead Basil Parmesan Spread
with Crostini

Prepare ahead Walnut Biscotti

Thaw Tomato Sauce in refrigerator
overnight

DAY OF PARTY (ABOUT 2 HOURS)

Buy groceries and create the ambience

Prepare ahead Caesar Salad

Prepare ahead Fish Milanese with Parsley Garlic Sauce

Prepare ahead Sautéed Red and Yellow Peppers

Prepare ahead Mixed Berries with Moscato

5:00 PM
Shower and dress

6:30 PM
Prepare coffeemaker

Open wines, turn on music,
light candles

Put out starter bowls, salad plates,
sorbet bowls, main course
plates, and dessert bowls

Prepare sugar and milk for coffee

7:00 PM
Preheat oven to 400°F/200°C

Put butter pats and rolls on
butter plates

Put a cucumber slice in each
water glass

Prepare ahead Sparkling Raspberry

Put out roasted almonds

Put water on to boil for Spaghetti

7:20 PM
Put Pepperoni Pinwheels in oven

7:30 PM (GUESTS ARRIVE)
Open and pour Champagne; garnish
with a raspberry (have water
ready for those who prefer water)

7:35 PM
Remove Pepperoni Pinwheels from
oven and serve

8:00 PM
Finish Spaghetti with Tomato Sauce

8:05 PM
Call people to table

Serve starter wine and water

8:10 PM
Serve Spaghetti with Tomato Sauce
according to Presentation Tip

8:30 PM
Finish salad and serve

Take sorbet out of freezer

8:45 PM
Serve sorbet, garnished with mint

Finish Mixed Berries with Moscato

9:05 PM
Finish Fish Milanese

Reheat Sautéed Red and Yellow
Peppers in microwave

Plate Fish Milanese according to
Presentation Tip

9:15 PM
Serve main course and wine

Turn on coffeemaker

9:45 PM
Serve Mixed Berries according to
Presentation Tip

Serve dessert and dessert wine
(if using)

10:00 PM
Serve coffee, tea, and
after-dinner cookies

Grocery List

ONE WEEK BEFORE PARTY

PANTRY ITEMS
2¹/₃ cups extra-virgin olive oil
Kosher salt
Freshly ground black pepper
³/₄ teaspoon dried thyme
¹/₂ teaspoon dried oregano
¹/₄ teaspoon dried rosemary
2¹/₄ cups sugar
3¹/₂ cups flour
¹/₂ teaspoon baking powder
¹/₂ teaspoon baking soda
1¹/₂ teaspoons vanilla extract
¹/₄ teaspoon almond extract
2 cups chopped walnuts
1 (28-ounce) can diced tomatoes
¹/₃ cup sun-dried tomatoes
in oil
5 teaspoons Dijon mustard
2 teaspoons honey
1 teaspoon anchovy paste
1 teaspoon Worcestershire sauce
1¹/₂ cups plain bread crumbs
1 pound spaghetti
1 (12-ounce) jar roasted almonds
Decaffeinated and regular coffee
Regular and herbal tea bags

ALCOHOL AND DRINKS
2 bottles Champagne or dry sparkling wine
2 bottles red wine for starter (Dolcetto)

2 bottles white wine for main course
(Soave)
1 bottle dessert wine for Mixed Berries
(Moscato d'Asti)
3 bottles sparkling water
9 tablespoons raspberry liqueur
1 tablespoon vodka

PRODUCE
8 lemons
16 ounces fresh strawberries
1 tablespoon chopped basil leaves
¹/₃ cup chopped mint leaves
(about ³/₄ ounce)
1 carrot
1 celery stalk
3 onions
8 cloves garlic

DAIRY
2¹/₈ cups grated Parmesan cheese
7 eggs
1³/₄ cups butter

MEAT, FISH AND DELI
24 pepperoni slices

FREEZER
¹/₂ (17.3-ounce) package frozen puff pastry
1 quart vanilla ice cream

TWO DAYS BEFORE PARTY

PRODUCE
6 ounces blackberries
6 ounces blueberries
12 ounces raspberries
12 ounces strawberries
1 orange
1 cup packed basil leaves
1 bunch basil leaves for garnish
1 bunch flat-leaf parsley
1 bunch fresh mint for sorbet
garnish
1 cup packed baby spinach leaves
1 head romaine (about 10 ounces)
4 ounces arugula
2 red bell peppers

2 yellow bell peppers
1 cucumber

DAIRY
1¹/₈ cups whole milk
8 ounces cream cheese
4 ounces goat cheese
¹/₃ cup shredded Parmesan cheese

MEAT, FISH AND DELI
6 skinless tilapia fillets

BAKERY
1 French baguette
3 slices country-style bread

DAY OF PARTY

BAKERY
6 rolls

Marinated Flank Steak
menu

SERVES 8

Cocktail & Hors d'Oeuvres

Amaretto and Peach Champagne

Shrimp Cocktail

Herbed Goat Cheese and Grape Crostini

Cashews and Party Mix

Starter

Potato Leek Soup

Rolls and Butter

Viognier

Salad

Baby Spinach with Pine Nuts and Goat Cheese

Palate Cleanser

Melon Sorbet

Main Course

Marinated Flank Steak

Wild Rice Salad

Summer Corn Salad

Zinfandel

Dessert

Strawberry-Glazed Cheesecake

Shortbread

Moscato D'Asti

Coffee & Tea

Amaretto and Peach Champagne

2	teaspoons peach schnapps	1/2	cup plus 2 tablespoons Champagne or dry sparkling wine
2	teaspoons amaretto	1/4	lemon slice for garnish

Preparation Time: 10 min.

Fill the bottom of a Champagne glass with the peach schnapps and amaretto. Fill the glass with Champagne or dry sparkling wine. Garnish with 1/4 of a lemon slice.

To Prepare Ahead: Pour the peach schnapps and the amaretto into the bottom of each Champagne glass and place the glasses near where you are going to serve the apéritif. Have a few empty glasses available in case some guests prefer water. Place the quartered lemon slices in a bowl, cover, and refrigerate.

To Finish: Pour the Champagne, garnish with 1/4 of a lemon slice, and serve.

Handy Tip: One bottle of Champagne makes enough to serve 6.

Shrimp Cocktail

1 1/2	pounds cooked jumbo shrimp, tails on	2	tablespoons horseradish, or to taste
		1	teaspoon Worcestershire sauce
		2	tablespoons lemon juice
Cocktail Sauce		Few drops of Tabasco sauce	
1	cup ketchup	Curly parsley for garnish	

Preparation Time: 10 min.

PRESENTATION TIP: Place the Cocktail Sauce in a bowl in the center of a platter; surround with the shrimp. Garnish with curly parsley.

Rinse the shrimp with cold water and pat dry. Place the shrimp on a plate, leaving a space in the middle for a bowl of cocktail sauce. Cover and refrigerate.

For the cocktail sauce: Mix together the ketchup, horseradish, Worcestershire sauce, lemon juice and Tabasco sauce.

To Prepare Ahead: You can make the cocktail sauce up to 5 days ahead and store, covered, in the refrigerator. Early on the day of the party, assemble the shrimp platter according to the Presentation Tip. Cover and refrigerate until ready to serve.

Substitution: If you prefer a chunkier cocktail sauce, substitute 1/2 cup chili sauce for 1/2 cup of the ketchup.

Herbed Goat Cheese and Grape Crostini

Preparation Time: 20 min.
Cooking Time: 20 min.
Total Time: 40 min.

PRESENTATION TIP:
You can either let your guests serve themselves, or you can make up the crostini with the goat cheese. If you are making them up, place a slice of Herbed Goat Cheese on each crostini. Top with half of a red grape and half of a green grape. Place on a platter. Garnish with bunches of grapes and serve.

HERBED GOAT CHEESE

1   tablespoon finely chopped fresh flat-leaf parsley
1   tablespoon finely chopped fresh chives
1 1/2   teaspoons finely chopped fresh thyme leaves
1/2   teaspoon freshly ground black pepper
1   (8-ounce) log fresh goat cheese

CROSTINI AND ASSEMBLY

French baguette
2   tablespoons extra-virgin olive oil for brushing
1/2   pound seedless red grapes
1/2   pound seedless green grapes

For the goat cheese: In a small bowl, mix together the flat-leaf parsley, chives, thyme and pepper. Spread the mixture on your work surface. Roll the goat cheese log in the herbs until well covered. Wrap the herbed goat cheese in plastic wrap and refrigerate until needed.

For the crostini: Preheat the oven to 350°F/180°C. Cut the baguette into 3/8-inch slices. Brush both sides of each slice with extra-virgin olive oil and place on an ungreased baking sheet. Bake for 10 minutes, turn the slices over and bake for 10 minutes more, or until lightly toasted. Remove to a wire rack to cool completely. Cut about 20 red and green grapes into halves and serve according to the Presentation Tip.

TO PREPARE AHEAD: You can make the Herbed Goat Cheese up to 2 days ahead, wrap in plastic wrap, and store in the refrigerator. You can toast the crostini up to 2 days ahead. When cool, store the crostini in a sealable plastic bag at room temperature. On the day of the party, slice the grapes and store, covered, in the refrigerator.

TO FINISH: Arrange a platter of crostini and grapes according to the Presentation Tip.

HANDY TIP: I like using plain dental floss to slice goat cheese. Give it a try.

Potato Leek Soup

2	tablespoons butter	4	cups chicken stock
3	cups sliced leeks (3 to 4 leeks), white part only	$1^1/_2$	cups whipping cream
			Kosher salt and white pepper to taste
1	cup chopped onion	$^1/_2$	cup grated white Cheddar cheese for garnish
4	or 5 russet or Idaho potatoes, peeled and cut into $^3/_4$-inch dice (about 4 cups)	2	tablespoons chopped fresh chives for garnish

Preparation Time: 20 min.
Cooking Time: 25 min.
Total Time: 45 min.

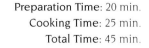

PRESENTATION TIP: Ladle the soup into bowls. Place a small amount of grated Cheddar cheese in the middle of each bowl and top with a pinch of chives.

Melt the butter in a large soup pot. Add the leeks and onions and sauté over medium heat for about 3 minutes. Add the potatoes and chicken stock. Turn up the heat and bring to a boil. Cover, turn down the heat to low and simmer for 15 minutes or until the potatoes are tender. Remove from the heat. Purée in batches in a blender until smooth.

Return to the cleaned-out soup pot. Stir in cream and season with salt and pepper. If serving cold, cool, cover and refrigerate. If serving warm, reheat gently over low heat, stirring constantly. Don't let the soup boil!

TO PREPARE AHEAD: You can make the Potato Leek Soup up to 2 days ahead. Cool, cover, and refrigerate. Prepare the grated Cheddar cheese, cover, and refrigerate.

TO FINISH: If serving the soup hot, reheat gently. Serve according to the Presentation Tip.

Baby Spinach with Pine Nuts and Goat Cheese

SERVES 6 TO 8

Preparation Time: 10 min.

SALAD
8	ounces baby spinach
1/3	cup pine nuts

DRESSING
2	tablespoons balsamic vinegar
1	teaspoon honey

2	teaspoons Dijon mustard
1/2	teaspoon kosher salt
1/4	teaspoon freshly ground black pepper
1/3	cup extra-virgin olive oil
4	ounces crumbled goat cheese

For the salad: Rinse and spin dry the spinach and place in a large bowl. Cover with a damp towel and refrigerate until needed.

Place the pine nuts in a small nonstick frying pan. Heat over medium heat, tossing occasionally, until the pine nuts start to turn golden brown, about 3 minutes. Watch them closely because when they go, they go quickly! Set aside.

For the dressing: In a small bowl, whisk together the balsamic vinegar, honey, Dijon mustard, salt and pepper. While continuing to whisk, add the extra-virgin olive oil in a steady stream. Continue whisking until the dressing thickens and emulsifies. Set aside

To serve family style, toss the spinach with enough dressing to coat. Sprinkle with the crumbled goat cheese and pine nuts.

TO PREPARE AHEAD: Follow the directions above, stopping before you toss the spinach with dressing. Cover and refrigerate the dressing. An hour before serving, remove the salad dressing from the refrigerator and return to room temperature.

TO FINISH: Whisk the dressing. Toss the spinach with enough dressing to coat and place on individual plates. Sprinkle with the goat cheese and pine nuts.

Melon Sorbet

1	large cantaloupe, seeded and cut into chunks	3	tablespoons fresh lemon juice	
1/2	cup sugar	2	tablespoons vodka	
			Mint sprigs for garnish	

Place the cantaloupe chunks in a blender and purée until smooth. You should have about 4 cups of purée. Discard any excess. Add the sugar, lemon juice and vodka. Blend briefly to combine. Cover and refrigerate for an hour.

Pour into an ice cream maker and process according to the manufacturer's directions. When finished, pour into an airtight plastic container and freeze until ready to serve.

Preparation Time: 10 min.
Ice Cream Maker: 20 min.
Total Time: 30 min. plus cooling time

TO PREPARE AHEAD: Prepare the sorbet up to a month ahead, place in an airtight container, and freeze.

TO FINISH: Remove the sorbet 15 minutes before serving to allow it to soften slightly. When ready, scoop into bowls, garnish with the mint, and serve.

Marinated Flank Steak

MARINADE

3/4	cup extra-virgin olive oil	2	tablespoons lemon juice	
2	tablespoons Worcestershire sauce	1	teaspoon dried parsley	
1/2	cup soy sauce			
1/4	cup balsamic vinegar	2 1/2	pounds flank steak	
2	cloves garlic, slivered	2	oranges, sliced, for spiral garnish	
1	teaspoon dry mustard		Flat-leaf parsley for garnish	

In a small bowl, combine the extra-virgin olive oil, Worcestershire sauce, soy sauce, balsamic vinegar, garlic, dry mustard, lemon juice and parsley. Place the marinade in a large sealable plastic bag. Add the flank steak to the marinade, making sure to coat the meat on all sides. Seal the bag, squeezing out as much excess air as possible. Marinate in the refrigerator overnight or for up to 2 days.

Remove the flank steak from the refrigerator about 20 minutes before cooking and discard the marinade. If cooking on a grill, grill for 4 to 5 minutes per side. If cooking in the oven, preheat the broiler. Place the flank steak on a broiler pan and broil for approximately 5 to 6 minutes per side for medium rare (an instant read thermometer should register 130°F/54°C) or until desired doneness.

Remove from the grill or oven and let rest for 5 minutes. Slice the flank steak on the diagonal across the grain in 3/8-inch strips.

Preparation Time: 10 min.
Cooking Time: 10 to 12 min.
Total Time: 20 to 22 min. plus marinating time

PRESENTATION TIP:
Place several slices of flank steak on each plate. Place a large spoonful of Summer Corn Salad and Wild Rice Salad on the plate. Garnish with an orange spiral and a sprig of flat-leaf parsley.

TO PREPARE AHEAD: Marinate the flank steak at least a day ahead and up to 2 days ahead. Remove the flank steak from the refrigerator about 20 minutes before cooking.

TO FINISH: Grill or broil the flank steak as directed above. While the steak is cooking, prepare the flat-leaf parsley garnish and slice the orange for the orange twists. Serve according to the Presentation Tip.

Wild Rice Salad

Preparation Time: 20 min.
Cooking Time: 50 min.
Total Time: 70 min. plus
cooling time

1	cup wild rice
2	cups long grain white rice
1/3	cup pine nuts
1/2	cup extra-virgin olive oil
1/2	cup apple cider vinegar
	Zest of 1 orange
1/2	cup orange juice
1	tablespoon sugar
3	tablespoons soy sauce
1/2	teaspoon kosher salt

1/4	teaspoon freshly ground black pepper
1/2	teaspoon dry mustard
2	cloves garlic, minced
1	tablespoon sesame oil
1/2	red bell pepper, cored and diced
1/2	cup sliced green onions
1/2	cup dried currants
1	teaspoon kosher salt
1	cup sugar snap peas

Bring 7 cups water to a boil in a large pot. Add the wild rice, cover and simmer for 30 minutes over low heat. Add the white rice and cook for 20 minutes longer or until the water has been absorbed. Uncover and set aside to cool.

While the rice is cooling, place the pine nuts in a small nonstick frying pan. Heat over medium heat, tossing occasionally, until the pine nuts start to turn golden brown, about 3 minutes. Watch them closely because when they go, they go quickly! Set aside.

In a small bowl, whisk together the extra-virgin olive oil, apple cider vinegar, orange zest, orange juice, sugar, soy sauce, salt, pepper, dry mustard, garlic and sesame oil.

Add the dressing to the cooled rice and stir until combined. Add the diced red pepper, sliced green onions, currants and toasted pine nuts.

Bring a medium pot of water to a boil. Add 1 teaspoon salt to the boiling water. Add the sugar snap peas and blanch for 2 minutes. Drain and plunge into cold water to stop the cooking process. Chop into 1/2-inch pieces.

Just prior to serving, add the cooled sugar snap peas to the rice and stir to combine.

TO PREPARE AHEAD: You can make the Wild Rice Salad up to 2 days ahead, stopping before adding the blanched sugar snap peas. Cover and refrigerate the salad and blanched sugar snap peas in separate containers.

TO FINISH: When ready to serve, stir in the sugar snap peas.

Summer Corn Salad

1	teaspoon kosher salt	2	tablespoons Champagne vinegar or white wine vinegar
8	ears corn	1/4	teaspoon kosher salt
12	ounces cherry tomatoes, quartered	1/4	teaspoon freshly ground black pepper
1	cup chopped green onions	1/4	cup extra-virgin olive oil
1/4	cup fresh basil chiffonade		

Preparation Time: 10 min.
Cooking Time: 7 min.
Total Time: 17 min.

Bring a large pot of water to a boil. Add 1 teaspoon salt to the boiling water. Add the corn and boil for 7 minutes. Remove from the water and cool.

Cut the kernels off the cob and place in a large bowl. Add the tomatoes, green onions and basil.

In a small bowl, combine the vinegar, salt and pepper. While continuing to whisk, add the extra-virgin olive oil in a steady stream. Continue whisking until the dressing thickens and emulsifies. Add to the corn salad and stir until combined.

Cover with plastic wrap and chill until ready to serve.

To Prepare Ahead: You can make the Summer Corn Salad a day ahead and store, covered, in the refrigerator.

Substitution: If you prefer, you can use a 28-ounce bag of frozen corn. Place the frozen corn in a large microwave-safe bowl. Cover with plastic wrap and make a few slits for vents. Microwave for 4 minutes; stir. If needed, microwave for an additional minute at a time until the corn is thawed but still cool. Place in a large bowl and proceed as directed above.

Shortbread

1	cup butter		Pinch of kosher salt
1/2	cup sugar	1	tablespoon sugar for sprinkling
2 1/2	cups all-purpose flour		

Preparation Time: 10 min.
Cooking Time: 30 min.
Total Time: 40 min.

Preheat the oven to 325°F/160°C.

In a large bowl, cream together the butter and 1/2 cup sugar with an electric mixer.

Add the flour and salt. Mix well. The dough will be crumbly. Use your hands to make sure it is well combined. Press the dough into an ungreased 9×13-inch baking pan.

Flatten the top by pressing on the surface with the base of another 9×13-inch pan or the base of a measuring cup. Score the dough where you want to cut. Prick the surface with a fork in a symmetrical pattern. Sprinkle with 1 tablespoon sugar.

Bake for 30 to 35 minutes or until lightly browned. Remove from the oven and let cool briefly. Cut the bars and remove to a wire rack. Cool completely.

To Prepare Ahead: You can make the Shortbread up to a week ahead. Place the cookies you are going to use on a small serving platter and cover securely with plastic wrap. Store the rest in an airtight container.

Strawberry-Glazed Cheesecake

Preparation Time: 30 min.
Cooking Time: 45 to 55 min.
Total Time: 75 to 85 min. plus refrigeration

PRESENTATION TIP:
Holding the squeeze bottle of reserved glaze and using a back and forth motion, make a zigzag pattern with the glaze on a dessert plate. Place a slice of the cheesecake in the middle of the plate and serve.

CRUST
3/4 cup walnuts, coarsely ground
3/4 cup graham cracker crumbs
3 tablespoons butter, melted

FILLING
32 ounces cream cheese, at room temperature
4 eggs
1 1/4 cups sugar
1 tablespoon freshly squeezed lemon juice
2 teaspoons vanilla extract

TOPPING
2 cups sour cream
1/2 cup sugar
1 teaspoon vanilla

STRAWBERRY GLAZE
4 cups medium strawberries
1 (12-ounce) jar strawberry jelly
1 tablespoon cornstarch
1/4 cup Cointreau or water

Preheat the oven to 350°F/180°C. Butter a 9- or 10-inch springform pan.

For the crust: In a medium bowl, combine the walnuts, graham cracker crumbs and butter. Press onto the bottom of the springform pan. Refrigerate until ready to fill.

For the filling: Using an electric mixer, beat the cream cheese in a large bowl until smooth. Add the eggs, sugar, lemon juice and vanilla. Beat thoroughly. Spoon over the crust.

Set the springform pan on a baking sheet. Bake a 10-inch cheesecake for 40 to 45 minutes or a 9-inch cheesecake for 50 to 55 minutes. The cheesecake will rise, and the top may crack in several places. Don't worry!

For the topping: While the cake is baking, combine the sour cream, sugar and vanilla. Blend well. Cover and refrigerate.

When the cheesecake is done, remove from the oven and let stand on a wire rack for 15 minutes. Then, spoon the topping over the cheesecake, starting at the center and extending to within 1/2 inch of the edge. Return to the oven and bake for an additional 5 minutes.

Remove from the oven and let cool. Refrigerate for at least 24 hours or up to 3 days.

For the glaze: Several hours before serving, rinse the strawberries and pat dry. In a small saucepan, combine a little of the jelly with the cornstarch and mix well. Add the remaining jelly and the Cointreau or water. Cook over medium heat, stirring frequently, until thickened and clear, about 5 minutes. Cool to lukewarm.

Using a knife, loosen the cheesecake from the side of the pan and remove the springform. Hull the strawberries. You can arrange the strawberries pointed end up over the top of the cheesecake, or slice them and arrange them in a radiating pattern over the top of the cheesecake for a more dramatic presentation. Spoon the glaze over the strawberries, allowing some to drip down the side of the cheesecake. Reserve about 1/3 cup of the glaze to use as a garnish. Place the reserved glaze in a plastic squeeze bottle and refrigerate. Return the cheesecake to the refrigerator until the glaze on the cheesecake has set, about an hour.

TO PREPARE AHEAD: You can make the cheesecake up to 3 days ahead, stopping before adding the strawberries and glaze. Cool, cover, and refrigerate.

TO FINISH: A few hours before serving, finish as directed above.

HANDY TIP: If you don't have a plastic squeeze bottle, you can put the reserved glaze in a sealable plastic bag. When ready to use, cut a very small piece of plastic off 1 corner of the bag and squeeze out the glaze to produce a zigzag pattern on the plate.

Timeline

ONE WEEK BEFORE (ABOUT 1/2 HOUR)

Buy groceries and create the ambience

Prepare ahead Melon Sorbet

TWO DAYS BEFORE (ABOUT 1 1/2 HOURS)

Buy groceries and create the ambience

Put sparkling water, Champagne, white wine, and dessert wine (if using) in refrigerator

Put out red wine

Prepare ahead Shortbread

Prepare ahead Strawberry-Glazed Cheesecake

ONE DAY BEFORE (ABOUT 1 3/4 HOURS)

Prepare ahead Wild Rice Salad

Prepare ahead Potato Leek Soup

Prepare ahead Marinated Flank Steak

DAY OF PARTY (ABOUT 1 1/2 HOURS)

Buy groceries and create the ambience

Prepare ahead Herbed Goat Cheese and Grape Crostini

Prepare ahead Shrimp Cocktail

Prepare ahead Summer Corn Salad

Prepare ahead Baby Spinach with Pine Nuts and Goat Cheese

Finish Strawberry-Glazed Cheesecake

5:00 PM
Shower and dress

6:30 PM
Prepare coffeemaker

Open wines, turn on music, light candles

Put out starter bowls, salad plates, sorbet bowls, main course plates, and dessert plates

Prepare sugar and milk for coffee

7:00 PM
Put butter pats and rolls on butter plates

Put a cucumber slice in each water glass

Prepare ahead Amaretto and Peach Champagne

Put out cashews and party mix

7:15 PM
Put out Shrimp Cocktail

Finish Herbed Goat Cheese Crostini and serve according to Presentation Tip

Remove salad dressing from refrigerator

7:30 PM (GUESTS ARRIVE)
Open and pour Champagne; garnish with lemon (have water ready for those who prefer water)

7:35 PM
If serving soup hot, start to reheat soup over medium-low heat; stir and check occasionally

8:00 PM
If serving soup hot, check soup is hot

8:05 PM
Call people to table

Serve starter wine and water

8:10 PM
Serve Potato Leek Soup, hot or cold, according to Presentation Tip

8:30 PM
Finish salad and serve

Take sorbet out of freezer

8:45 PM
Remove Marinated Flank Steak from refrigerator

Serve sorbet, garnished with mint

Turn on grill or oven broiler

9:00 PM
Finish Marinated Flank Steak

Add sugar snap peas to Wild Rice Salad

Remove Summer Corn Salad from refrigerator

Plate Marinated Flank Steak according to Presentation Tip

9:15 PM
Serve main course and wine

Turn on coffeemaker

9:45 PM
Serve Strawberry-Glazed Cheesecake according to Presentation Tip

Serve dessert wine (if using)

10:00 PM
Serve coffee, tea, and after-dinner cookies

Grocery List

ONE WEEK BEFORE PARTY

PANTRY ITEMS

2 cups extra-virgin olive oil
1 tablespoon sesame oil
2 1/4 tablespoons good-quality balsamic vinegar
2 tablespoons Champagne vinegar or white wine vinegar
1/2 cup cider vinegar
Kosher salt
Freshly ground black pepper
1 1/2 teaspoons dry mustard
1 teaspoon dried parsley
3 3/8 cups sugar
2 1/2 cups flour
3 teaspoons vanilla extract
1 tablespoon cornstarch
1 cup ketchup
2 teaspoons Dijon mustard
2 tablespoons horseradish
2 1/3 tablespoons Worcestershire sauce
3/4 cup soy sauce
Few drops of Tabasco sauce
4 cups chicken stock
1 teaspoon honey
1 cup wild rice
2 cups long grain white rice

2/3 cup pine nuts
3/4 cup coarsely ground walnuts
1/2 cup dried currants
3/4 cup graham cracker crumbs
12 ounces strawberry jelly
1 (12-ounce) jar cashews
1 (8.75-ounce) package party mix
Decaffeinated and regular coffee
Regular and herbal tea bags

ALCOHOL AND DRINKS

2 bottles Champagne or sparkling wine
2 bottles white wine for starter (Viognier)
2 bottles red wine for main (Zinfandel)
1 bottle dessert wine, if using (Moscato d'Asti)
4 bottles sparkling water
1/3 cup peach schnapps
1/3 cup Disaronno amaretto or other amaretto
2 tablespoons vodka
1/4 cup Cointreau (optional)

PRODUCE

5 lemons
1 cantaloupe

TWO DAYS BEFORE PARTY

PRODUCE

4 cups medium strawberries
1/2 pound seedless red grapes
1/2 pound seedless green grapes
3 oranges
1 tablespoon chopped fresh flat-leaf parsley
1 bunch flat-leaf parsley for main garnish
1 bunch curly parsley for appetizer garnish
3 tablespoons chopped fresh chives
1 1/2 teaspoons chopped fresh thyme
1/4 cup fresh basil chiffonade
1 bunch fresh mint for sorbet garnish
8 ounces baby spinach
4 leeks
1 onion
5 russet or Idaho potatoes
4 cloves garlic
8 ears fresh corn
12 ounces cherry tomatoes
1 1/2 cups green onions
1/2 red bell pepper

1 cup sugar snap peas
1 cucumber

DAIRY

1 cup whole milk
2 cups butter
4 eggs
1 (8-ounce) log fresh goat cheese
4 ounces crumbled goat cheese
1/2 cup grated white Cheddar cheese
1 1/2 cups whipping cream
32 ounces cream cheese
2 cups sour cream
1/2 cup orange juice

MEAT, FISH AND DELI

1 1/2 pounds cooked jumbo shrimp with tails on
2 1/2 pounds flank steak

BAKERY

1 French baguette

DAY OF PARTY

BAKERY

8 rolls

Lemon Chicken with Rosemary

menu

SERVES 8

Cocktail & Hors d'Oeuvres

Peach Champagne

Tzatziki with Pita and Vegetables

Stuffed Mushrooms with Provolone

Party Mix

Starter

Shells with Garlic, Tomato and Basil

Rolls and Butter

Chianti

Salad

Mixed Greens with Goat Cheese Rounds

Palate Cleanser

Blackberry Sorbet

Main Course

Lemon Chicken with Rosemary

Tabbouleh

Roasted Asparagus

Verdicchio

Dessert

Panna Cotta with Fresh Berries

Lemon Wafers

Moscato d'Asti

Coffee & Tea

Peach Champagne

2 tablespoons peach nectar
1 teaspoon peach schnapps

½ cup plus 2 tablespoons Champagne or dry sparkling wine

Preparation Time: 5 min.

Fill the bottom of a Champagne glass with the peach nectar and peach schnapps. Fill the glass with Champagne or dry sparkling wine.

TO PREPARE AHEAD: Pour the peach nectar and the peach schnapps into the bottom of each Champagne glass and place the glasses near where you are going to serve the apéritif. Have a few empty glasses available in case some guests prefer water.

TO FINISH: Pour the Champagne and serve.

HANDY TIP: One bottle of Champagne makes enough to serve 6.

Tzatziki

2 cups plain full-fat yogurt
1 pound cucumbers
½ teaspoon kosher salt
2 teaspoons chopped fresh dill
2 cloves garlic, minced
1 tablespoon extra-virgin olive oil
1 tablespoon lemon juice

Kosher salt to taste
Pita bread, cut into triangles
½ pound carrots, peeled and cut into strips
1 red bell pepper, cored, seeded and cut into strips

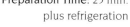

Preparation Time: 25 min. plus refrigeration

PRESENTATION TIP: Serve the Tzatziki with the pita triangles, carrots, and red pepper.

Place the yogurt in a cheesecloth-lined sieve. Place over a bowl, cover and refrigerate for 6 hours or overnight.

Peel, seed and grate the cucumbers on the large holes of a grater. Place the cucumbers in a sieve, sprinkle with ½ teaspoon salt and let drain for 15 minutes. Squeeze out the excess liquid.

Place the strained yogurt in a medium bowl. Stir in the chopped dill, minced garlic, extra-virgin olive oil, lemon juice and salt to taste. Stir in the grated cucumbers. Chill, covered, for at least 2 hours before serving.

TO PREPARE AHEAD: The day before your party, place the yogurt in the cheesecloth-lined sieve over a bowl, cover, and refrigerate.

TO FINISH: Complete the Tzatziki according to the directions. Prepare the vegetable platter with the Tzatziki, cover, and refrigerate. Cut the pita bread into triangles and place in a plastic bag until ready to serve. Serve according to the Presentation Tip.

HANDY TIP: If you are short on time, skip straining the yogurt. This will result in a slightly less firm Tzatziki, but it will still taste fine.

Stuffed Mushrooms with Provolone

Preparation Time: 10 min.
Cooking Time: 10 min.
Total Time: 20 min.

1	(8-ounce) package large fresh button mushrooms
4	ounces cream cheese, at room temperature
2	green onions, chopped
3	slices provolone cheese

Preheat the oven to 350°F/180°C.

Wipe any remaining dirt off the mushrooms with a damp cloth and snap out the stems.

In a small bowl, mix together the cream cheese and the green onions. Fill each mushroom cap with the cream cheese mixture.

Cut the provolone cheese into small squares to cover each mushroom. Place on an ungreased baking sheet. Bake for 10 minutes or until heated through.

TO PREPARE AHEAD: On the day of the party, make the mushrooms, stopping before baking. Arrange on an ungreased baking sheet, cover, and refrigerate.

TO FINISH: Bake, uncovered, as directed above.

Shells with Garlic, Tomato and Basil

Preparation Time: 10 min.
Cooking Time: 10 min.
Total Time: 20 min. plus 1 hour marinating time

3	green onions, coarsely chopped
3	cloves garlic, minced
1/4	cup fresh basil chiffonade
1/2	teaspoon kosher salt
1/2	teaspoon freshly ground black pepper
1/3	cup extra-virgin olive oil
12	ounces cherry tomatoes, quartered
1	pound medium shells
1	cup grated Parmesan cheese, divided

In a medium bowl, combine the green onions, garlic, basil, salt, pepper and extra-virgin olive oil. Gently stir in the tomatoes. Cover and let marinate at room temperature for 1 hour.

Cook the pasta according to the package directions. Drain and return to the pot.

Add the tomato mixture and 1/3 cup of the Parmesan cheese to the pasta. Stir until combined. Spoon into bowls and serve with the remaining 2/3 cup grated Parmesan cheese on the side.

TO PREPARE AHEAD: You can prepare the tomato mixture up to 8 hours in advance. Cover and refrigerate. An hour before serving, remove from the refrigerator and return to room temperature.

TO FINISH: Cook the pasta according to the package directions, drain, and serve as directed above.

HANDY TIP: To make the basil chiffonade, stack several basil leaves and roll into a cigar shape. Then, slice crosswise into 1/8-inch strips.

Mixed Greens with Goat Cheese Rounds

Preparation Time: 15 min.
Cooking Time: 5 min.
Total Time: 20 min.

8   ounces mixed baby greens

DRESSING
1 1/2 tablespoons fresh lemon juice
1 1/2 tablespoons Champagne vinegar
1   tablespoon minced shallot
1   clove garlic, crushed
2   teaspoons Dijon mustard
1   tablespoons finely chopped
     flat-leaf parsley
1/4   teaspoon kosher salt

1/8   teaspoon freshly ground
     black pepper
1/3   cup walnut oil

GOAT CHEESE ROUNDS
1   (11-ounce) log goat cheese
2   egg whites
1   tablespoon water
1/2   cup plain bread crumbs
1   tablespoon extra-virgin olive oil
1   tablespoon butter

Rinse and spin dry the mixed greens. Place in a large bowl, cover with a damp towel and refrigerate until needed.

For the dressing: In a small bowl, whisk together the lemon juice, Champagne vinegar, minced shallot, crushed garlic, Dijon mustard, chopped parsley, salt and pepper. Add the walnut oil in a stream, whisking continuously until the dressing thickens and emulsifies. Set aside.

For the rounds: Cut the goat cheese into 16 slices. In a small bowl, beat the egg whites and water until frothy. Dip the goat cheese slices into the egg white mixture and then coat with the bread crumbs. Place on a parchment-lined plate and chill for 15 minutes or longer.

In a frying pan large enough to hold the rounds, heat the extra-virgin olive oil and butter until hot. Fry the goat cheese rounds until lightly golden, about 1 minute per side, turning halfway through. The rounds should be warm but not runny. Drain on paper towels. Toss the mixed greens with enough dressing to coat. Place on individual plates and top each with 2 goat cheese rounds.

TO PREPARE AHEAD: On the day of the party, follow the directions above, covering and refrigerating the dressing and stopping after you put the goat cheese rounds in the refrigerator to chill. An hour before serving, remove the salad dressing from the refrigerator and return to room temperature.

TO FINISH: Just before serving, fry the goat cheese rounds and serve as directed above.

HANDY TIP: Plain dental floss is a great way to slice goat cheese. Give it a try.

Blackberry Sorbet

1	cup sugar	2	tablespoons crème de cassis
1	cup water		Mint sprigs for garnish
16	ounces fresh blackberries		

Preparation Time: 10 min.
Cooking Time: 5 min.
Ice Cream Maker: 20 min.
Total Time: 35 min. plus cooling time

In a medium saucepan, heat the sugar and water until the sugar melts and the mixture starts to boil. Boil for 2 minutes. Remove from the heat and cool completely.

Rinse and pat dry the blackberries. Place the blackberries in the bowl of a blender. Add the sugar syrup and crème de cassis. Purée until smooth.

Pour the blackberry mixture through a fine sieve, using the back of a spoon to help push the mixture through.

Pour the strained mixture into an ice cream maker and process according to the manufacturer's directions. When finished, pour into an airtight container and freeze until ready to serve.

TO FREEZE: Prepare the sorbet up to a month ahead, place in an airtight container, and freeze.

TO FINISH: Remove the sorbet 15 minutes before serving to allow it to soften slightly. When ready, scoop into bowls, garnish with the mint, and serve.

HANDY TIP: By making and storing a big batch of sugar syrup, you can save preparation time when making many sorbets. In a large saucepan, heat 4 cups sugar and 4 cups water until the sugar melts and the mixture starts to boil. Boil for 2 minutes. Remove from the heat and cool. Store the sugar syrup in a bottle in the refrigerator. It will keep for several months. As a simple rule of thumb, if a sorbet recipe calls for 1 cup sugar and 1 cup water, use 1 1/2 cups of the prepared sugar syrup, or 75 percent of the 2 ingredients added together.

Summer

Lemon Chicken with Rosemary

Preparation Time: 5 min.
Cooking Time: 20 to 25 min.
Total Time: 25 to 30 min. plus marinating time

PRESENTATION TIP:
Place a breast of chicken on a plate and spoon over the Lemon Rosemary Sauce. Garnish with a sprig of rosemary. Serve the chicken accompanied with Tabbouleh and Roasted Asparagus.

MARINADE

1/2	cup extra-virgin olive oil
1/2	cup lemon juice (2 or 3 lemons)
1	tablespoon chopped fresh rosemary
1	teaspoon kosher salt
1/2	teaspoon freshly ground black pepper
8	boneless skinless chicken breasts
3	tablespoons extra-virgin olive oil, divided

LEMON ROSEMARY SAUCE

1/2	cup butter, melted
	Grated zest of 1 lemon
1	tablespoon lemon juice
1	tablespoon chopped fresh rosemary
	Rosemary sprigs for garnish

For the marinade: In a small bowl, mix together the extra-virgin olive oil, lemon juice, rosemary, salt and pepper. Place the marinade in a sealable plastic bag. Add the boneless chicken breasts. Squeeze out as much air as possible and seal the plastic bag. Move the breasts around until well coated with the marinade. Place in the refrigerator for at least 4 hours or overnight.

Preheat the oven to 375°F/190°C. Lightly oil a baking sheet.

Heat 1 tablespoon extra-virgin olive oil in a large frying pan over medium heat. When hot, remove the chicken breasts from the marinade and sauté for 2 1/2 minutes per side. Discard the marinade. Place the seared breasts on the prepared baking sheet. Repeat with the remaining breasts and extra-virgin olive oil. Place in the preheated oven and roast for 15 to 20 minutes, or until cooked through.

For the sauce: While the chicken is baking, combine the melted butter, lemon zest, lemon juice and rosemary in a small microwave-safe bowl. Before serving, heat in the microwave. Serve according to the Presentation Tip.

TO PREPARE AHEAD: Make the marinade the night before the party and marinate the chicken breasts overnight in the refrigerator.

TO SEAR: On the day of the party, sear the breasts as directed above. After searing, place the breasts on an oiled baking sheet, cool, cover, and refrigerate. Make the Lemon Rosemary Sauce, cool, cover, and refrigerate.

TO FINISH: When ready to roast, place the uncovered chicken breasts in a preheated 375°F/190°C oven for 20 to 30 minutes or until done. Reheat the Lemon Rosemary Sauce in the microwave. Serve according to the Presentation Tip.

Tabbouleh

1	cup bulgur wheat		1/2	cup chopped mint leaves
1	cup boiling water		1	cup chopped flat-leaf parsley
Juice of 1 lemon			1	cup minced green onions
1/4	cup extra-virgin olive oil		1	English cucumber, seeded and diced
1/2	teaspoon kosher salt		12	ounces cherry tomatoes, halved
1/4	teaspoon freshly ground black pepper			

Preparation Time: 20 min. plus 2 hours resting and refrigeration

In a large bowl, combine the bulgur wheat, boiling water, lemon juice and extra-virgin olive oil. Cover and let soak for 1 hour.

Add the salt, pepper, mint, parsley, green onions, cucumber and tomatoes. Cover and refrigerate for at least an hour.

TO PREPARE AHEAD: You can make the Tabbouleh up to a day ahead and store, covered, in the refrigerator.

Roasted Asparagus

2	pounds pencil-thin asparagus		2	teaspoons freshly ground black pepper
2	tablespoons extra-virgin olive oil			
2	teaspoons kosher salt			

Preparation Time: 5 min.
Cooking Time: 5 to 10 min.
Total Time: 10 to 15 min.

Preheat the oven to 400°F/200°C. Wash the asparagus and snap off the woody stems.

Place the asparagus on a baking sheet. Toss with the extra-virgin olive oil. Sprinkle with the salt and pepper. Spread the asparagus into a single layer. Roast in the oven for 5 to 10 minutes or until tender-crisp.

TO PREPARE AHEAD: You can make the asparagus ahead on the day. Cool to room temperature.

TO FINISH: Either serve at room temperature or reheat in a 400°F/200°C oven for 3 to 5 minutes to heat through.

Summer

Panna Cotta with Fresh Berries

Preparation Time: 15 min.
Cooking Time: 5 min.
Total Time: 20 min.
plus refrigeration

PRESENTATION TIP:
Spoon the berries over
the top of each dessert
dish and serve.

1	cup whole milk	2	teaspoons vanilla extract
2½	teaspoons unflavored gelatin	6	ounces blackberries
	(1 envelope)	6	ounces blueberries
3	cups whipping cream	6	ounces raspberries
⅓	cup sugar	2	tablespoons sugar
	Pinch of kosher salt		

Place the milk in a medium saucepan and sprinkle with the unflavored gelatin. Let stand for 5 minutes. Heat the milk and gelatin over medium heat until hot but not boiling, about 5 minutes. The gelatin should be dissolved. Add the cream, ⅓ cup sugar and the salt. Stir until the sugar has dissolved. Stir in the vanilla. Remove from the heat and let cool for 5 minutes. Pour into 6 to 8 glass dessert dishes. Cover and refrigerate for at least 6 hours or up to 4 days. When ready to serve, rinse the berries and pat dry. Place the berries in a bowl and sprinkle with 2 tablespoons sugar.

TO PREPARE AHEAD: You can make the Panna Cotta up to 4 days ahead and store, covered, in the refrigerator. On the day of the party, rinse the berries and pat dry. Place in a bowl and refrigerate until needed.

TO FINISH: When ready to serve, sprinkle the berries with sugar and serve according to the Presentation Tip.

Lemon Wafers

Preparation Time: 15 min.
Cooking Time: 8 to
10 min. per batch

1	cup butter	1	teaspoon vanilla extract
1	cup sugar	2½	cups flour
1	egg	½	teaspoon baking soda
	Grated zest of 1 lemon	½	teaspoon kosher salt
2	tablespoons lemon juice	½	cup sugar for coating

Preheat the oven to 375°/190°C. In a large bowl, cream together the butter and 1 cup sugar with an electric mixer. Beat in the egg, lemon zest, lemon juice and vanilla.

In a small bowl, combine the flour, baking soda and salt. Blend the flour mixture into the butter mixture until thoroughly combined. If baking immediately, shape into 1-inch balls. Roll each ball in ½ cup sugar to coat. Arrange the balls 2 inches apart on an ungreased cookie sheet. Bake for 8 to 10 minutes or until the edges of the cookies are golden brown. Remove from the oven and transfer the cookies to a wire rack to cool.

TO PREPARE AHEAD: Make the dough as directed above and shape into 4 logs. Wrap in plastic wrap and place in a sealable plastic bag. Freeze for up to 3 months.

TO FINISH: Thaw the dough for 30 minutes (or briefly in the microwave). Cut into ⅜-inch-thick slices. Dip 1 side of each slice in the sugar and place sugar side up on an ungreased cookie sheet. Bake as directed above. When cool, place on a small serving platter and cover securely with plastic wrap.

Timeline

ONE WEEK BEFORE (ABOUT 1 HOUR)

Buy groceries and create the ambience

Prepare ahead Blackberry Sorbet

Prepare ahead Lemon Wafers

TWO DAYS BEFORE (ABOUT 1/4 HOUR)

Buy groceries and create the ambience

Put sparkling water, Champagne, white wine, and dessert wine (if using) in refrigerator

Put out red wine

ONE DAY BEFORE (ABOUT 1/2 HOUR)

Prepare ahead Panna Cotta

Prepare ahead Tzatziki

Prepare ahead Lemon Chicken with Rosemary

DAY OF PARTY (ABOUT 2 1/2 HOURS)

Buy groceries and create the ambience

Prepare ahead Tabbouleh

Finish Tzatziki

Prepare ahead Stuffed Mushrooms with Provolone

Prepare ahead Shells with Garlic, Tomato and Basil

Prepare ahead Mixed Greens with Goat Cheese Rounds

Prepare ahead Roasted Asparagus

Sear Lemon Chicken with Rosemary

Rinse and pat dry berries for Panna Cotta

Finish Lemon Wafers

5:00 PM
Shower and dress

6:30 PM
Prepare coffeemaker

Open wines, turn on music, light candles

Put out starter bowls, salad plates, sorbet bowls, main course plates, and dessert plates

Prepare sugar and milk for coffee

7:00 PM
Preheat oven to 350°F/180°C

Put butter pats and rolls on butter plates

Put a cucumber slice in each water glass

Prepare ahead Peach Champagne

Put out party mix

Put water on to boil for pasta shells

7:15 PM
Serve Tzatziki according to Presentation Tip

Remove salad dressing from refrigerator

7:25 PM
Put Stuffed Mushrooms with Provolone in oven

7:30 PM (GUESTS ARRIVE)
Open and pour Champagne (have water ready for those who prefer water)

7:35 PM
Take Stuffed Mushrooms with Provolone out of oven and serve

Turn up oven to 375°F/190°C

7:55 PM
Add pasta shells to boiling water

8:05 PM
Call people to table

Serve starter wine and water

8:10 PM
Finish Shells with Garlic, Tomato and Basil and serve

8:30 PM
Finish salad and serve

Take sorbet out of freezer

8:45 PM
Serve sorbet, garnished with mint

Put Lemon Chicken with Rosemary in oven

9:05 PM
Remove Lemon Chicken with Rosemary from oven

Put Roasted Asparagus in oven to warm (if serving warm)

Take Tabbouleh out of refrigerator

Plate Lemon Chicken with Rosemary according to Presentation Tip

9:15 PM
Serve main course and wine

Turn on coffeemaker

9:45 PM
Serve Panna Cotta according to Presentation Tip

Serve dessert wine (if using)

10:00 PM
Serve coffee, tea, and after-dinner cookies

Grocery List

ONE WEEK BEFORE PARTY

Pantry Items
1²/₃ cups extra-virgin olive oil
¹/₃ cup walnut oil
1¹/₂ tablespoons Champagne vinegar
Kosher salt
Freshly ground black pepper
3 cups sugar
2¹/₂ cups flour
¹/₂ teaspoon baking soda
3 teaspoons vanilla extract
2¹/₂ teaspoons unflavored gelatin
    (1 envelope)
1 pound medium pasta shells
1 cup bulgur wheat
¹/₂ cup plain bread crumbs
2 teaspoons Dijon mustard
1 package party mix
Decaffeinated and regular coffee
Regular and herbal tea bags

Alcohol and Drinks
2 bottles Champagne or sparkling wine
2 bottles red wine for starter (Chianti)
2 bottles white wine for main (Verdicchio)
1 bottle dessert wine, if using
    (Moscato d'Asti)
4 bottles sparkling water
1 cup peach nectar
3 tablespoons peach schnapps
2 tablespoons crème de cassis

Produce
16 ounces blackberries
8 lemons

Dairy
1²/₃ cups butter
3 eggs

TWO DAYS BEFORE PARTY

Produce
6 ounces blackberries
6 ounces blueberries
6 ounces raspberries
2 teaspoons chopped fresh dill
¹/₄ cup fresh basil chiffonade
1 bunch chopped fresh mint
1 bunch fresh mint for garnish
1 bunch chopped fresh rosemary and
    sprigs for garnish
1¹/₄ cups chopped fresh flat-leaf parsley
8 ounces mixed baby greens
24 ounces cherry tomatoes
6 cloves garlic
¹/₂ pound carrots
1 red bell pepper
8 ounces white button mushrooms
11 green onions
2 shallots

2 pounds pencil-thin asparagus
1 English cucumber
3 cucumbers

Dairy
2 cups whole milk
2 cups plain full-fat yogurt
4 ounces cream cheese
3 slices provolone cheese
1 cup grated Parmesan cheese
1 (11-ounce) log goat cheese
3 cups whipping cream

Meat, Fish and Deli
8 boneless skinless chicken breasts

Bakery
1 package pita bread

DAY OF PARTY

Bakery
8 rolls

Mahi Mahi with Mango Salsa

menu

SERVES 8

Cocktail & Hors d'Oeuvres

Margarita Champagne

Guacamole, Tomato Salsa and Chips

Peanuts

Starter

Zucchini Soup

Rolls and Butter

🍇 Sémillion

Salad

Mixed Greens with Citrus Vinaigrette

Palate Cleanser

Pineapple Sorbet

Main Course

Mahi Mahi with Mango Salsa

Sugar Snap Peas

Baby New Potatoes

🍇 Torrontes

Dessert

Lime Pie

Sugar Cookies

🍇 Moscato D'Asti or Late Harvest Riesling

Coffee & Tea

Margarita Champagne

1 1/2 teaspoons tequila
1 1/2 teaspoons Triple Sec
1/2 teaspoon lime juice

1/2 teaspoon sugar
1/2 cup plus 2 tablespoons Champagne or dry sparkling wine

Preparation Time: 10 min.

Fill the bottom of a Champagne glass with the tequila, Triple Sec, lime juice and sugar. Fill the glass with Champagne or dry sparkling wine and stir.

TO PREPARE AHEAD: Pour the tequila, Triple Sec, lime juice, and sugar into the bottom of each Champagne glass and place the glasses near where you are going to serve the apéritif. Have a few empty glasses available in case some guests prefer water.

TO FINISH: Pour the Champagne and serve.

HANDY TIP: One bottle of Champagne makes enough to serve 6.

Guacamole

4 avocados
1 jalapeño pepper, cored and minced
1/3 cup chopped cilantro
1/2 teaspoon kosher salt

3/4 teaspoon cumin
Juice of 1/2 lime
Tortilla chips to serve

Preparation Time: 15 min.

Peel, core and mash the avocados in a medium bowl. Add the jalapeño pepper and cilantro. Add the salt, cumin and lime juice. Mix until combined.

TO PREPARE AHEAD: You can make the Guacamole ahead on the day of the party. Put an avocado pit in the bowl with the Guacamole and cover tightly with plastic wrap. Refrigerate until needed.

TO FINISH: Remove the avocado pit and serve with the tortilla chips.

HANDY TIP: Be careful not to touch your eyes when you're chopping the jalapeño pepper, and wash your hands afterwards!

Summer

Tomato Salsa

Preparation Time: 15 min.

4	medium tomatoes, chopped	1	tablespoon extra-virgin olive oil
2	green onions, chopped		Juice of 1/2 lime
1/4	cup chopped onion		Few drops of Tabasco sauce
1/4	cup chopped cilantro		Kosher salt to taste
1	jalapeño pepper, cored and minced		Tortilla chips to serve

Place the tomatoes in a medium bowl. Add the green onions, onion, cilantro and jalapeño pepper. Stir in the extra-virgin olive oil, lime juice, Tabasco sauce and salt.

TO PREPARE AHEAD: You can make the salsa up to 2 days ahead and store, covered, in the refrigerator.

SUBSTITUTION: This recipe really tastes best when tomatoes are at their peak. If you can't get good tomatoes, try using a 14.5-ounce can of diced tomatoes instead. Or, if you're in a pinch, buy a good-quality ready-made salsa.

Zucchini Soup

Preparation Time: 20 min.
Cooking Time: 10 to 16 min.
Total Time: 30 to 36 min. plus refrigeration (if serving cold)

PRESENTATION TIP: Ladle the soup into bowls and garnish with a small amount of grated zucchini.

1 1/2	cups chopped onions	1	teaspoon kosher salt
2	tablespoons butter		White pepper to taste
2	pounds zucchini, sliced	1	cup milk
3	cups chicken stock	1	cup half-and-half
1/4	teaspoon nutmeg	1/2	cup grated zucchini for garnish

In a large soup pot, sauté the onions in butter over medium heat until translucent, about 5 to 8 minutes. Add the sliced zucchini to the onions. Add the chicken stock. Turn up the heat and bring to a boil. Cook until the zucchini is tender but not mushy, about 5 to 8 minutes.

Let cool slightly. Then, purée in batches in a blender until smooth. Add the nutmeg. Add the salt and white pepper.

If serving hot, add the milk and half-and-half and reheat gently. If serving cold, cool to room temperature, add the milk and half-and-half, cover and refrigerate.

TO PREPARE AHEAD: You can make the soup up to 2 days ahead, cool, cover, and refrigerate.

TO FINISH: If serving the soup hot, reheat gently. Serve according to the Presentation Tip.

HANDY TIP: If you can, use freshly ground nutmeg. It has a more intense flavor than prepared ground nutmeg. You can grate the nutmeg on your microplane or the finest blades of your hand grater.

SUBSTITUTION: For a lighter soup, you can substitute milk for the half-and-half. Or, if you prefer a richer soup, substitute whipping cream for the half-and-half.

Mixed Greens with Citrus Vinaigrette

3/4 cup walnut halves
8   ounces mixed baby greens
1   red onion, sliced

DRESSING
2   tablespoons orange juice
1 1/2 tablespoons Champagne vinegar
1   teaspoon Dijon mustard

1/4 teaspoon kosher salt
1/8 teaspoon freshly ground
     black pepper
1/3 cup extra-virgin olive oil
1   (15-ounce) can mandarin oranges in
     light syrup, drained

Preparation Time: 10 min.
Cooking Time: 3 min.
Total Time: 13 min.

Place the walnuts in a nonstick frying pan over medium heat. Cook, stirring often, until lightly browned, about 3 minutes. Remove from the heat and set aside.

Rinse and spin dry the mixed greens. In a large bowl, toss the mixed greens and red onion. Cover with a damp towel and refrigerate until needed.

For the dressing: In a small bowl, combine the orange juice, Champagne vinegar, Dijon mustard, salt and pepper. While whisking constantly, add the extra-virgin olive oil in a steady stream until the mixture thickens and emulsifies. Set aside.

Toss the mixed greens with enough dressing to coat. To serve family style, sprinkle the dressed mixed greens with the walnuts and the sections of mandarin orange.

TO PREPARE AHEAD: Follow the directions above, stopping after making the salad dressing. Cover the dressing and refrigerate. Set aside the can of mandarin oranges.

TO FINISH: Toss the mixed greens with enough dressing to coat and place on individual plates. Top with some walnuts and a few sections of mandarin orange.

SUBSTITUTION: If you don't have Champagne vinegar, feel free to substitute white wine vinegar or rice vinegar instead.

Pineapple Sorbet

Preparation Time: 10 min.
Cooking Time: 5 min.
Ice Cream Maker: 20 min.
Total Time: 35 min. plus
cooling time

1   cup water
1   cup sugar
1   (20-ounce) can sliced pineapple
    packed in its own juice, drained

1   tablespoon vodka
Mint sprigs for garnish

In a medium saucepan, heat the water and sugar until the sugar melts and the mixture starts to boil. Boil for 2 minutes. Remove from the heat and cool completely.

Purée the drained pineapple, sugar syrup and vodka in a blender until smooth. Pour into an ice cream maker and process according to the manufacturer's directions.

When finished, pour into an airtight container and freeze until ready to serve.

TO FREEZE: Prepare the sorbet up to a month ahead, place in an airtight container, and freeze.

TO FINISH: Remove the sorbet 15 minutes before serving to allow it to soften slightly. When ready, scoop into bowls, garnish with the mint, and serve.

Mahi Mahi with Mango Salsa

8   (6-ounce) skinless mahi mahi fillets
2   cups milk

MANGO SALSA AND ASSEMBLY
4   mangoes, peeled and diced
1   red bell pepper, cored and diced
1/2   cup chopped red onion
1/4   cup chopped cilantro
1/4   cup rice vinegar
1/4   cup lime juice
1/4   teaspoon red pepper flakes
Kosher salt and freshly ground
      black pepper to taste
Juice of 1 lemon

Preparation Time: 20 min.
Cooking Time: 12 to
15 min.
Total Time: 32 to 35 min.
plus marinating time

PRESENTATION TIP:
Place a fillet on each
plate. Top with the
Mango Salsa and serve
with the Sugar Snap
Peas and the Baby
New Potatoes.

Rinse and pat dry the fish. Place the fish in a sealable plastic bag and add the milk, turning to make sure the fish is coated on all sides. Seal and refrigerate for 1 to 4 hours.

To make the salsa: In a small bowl, combine the mangoes, bell pepper, onion, cilantro, vinegar, lime juice and red pepper flakes. Cover and let rest at room temperature for 30 minutes.

Preheat the oven to 350°F/180°C. Remove the fish from the milk bath and place on a wire rack on top of a rimmed baking sheet. Season generously with salt and pepper. Drizzle with the lemon juice. Bake in the preheated oven for about 12 to 15 minutes or until the fish is opaque and cooked through. Remove from the oven and serve topped with the Mango Salsa.

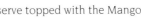

TO PREPARE AHEAD: On the day of the party, 1 to 4 hours before serving, place the fish in a sealable plastic bag with the milk and refrigerate. Prepare the Mango Salsa, cover, and refrigerate.

TO FINISH: Prepare and bake the fish as directed above. Serve according to the Presentation Tip.

SUBSTITUTION: If you can't find mahi mahi, try salmon (boneless with skin on) or tilapia instead. Season with salt and pepper. Sprinkle with the juice of 1 lemon and bake on a lightly oiled baking sheet. For both the salmon and the tilapia, preheat the oven to 350°F/180°C and bake for 12 to 15 minutes or until done.

Sugar Snap Peas

1 1/2   pounds sugar snap peas
1/4   cup butter

Kosher salt to taste

Preparation Time: 10 min.
Cooking Time: 2 to 3 min.
Total Time: 12 to 13 min.

Rinse the sugar snap peas with water and drain. Peel the string at 1 end along the ridge of the pod. Peel the string at the other end along the other ridge of the pod.

Melt the butter in a large frying pan with a lid. Stir in the sugar snap peas, cover and cook over medium heat for 2 to 3 minutes. Shake the pan occasionally. When done, season with salt.

TO PREPARE AHEAD: You can string the peas ahead on the day and store, covered, in the refrigerator until ready to use.

TO FINISH: Sauté as directed above.

Baby New Potatoes

3	pounds baby new potatoes	2	tablespoons chopped fresh chives
2	tablespoons butter		Kosher salt to taste

Rinse the potatoes and place in a large pot of water. Bring to a boil. Boil for 12 to 15 minutes or until tender. Remove from the heat and drain. Add the butter and chives. Toss gently to coat. Season with salt.

To Prepare Ahead: You can boil the potatoes up to a day ahead. After draining, plunge in cold water to stop the cooking process. Cool, cover, and refrigerate.

To Finish: When ready to serve, add the butter and reheat in the microwave. Sprinkle with the chopped chives and season with salt.

Sugar Cookies

1	cup butter	4	teaspoons baking powder
2	cups sugar	1 1/2	teaspoons baking soda
4	eggs	1	cup sour cream
1	teaspoon vanilla extract	1/2	cup sugar for sprinkling
6	cups flour		

In a large bowl, cream together the butter and 2 cups sugar with an electric mixer. Add the eggs 1 at a time, beating after each addition. Add the vanilla.

In a separate bowl, stir together the flour, baking powder and baking soda. Add the dry ingredients to the egg mixture alternately with the sour cream. Cover and chill in the refrigerator for 4 hours or overnight.

Preheat the oven to 350°F/180°C. Roll out half the dough on a floured surface until it is about 3/8 inch thick.

Cut out rounds or shapes with a cookie cutter. Place on an ungreased cookie sheet, sprinkle with 1/2 cup sugar and then bake in the preheated oven for 8 to 10 minutes. Repeat with the rest of the dough.

To Prepare Ahead: Prepare and bake the cookies as directed above. When the cookies have cooled completely, place in an airtight container, separating the layers with parchment paper, and freeze. At least an hour before serving, remove from the freezer and bring to room temperature.

Lime Pie

CRUST
1¼   cups finely crushed graham crackers
3   tablespoons sugar
6   tablespoons butter, melted

FILLING
1   (14-ounce) can sweetened
     condensed milk
4   teaspoons lime zest (about 2 limes)
½   cup fresh lime juice (about 3 or
     4 limes)
2   large eggs

TOPPING
1   cup sour cream
¼   cup sugar
½   teaspoon vanilla

WHIPPED CREAM
1   cup whipping cream
2   tablespoons sugar
2   limes, sliced for spirals,
     for garnish

Preparation Time: 20 min.
Cooking Time: 22 to
24 min.
Total Time: 42 to 44 min.

PRESENTATION TIP:
Place a piece of pie on a
plate. Top with a dollop
of Whipped Cream. Make
a small cut to the center
of each lime slice. Twist
the two ends, making a
spiral, and place on top
of the Whipped Cream.
The twisted lime slice
will form either an "s" or
a "z" shape depending on
which way you twist.

Preheat the oven to 350°F/180°C.

For the crust: In a small bowl, mix together the graham cracker crumbs and sugar. Add the melted butter and toss until well combined. Press over the bottom and side of a 9-inch pie plate. Bake until the crust is crisp and golden, about 7 to 9 minutes. Cool completely before filling.

For the filling: In a medium bowl, whisk together the sweetened condensed milk, lime zest, lime juice and eggs. Pour the filling into the cooled graham cracker crust. Bake on the center rack for 10 minutes or until the pie starts to set.

For the topping: While the pie is baking, stir together the sour cream, sugar and vanilla in a small bowl. Remove the pie from the oven and spread with the topping. Return to the oven for 5 minutes. Remove from the oven. Cool the pie on a wire rack and then refrigerate for 6 hours or overnight.

For the whipped cream: In a small bowl, whip the cream and sugar with an electric mixer until it forms stiff peaks. Cut the lime into thin slices.

Serve according to the Presentation Tip.

TO PREPARE AHEAD THE LIME PIE: You can make up the Lime Pie a day ahead and store, covered, in the refrigerator.

TO PREPARE AHEAD THE WHIPPED CREAM AND LIMES: On the day of the party, whip the cream and sugar, cover, and refrigerate. Slice the limes for the spirals, cover, and refrigerate.

TO FINISH: Re-whip the Whipped Cream, if necessary, and serve according to the Presentation Tip.

HANDY TIP: You can buy a box of graham cracker crumbs at most grocery stores. Or, you can place graham crackers in the bowl of a food processor and process until crumbled. Another option is to place the graham crackers in a sealable plastic bag, squeeze out the excess air, seal, and crush with a rolling pin or mallet. Any method will do!

HANDY TIP #2: Place your fresh limes in the microwave for 30 to 60 seconds before squeezing. You'll be amazed how much more juice you'll get from each lime.

Timeline

ONE WEEK BEFORE
(ABOUT 1 1/2 HOURS)

Buy groceries and create the ambience

Prepare ahead Pineapple Sorbet

Prepare ahead Sugar Cookies

TWO DAYS BEFORE
(ABOUT 1/4 HOUR)

Buy groceries and create the ambience

Put sparkling water, Champagne,
white wines, and dessert wine (if using)
in refrigerator

ONE DAY BEFORE
(ABOUT 1 1/2 HOURS)

Prepare ahead Zucchini Soup

Prepare ahead Lime Pie

DAY OF PARTY (ABOUT 2 HOURS)

Buy groceries and create the ambience

Remove Sugar Cookies from freezer

Prepare ahead Baby New Potatoes

Prepare ahead Sugar Snap Peas

Prepare ahead Mixed Greens with Citrus Vinaigrette

Prepare ahead Guacamole and Tomato Salsa

Prepare ahead Mahi Mahi with Mango Salsa

5:00 PM
Shower and dress

6:30 PM
Prepare coffeemaker

Open wines, turn on music,
  light candles

Put out starter bowls, salad plates,
  sorbet bowls, main course
  plates, and dessert plates

Prepare sugar and milk for coffee

Prepare ahead Whipped Cream and
  limes for Lime Pie

7:00 PM
Put butter pats and rolls on
  butter plates

Put a cucumber slice in each
  water glass

Prepare ahead Margarita Champagne

Put out peanuts

Remove salad dressing
  from refrigerator

7:25 PM
Put out Guacamole, Tomato Salsa
  and Chips

7:30 PM (GUESTS ARRIVE)
Open and pour Champagne (have
  water ready for those who
  prefer water)

7:35 PM
If serving soup hot, start to reheat
  soup over medium-low heat;
  stir and check occasionally

8:00 PM
If serving soup hot, check soup is hot

8:05 PM
Call people to table

Serve starter wine and water

8:10 PM
Serve Zucchini Soup, hot or cold,
  according to Presentation Tip

Preheat oven to 350°F/180°C

8:30 PM
Finish salad and serve

Take sorbet out of freezer

Remove Mango Salsa from
  refrigerator

8:45 PM
Serve sorbet, garnished with mint

Finish Mahi Mahi

9:05 PM
Reheat Baby New Potatoes in
  microwave; sprinkle with chives
  and season with salt

Finish Sugar Snap Peas

Remove Mahi Mahi from oven
  and plate according to
  Presentation Tip

9:15 PM
Serve main course and wine

Turn on coffeemaker

9:45 PM
Serve Lime Pie according to
  Presentation Tip

Serve dessert wine (if using)

10:00 PM
Serve coffee, tea, and
  after-dinner cookies

Grocery List

PANTRY ITEMS

1/2   cup extra-virgin olive oil
1 1/2 tablespoons Champagne vinegar
1/4   cup rice vinegar
Kosher salt
Freshly ground black pepper
1/8   teaspoon white pepper
3/4   teaspoon ground cumin
1/4   teaspoon ground nutmeg
1/4   teaspoon red pepper flakes
4 1/4 cups sugar
6   cups flour
4   teaspoons baking powder
1 1/2 teaspoons baking soda
1 1/2 teaspoons vanilla extract
3   cups chicken stock
3/4   cup walnuts
1   teaspoon Dijon mustard
1 1/4 cups graham cracker crumbs
1   (14-ounce) can sweetened
      condensed milk
1   (20-ounce) can sliced pineapple in
      own juice

1   (15-ounce) can mandarin oranges
Few drops of Tabasco sauce
1   (13- to 15-ounce) package tortilla chips
1   (12-ounce) jar peanuts
Decaffeinated and regular coffee
Regular and herbal tea bags

ALCOHOL AND DRINKS

2   bottles Champagne or sparkling wine
2   bottles white wine for starter (Semillon)
2   bottles white wine for main (Torrontes)
1   bottle dessert wine, if using (Moscato
      d'Asti or Late Harvest Riesling)
4   bottles sparkling water
1/4   cup tequila
1/4   cup Triple Sec
1   tablespoon vodka

DAIRY

2 2/3 cups butter
6   eggs
2   cups sour cream

PRODUCE

1   lemon
8   limes
1   cup chopped fresh cilantro
2   tablespoons chopped fresh chives
1   bunch fresh mint for sorbet garnish
4   avocados
2   jalapeño peppers
4   tomatoes
2   green onions
1 1/2 red onions
2 1/4 onions
2 1/2 pounds zucchini
8   ounces mixed baby greens
4   mangoes

1   red bell pepper
1 1/2 pounds sugar snap peas
3   pounds baby new potatoes
      (red or white)
1   cucumber

DAIRY

1   cup whipping cream
2   tablespoons orange juice
1   cup half-and-half
4   cups whole milk

MEAT, FISH AND DELI

8   (6-ounce) skinless mahi mahi fillets

BAKERY

8   rolls

Fall

Chicken Parmesan with Angel Hair Pasta

SERVES 8

Black Currant and Amaretto Champagne • Puff Pastry with Fig, Goat Cheese and Prosciutto • Basil Shrimp with Lemon • Mixed Greens with Roasted Portobello Mushrooms • Apricot Sorbet • Chicken Parmesan with Angel Hair Pasta • Poached Pears with Orange Butterscotch Sauce • Orange Almond Wafers

Salmon with Charmoula and Olives

SERVES 8

Pomegranate Champagne • Spinach Cheese Balls • Eggplant Dip with Pita and Vegetables • Tomato and Goat Cheese Galettes with Raspberry Vinaigrette • Mesclun Greens with Chive Mustard Vinaigrette • Orange Sorbet • Salmon with Charmoula and Olives • Rice with Lemon and Parsley • Sugar Snap Peas and Peas • Chocolate Ganache Cake with Fresh Raspberries • Almond Tuiles

Pork with Dry Herb Rub and Orange Sauce

SERVES 8

Cranberry Champagne • Spinach Phyllo Triangles • Thyme Dip with Gourmet Chips and Fresh Vegetables • Butternut Squash Soup • Endive, Gorgonzola and Walnuts • Cranberry Orange Sorbet • Pork with Dry Herb Rub and Orange Sauce • Mushroom Risotto • Brussels Sprouts • Apple Cranberry Crisp • Oatmeal Raisin Cookies

Thanksgiving Turkey

SERVES 10

Dill Dip and Vegetables • Roast Turkey with Pork and Herb Stuffing • Cranberry Chutney • Mashed Potato Casserole • Candied Yams • Green Beans with Almonds • Corn Bread Pudding • Banana Bread • Pumpkin Cake • Chocolate-Covered Peanut Butter Balls • Chewy Molasses Cookies

Chicken Parmesan with Angel Hair Pasta

menu

SERVES 8

Cocktail & Hors d'Oeuvres

Black Currant and Amaretto Champagne

Puff Pastry with Fig, Goat Cheese and Prosciutto

Mixed Nuts

Starter

Basil Shrimp with Lemon

Rolls and Butter

 Gavi

Salad

Mixed Greens with Roasted Portobello Mushrooms

Palate Cleanser

Apricot Sorbet

Main Course

Chicken Parmesan with Angel Hair Pasta

 Barbera or Chianti

Dessert

Poached Pears with Orange Butterscotch Sauce

Orange Almond Wafers

 Moscato d'Asti

Coffee & Tea

Black Currant and Amaretto Champagne

2 teaspoons amaretto
2 teaspoons crème de cassis

$^1/_2$ cup plus 2 tablespoons Champagne or dry sparkling wine

Preparation Time: 10 min.

Fill the bottom of a Champagne glass with amaretto and crème de cassis. Fill the glass with Champagne or dry sparkling wine.

TO PREPARE AHEAD: Pour the amaretto and crème de cassis into the bottom of each Champagne glass and place the glasses near where you are going to serve the apéritif. Have a few empty glasses available in case some guests prefer water.

TO FINISH: Pour the Champagne and serve.

HANDY TIP: One bottle of Champagne makes enough to serve 6.

Puff Pastry with Fig, Goat Cheese and Prosciutto

SERVES 8 TO 10

1 sheet frozen puff pastry, thawed ($^1/_2$ of a 17.3-ounce package)
$^1/_2$ cup fig spread

4 ounces crumbled goat cheese
4 pieces thinly sliced good-quality imported prosciutto

Preparation Time: 15 min.
Cooking Time: 25 to 32 min.
Total Time: 40 to 47 min.

Preheat the oven to 400°F/200°C.

Roll out the sheet of puff pastry on a floured surface to form a rectangle of 10×14 inches. Brush a $^1/_2$-inch border around the edge of the pastry with water. Fold this edge over and seal.

Place on an ungreased baking sheet. Prick with a fork in a dozen places and bake for 10 to 12 minutes or until a light golden brown. Turn down the oven to 350°F/180°C and bake for an additional 10 to 12 minutes. Remove from the oven.

With a knife, cover the pastry with the fig spread. Sprinkle with the crumbled goat cheese. Using a pair of scissors, snip the prosciutto into $^1/_2$-inch pieces and distribute over the top of the pastry.

Return to the oven for 5 to 8 minutes or until heated through. Remove from the oven and let cool for 5 minutes. Cut into 20 squares. Serve warm or at room temperature.

TO PREPARE AHEAD: You can bake the pastry ahead on the day, stopping before the addition of the fig spread. Cool on a wire rack.

TO FINISH: Place the pastry on an ungreased baking sheet, top with the fig spread, goat cheese, and prosciutto, and bake as directed above.

HANDY TIP: If your fig spread has fig chunks in it, process until smooth. It will be easier to spread.

Basil Shrimp with Lemon

PRESENTATION TIP:
Place 3 slices of lemon in a half circle on a plate. Add several basil shrimp in a mound in the center of the plate, partially overlapping the lemons.

2   pounds raw shrimp, peeled and deveined with tails on

PESTO
2   cups loosely packed basil leaves (about 3 ounces)
3   tablespoons pine nuts

3   cloves garlic
1/2   cup extra-virgin olive oil
1/4   cup grated Parmesan cheese
Kosher salt and freshly ground black pepper to taste
3   lemons, thinly sliced and seeded

Preheat the oven to 400°F/200°C. Line 2 baking sheets with parchment paper. Rinse and pat dry the shrimp.

For the pesto: In the bowl of a food processor, place the basil leaves, pine nuts and garlic. Pulse until chopped. While continuing to process, slowly add the extra-virgin olive oil in a constant stream. Add the Parmesan cheese and pulse until blended. Season with salt and pepper.

In a large bowl, combine the shrimp and pesto. Stir gently until well coated. Place the shrimp on the parchment-lined baking sheets in a single layer. Bake for 8 to 10 minutes or until the shrimp are opaque.

TO PREPARE AHEAD: You can prepare the basil shrimp a day ahead, stopping before baking. Cover the bowl of pesto-coated shrimp with plastic wrap and store in the refrigerator. Thinly slice the lemons, removing all seeds, and refrigerate in an airtight container.

TO FINISH: Bake as directed above and serve according to the Presentation Tip.

HANDY TIP: If you want to spice up your shrimp, sprinkle the shrimp with 1/4 teaspoon red pepper flakes just before baking.

Mixed Greens with Roasted Portobello Mushrooms

8   ounces mixed baby greens

DRESSING

1 1/2   tablespoons finely minced shallots
1   tablespoon sherry vinegar
1   tablespoon lemon juice
1   teaspoon Dijon mustard
1/4   teaspoon salt
1/8   teaspoon freshly ground
    black pepper

1/3   cup extra-virgin olive oil
4   large portobello mushrooms,
    stemmed
2   tablespoons extra-virgin olive oil
    for brushing
Kosher salt and freshly ground black
    pepper to taste
1/2   cup shaved Parmesan cheese

Preparation Time: 10 min.
Cooking Time: 20 min.
Total Time: 30 min.

Preheat the oven to 425°F/220°C.

Rinse and spin dry the mixed greens. Place in a large bowl, cover with a damp towel and refrigerate until needed.

For the dressing: In a small bowl, whisk together the shallots, sherry vinegar, lemon juice, Dijon mustard, 1/4 teaspoon salt and 1/8 teaspoon pepper. While continuing to whisk, add the extra-virgin olive oil in a steady stream. Continue whisking until the dressing thickens and emulsifies. Set aside.

Place the mushrooms cap side up on a baking sheet. Brush with extra-virgin olive oil and season with salt and pepper. Roast for 20 minutes. Remove from the oven and slice.

Toss the mixed greens with enough dressing to coat. To serve family style, top with the roasted mushrooms and sprinkle with the Parmesan cheese.

TO PREPARE AHEAD: On the day of the party, follow the directions above, stopping after you slice the mushrooms. Set aside in a microwave-safe bowl. Cover and refrigerate the salad dressing. Shave the Parmesan cheese, cover, and refrigerate. An hour before serving, remove the salad dressing from the refrigerator and return to room temperature.

TO FINISH: If desired, reheat the mushrooms briefly in the microwave. Whisk the dressing. Toss the mixed greens with enough dressing to coat and place on individual plates. Top with the roasted mushrooms and sprinkle with the Parmesan cheese.

Apricot Sorbet

Preparation Time: 10 min.
Cooking Time: 20 min.
Ice Cream Maker: 20 min.
Total Time: 50 min. plus cooling time

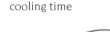

8	apricots, pitted	2	tablespoons fresh lemon juice
1/2	cup sugar	1	tablespoon apricot brandy
1/2	cup water	Mint sprigs for garnish	
1/4	cup orange juice		

Place the apricots, sugar, water, orange juice and lemon juice in a medium saucepan. Bring to a boil. Reduce the heat, cover and simmer for 15 minutes. Remove from the heat and let cool.

Place the apricot mixture in the bowl of a blender. Add the apricot brandy. Purée until smooth. Pour into an ice cream maker and process according to the manufacturer's directions.

When finished, pour into an airtight container and freeze until ready to serve.

TO FREEZE: Prepare the sorbet up to a month ahead, place in an airtight container, and freeze.

TO FINISH: Remove the sorbet 15 minutes before serving to allow it to soften slightly. When ready, scoop into bowls, garnish with the mint, and serve.

Chicken Parmesan with Angel Hair Pasta

Preparation Time: 30 min.
Cooking Time: 1 1/2 hours
Total Time: 2 hours

PRESENTATION TIP:
Place a mound of angel hair pasta in the middle of a plate. Place a chicken cutlet on top and garnish with the flat-leaf parsley.

TOMATO SAUCE
2	tablespoons extra-virgin olive oil
1 1/2	cups chopped onions
2	celery stalks, chopped
2	red bell peppers, cored, seeded and chopped
2	cloves garlic, minced
1	(28-ounce) can crushed tomatoes
1	tablespoon sugar
2	tablespoons tomato paste
1	(14-ounce) can chicken broth
2	teaspoons dried parsley
2	teaspoons dried basil
Kosher salt and freshly ground black pepper to taste	

CHICKEN
1	cup flour
3	eggs
2	tablespoons milk
1 1/2	cups bread crumbs
8	boneless chicken cutlets
6	tablespoons butter, divided
6	tablespoons extra-virgin olive oil, divided

ASSEMBLY
3	cups grated mozzarella cheese
1	cup shredded Parmesan cheese
1/4	cup extra-virgin olive oil
1	pound angel hair pasta
Flat-leaf parsley for garnish	

For the sauce: Heat the extra-virgin olive oil in a large saucepan. Add the onions, celery, red peppers and garlic and cook over medium heat, stirring often, until the onions are translucent, about 5 to 8 minutes. Add the crushed tomatoes, sugar, tomato paste, chicken broth, parsley and basil. Turn up the heat and bring to a boil. Reduce the heat to low, partially cover and simmer for 1 hour. Season with salt and pepper. Preheat the oven to 350°F/180°C.

For the chicken: Place the flour on a plate. In a medium bowl, beat together the eggs and milk. Place the bread crumbs on another plate. Coat a chicken cutlet in the flour, shaking off the excess. Dip the cutlet in the egg mixture. Dredge both sides of the cutlet in the bread crumbs, making sure to press the bread crumbs on firmly. Repeat with the remaining cutlets.

Heat 2 tablespoons of the butter and 2 tablespoons of the extra-virgin olive oil in a large frying pan over medium heat. Place as many cutlets as will fit in the frying pan and cook for 2 to 3 minutes per side, until browned and cooked through. Place on paper towels to drain. Repeat with the remaining cutlets, adding butter and extra-virgin olive oil to the pan with each batch.

To assemble: Place the chicken cutlets on the bottom of a 9×13-inch baking pan. Top the chicken cutlets with the grated mozzarella cheese. Spoon the Tomato Sauce over the mozzarella cheese. Sprinkle with the Parmesan cheese and drizzle with the extra-virgin olive oil. Bake, uncovered, for 20 to 30 minutes or until heated through.

Bring a large pot of water to a boil. Just before removing the chicken from the oven, cook the angel hair pasta according to the package directions; drain.

To Prepare Ahead Tomato Sauce: You can make the Tomato Sauce, cool, and freeze in an airtight container for up to 3 months. Remove from the freezer the night before the party and thaw in the refrigerator overnight. If you forget to thaw the sauce, you can always thaw it in the microwave.

To Prepare Ahead Chicken Parmesan: On the day of the party, cook the chicken cutlets and assemble the Chicken Parmesan as directed above, stopping before baking. Cover and refrigerate.

To Finish: When ready to serve, preheat the oven to 350°F/180°C and bake, uncovered, until heated through, about 30 to 40 minutes. Just before removing the Chicken Parmesan from the oven, cook the angel hair pasta according to the package directions. Drain. Serve according to the Presentation Tip.

Substitution: If you want to make Veal Parmesan, substitute 8 thinly sliced veal cutlets for the chicken. Follow the directions above but cook the veal cutlets over medium heat for only 1 to 2 minutes per side.

Poached Pears with Orange Butterscotch Sauce

SERVES 8

Preparation Time: 15 min.
Cooking Time: 15 to 20 min.
Total ime: 30 to 35 min.

PRESENTATION TIP:
To serve, place the pears on individual dessert plates. Spoon the Orange Butterscotch Sauce over the pears until you create a small puddle around the base of the pear. Garnish with a dollop of Mascarpone Cream on the side.

8   pears
2   tablespoons lemon juice
5   cups water
3/4   cup sugar

ORANGE BUTTERSCOTCH SAUCE
1/2   cup butter
1/2   cup packed light brown sugar
1/2   cup whipping cream

Zest of 1 orange
2   tablespoons Cointreau

MASCARPONE CREAM
1/3   cup whipping cream
4   ounces mascarpone cheese
3   tablespoons confectioners' sugar
1 1/2 teaspoons Cointreau

Core the pears, using a small knife or the small end of a melon ball cutter. Peel the pears, leaving the stems intact. Cut a small slice off the bottom of each pear so they stand upright. Rub each pear with the lemon juice to prevent discoloration.

In a large 6-quart pot, heat the water and sugar over medium heat until the sugar melts. Add the pears and bring the mixture to a boil. You may have to weight down the pears with a lid from a small saucepan. Turn down the heat and simmer for 15 to 20 minutes or until the pears are just tender. Remove the pears from the pot with a slotted spoon and set aside in a bowl to cool.

For the sauce: In a small saucepan while the pears are simmering, combine the butter, brown sugar, cream, orange zest and Cointreau. Heat over medium heat, stirring constantly, until the sugar dissolves and the butter melts. Bring to a boil. Turn down the heat and boil for 3 minutes without stirring. Remove from the heat, strain through a sieve to remove the orange zest and cool.

For the cream: In a small bowl, beat the cream, mascarpone cheese and confectioners' sugar with an electric mixer until firm peaks form. Stir in the Cointreau. Serve according to the Presentation Tip.

TO PREPARE AHEAD: You can poach the pears up to 2 days ahead. Remove from the poaching liquid, place in a container, and cool to room temperature. Cover and refrigerate until needed. You can make the Orange Butterscotch Sauce up to 2 days ahead and store, covered, in the refrigerator.

TO PREPARE AHEAD THE MASCARPONE CREAM: You can make the Mascarpone Cream ahead on the day and store, covered, in the refrigerator.

TO FINISH: Warm the Orange Butterscotch Sauce in the microwave, re-whip the Mascarpone Cream if needed, and serve according to the Presentation Tip.

Orange Almond Wafers

1	cup butter, softened	Zest of 1 orange
1	cup sugar	1½ cups flour
2	eggs	1 cup sliced almonds
1	teaspoon almond extract	

Preparation Time: 10 min.
Cooking Time: 7 to
9 min. per batch

Preheat the oven to 375°/190°C. Grease a cookie sheet.

In a medium bowl, blend the butter and sugar with an electric mixer until light and fluffy.

Add the eggs, almond extract and orange zest and beat until combined. Stir in the flour and then the almonds.

Drop by teaspoonfuls about 2 inches apart onto the greased cookie sheet. Bake for 7 to 9 minutes per batch. Cool on the cookie sheet for about 2 minutes. Then remove to a wire rack and cool completely. Store in an airtight container.

TO PREPARE AHEAD: You can make the cookies up to a week ahead. You'll only need about 16 cookies for your dinner party. Freeze the extra cookie dough or bake the cookies and store in an airtight container.

TO FINISH: Place the cookies you need for your party on a small serving platter and cover securely with plastic wrap until ready to serve.

TO FREEZE: Refrigerate unbaked cookie dough until firm enough to handle, about 15 minutes. Place a piece of plastic wrap on your work surface. Separate the dough into 2 equal pieces. Shape each piece into a log with a 1½-inch diameter. Roll each log in plastic wrap, sealing the ends. Place the logs in a sealable plastic bag and freeze for up to 3 months. When ready to bake, thaw for 30 minutes at room temperature (or briefly in the microwave) and bake as directed above.

Fall

Timeline

ONE WEEK BEFORE
(ABOUT 1½ HOURS)

Buy groceries and create the ambience

Prepare ahead Apricot Sorbet

Prepare ahead Tomato Sauce for Chicken Parmesan

TWO DAYS BEFORE
(ABOUT ¼ HOUR)

Buy groceries and create the ambience

Put sparkling water, Champagne, white wine, and dessert wine (if using) in refrigerator

Put out red wine

ONE DAY BEFORE
(ABOUT 1½ HOURS)

Prepare ahead Poached Pears

Prepare ahead Orange Almond Wafers

Thaw Tomato Sauce for Chicken Parmesan in refrigerator overnight

---

DAY OF PARTY (ABOUT 2 HOURS)

Buy groceries and create the ambience

Prepare ahead Puff Pastry with Fig, Goat Cheese and Prosciutto

Prepare ahead Basil Shrimp with Lemon

Prepare ahead Mixed Greens with Roasted Portobello Mushrooms

Prepare ahead Chicken Parmesan

Prepare ahead Mascarpone Cream for Poached Pears

5:00 PM
Shower and dress

6:30 PM
Prepare coffeemaker

Open wines, turn on music, light candles

Put out starter plates, salad plates, sorbet bowls, main course plates, and dessert plates

Prepare sugar and milk for coffee

7:00 PM
Preheat oven to 350°F/180°C

Put butter pats and rolls on butter plates

Put a cucumber slice in each water glass

Prepare ahead Black Currant and Amaretto Champagne

Put out mixed nuts

Finish Puff Pastry with Fig, Goat Cheese and Prosciutto

Remove salad dressing from refrigerator

7:25 PM
Cut Puff Pastry into squares, arrange on a serving platter, and put out for guests

Turn up oven to 400°F/200°F

7:30 PM (GUESTS ARRIVE)
Open and pour Champagne (have water ready for those who prefer water)

7:55 PM
Finish Basil Shrimp with Lemon

8:05 PM
Call people to table

Serve starter wine and water

Put on water to boil for angel hair pasta

8:10 PM
Serve Basil Shrimp according to Presentation Tip

8:30 PM
Finish salad and serve

Turn down oven to 350°F/180°C

Put Chicken Parmesan, uncovered, in oven

Take sorbet out of freezer

8:45 PM
Serve sorbet, garnished with mint

9:00 PM
Add angel hair pasta to boiling water, cook, and drain according to package directions

Remove Chicken Parmesan from oven; finish and plate according to Presentation Tip

9:15 PM
Serve main course and wine

Turn on coffeemaker

9:45 PM
Finish Poached Pears and serve according to Presentation Tip

Serve dessert wine (if using)

10:00 PM
Serve coffee, tea, and after-dinner cookies

Grocery List

ONE WEEK BEFORE PARTY

PANTRY ITEMS
2 cups extra-virgin olive oil
1 tablespoon sherry vinegar
Kosher salt
Freshly ground black pepper
2 teaspoons dried parsley
2 teaspoons dried basil
$2^1/_3$ cups sugar
$^1/_2$ cup light brown sugar
3 tablespoons confectioners' sugar
$2^1/_2$ cups flour
1 teaspoon almond extract
3 tablespoons pine nuts
1 cup sliced almonds
1 teaspoon Dijon mustard
$^1/_2$ cup fig spread
1 (28-ounce) can crushed tomatoes
2 tablespoons tomato paste
1 (14-ounce) can chicken broth
$1^1/_2$ cups plain bread crumbs
1 pound angel hair pasta
1 (12-ounce) jar mixed nuts
Decaffeinated and regular coffee
Regular and herbal tea bags

ALCOHOL AND DRINKS
2 bottles Champagne or sparkling wine
2 bottles white wine for starter (Gavi)
2 bottles red wine for main
(Barbera or Chianti)
1 bottle dessert wine, if using
(Moscato d'Asti)
4 bottles sparkling water
$^1/_3$ cup Disaronno amaretto
$^1/_3$ cup crème de cassis
1 tablespoon apricot brandy
$2^1/_2$ tablespoons Cointreau

PRODUCE
8 apricots
1 orange
2 onions
2 celery stalks
2 red bell peppers
5 cloves garlic

DAIRY
5 eggs
$2^2/_3$ cups butter
1 cup whipping cream
4 ounces mascarpone cheese
$^1/_4$ cup orange juice

FREEZER
$^1/_2$ (17.3-ounce) package frozen puff pastry

TWO DAYS BEFORE PARTY

PRODUCE
6 lemons
1 orange
8 pears
3 ounces basil leaves
1 bunch flat-leaf parsley sprigs for
main garnish
1 bunch fresh mint for sorbet garnish
8 ounces mixed baby greens
1 shallot
4 large portobello mushrooms
1 cucumber

DAIRY
$1^1/_8$ cups whole milk
4 ounces crumbled goat cheese
$^1/_4$ cup grated Parmesan cheese
1 cup shredded Parmesan cheese
$^1/_2$ cup shaved Parmesan cheese
3 cups grated mozzarella cheese

MEAT, FISH AND DELI
4 slices good-quality imported prosciutto
2 pounds raw shrimp, peeled and
deveined with tails on
8 boneless chicken cutlets

DAY OF PARTY

BAKERY
8 rolls

Salmon with Charmoula and Olives

menu

SERVES 8

Cocktail & Hors d'Oeuvres

Pomegranate Champagne

Spinach Cheese Balls

Eggplant Dip with Pita and Vegetables

Cashews

Starter

Tomato and Goat Cheese Galettes with Raspberry Vinaigrette

Rolls and Butter

Oregon Pinot Gris

Salad

Mesclun Greens with Chive Mustard Vinaigrette

Palate Cleanser

Orange Sorbet

Main Course

Salmon with Charmoula and Olives

Rice with Lemon and Parsley

Sugar Snap Peas and Peas

Rioja or Beaujolais-Villages

Dessert

Chocolate Ganache Cake with Fresh Raspberries

Almond Tuiles

Tawny Port

Coffee & Tea

Pomegranate Champagne

1	teaspoon sugar	1/2	cup plus 2 tablespoons Champagne	
2	tablespoons pomegranate juice		or dry sparkling wine	

Preparation Time: 5 min

Fill the bottom of a Champagne glass with the sugar and pomegranate juice. Fill the glass with Champagne or dry sparkling wine.

TO PREPARE AHEAD: Place the sugar and the pomegranate juice in the bottom of each Champagne glass and place the glasses near where you are going to serve the apéritif. Have a few empty glasses available in case some guests prefer water.

TO FINISH: Pour the Champagne and serve.

HANDY TIP: One bottle of Champagne makes enough to serve 6.

SUBSTITUTION: If you prefer, you can use 1 1/2 tablespoons PAMA Pomegranate Liqueur instead of the pomegranate juice and sugar.

Spinach Cheese Balls

2	(10-ounce) packages frozen chopped spinach	1/2	teaspoon kosher salt
4	eggs	1/4	teaspoon freshly ground black pepper
1	medium onion, finely chopped	1/2	cup butter, melted
1	cup grated Parmesan cheese	2	cups herb stuffing mix or herb-seasoned bread crumbs
1/4	teaspoon ground nutmeg		

Preparation Time: 20 min.
Cooking Time: 10 to 15 min.
Total Time: 30 to 35 min. plus 15 min. refrigeration

Preheat the oven to 350°F/180°C.

Thaw the frozen spinach in the microwave. The easiest way is to put the spinach in a bowl, cover with plastic wrap, making a few slits with a knife, and microwave for about 3 minutes. Then let sit for a minute. If it's not yet thawed, microwave for another minute. When the spinach has thawed, squeeze out the excess liquid; a cheesecloth works best, but your hands will do in a pinch.

Beat the eggs in a large bowl. Add the chopped onion to the eggs. Add the Parmesan cheese, nutmeg, salt and pepper and mix. Add the spinach to the egg mixture. Stir in the melted butter. Stir in the stuffing mix. Cover and refrigerate for about 15 minutes or until firm enough to handle. Shape into 1-inch balls and arrange on an ungreased baking sheet. Bake for 10 to 15 minutes or until lightly browned.

TO PREPARE AHEAD: You can freeze the unbaked Spinach Cheese Balls for up to 3 months. Follow the directions above but place the 1-inch balls on an ungreased baking sheet and freeze. When frozen, transfer the balls to a sealable plastic bag, squeezing out any excess air. Return to the freezer. When needed, place on an ungreased baking sheet and bake at 350°F/180°C for 15 to 20 minutes or until lightly browned. Serve warm.

Eggplant Dip with Pita and Vegetables

Preparation Time: 20 min.
Cooking Time: 60 min.
Total Time: 80 min.

PRESENTATION TIP:
Place the Eggplant Dip on an appetizer platter and surround with the red pepper and carrots. You can prepare the platter, without the pita triangles, early in the day and store, covered, in the refrigerator. Just before serving, place the pita triangles on the platter with the vegetables or in a separate basket.

1	large eggplant		2	tablespoons tahini
3	pita bread rounds		1/4	teaspoon kosher salt
1 1/2	tablespoons extra-virgin olive oil		1	tablespoon lemon juice
1/2	teaspoon kosher salt		1/2	cup full-fat yogurt
1/2	teaspoon freshly ground black pepper			Curly parsley for garnish
1/2	teaspoon dried oregano		1	red bell pepper, cored, seeded and sliced
2	cloves garlic, minced		1/2	pound carrots, peeled and sliced

Preheat the oven to 400°F/200°C.

Prick the eggplant with a fork in several places. Place on an ungreased baking sheet. Bake for an hour or until the outer skin is crisp and the inside is soft. Remove from the oven and let cool.

Meanwhile, make the pita triangles. Place a pita round on your work surface. Brush with 1/3 of the extra-virgin olive oil and sprinkle with 1/3 of the salt, pepper and oregano. Cut into triangles. Place on a baking sheet. Repeat with the other pita rounds, extra-virgin olive oil, salt, pepper and oregano. Bake for 8 minutes and then turn the pita triangles over and bake for another 8 minutes. Remove from the oven, cool and store in an airtight container until needed.

When the eggplant has cooled, spoon the insides into the bowl of a food processor. Discard the skin. Add the garlic, tahini, 1/4 teaspoon salt, lemon juice and yogurt. Purée until creamy. Spoon into a serving dish and garnish with parsley. Refrigerate, covered, until needed.

TO PREPARE AHEAD: You can make the Eggplant Dip up to 2 days ahead and store, covered, in the refrigerator. You can make the pita triangles up to 2 days ahead, cool, and store in an airtight container. You can prepare the vegetables up to a day ahead and store, covered, in the refrigerator.

TO FINISH: Serve according to the Presentation Tip.

HANDY TIP: If you can find it, use full-fat Greek yogurt, as it makes for a richer and creamier texture.

Tomato and Goat Cheese Galettes with Raspberry Vinaigrette

1   egg yolk
1   teaspoon water
1   sheet frozen puff pastry, thawed
    (¹/2 of a 17.3-ounce package)

RASPBERRY VINAIGRETTE
2   cloves garlic, minced
3   tablespoons raspberry vinegar

1   tablespoon Dijon mustard
1   tablespoon chopped fresh thyme
1   tablespoon sugar
¹/2 cup extra-virgin olive oil

¹/2 cup walnuts, toasted and chopped
8   medium vine-ripened tomatoes
1   (11-ounce) log goat cheese

Preparation Time: 20 min.
Cooking Time: 15 to 20 min.
Total Time: 35 to 40 min.

PRESENTATION TIP:
Transfer each Tomato and Goat Cheese Galette to a plate. Sprinkle with the walnuts and drizzle with the Raspberry Vinaigrette.

Preheat the oven to 400°F/200°C. In a small bowl, beat together the egg yolk and water.

Place the pastry sheet on a floured work surface. Using a 3-inch pastry cutter, cut out 8 rounds. If you don't have a 3-inch pastry cutter, a clean empty 6-ounce tuna can will do. Place the rounds on an ungreased baking sheet. Brush the tops with the egg mixture and prick each a few times with a fork. Bake, uncovered, for 10 to 12 minutes or until browned slightly.

For the vinaigrette: While the pastry is baking, whisk together the garlic, raspberry vinegar, Dijon mustard, thyme and sugar in a small bowl. While continuing to whisk, add the extra-virgin olive oil in a steady stream. Whisk until the dressing thickens and emulsifies. Set aside.

Place the walnuts in a small nonstick frying pan. Heat over medium heat, tossing occasionally, until the walnuts are toasted, about 3 minutes. When cool, chop coarsely.

To assemble and bake: Slice the tomatoes into twenty-four ³/8-inch-thick slices. Discard the ends. Slice the log of goat cheese into 24 slices. On an ungreased baking sheet, place 1 slice of tomato on each pastry round and top with a slice of goat cheese. Repeat with another layer of tomato and goat cheese and then a third layer of tomato and goat cheese. Return to the oven for 5 minutes, or until just heated through.

TO PREPARE AHEAD: On the day of the party, make the pastry rounds and cool on a wire rack. When cool, place the rounds in a sealable plastic bag until ready to use. Toast the walnuts and set aside. Make the Raspberry Vinaigrette, cover, and refrigerate. Slice the tomatoes and goat cheese, cover, and store separately in the refrigerator.

TO FINISH: Assemble and bake as directed above. Serve according to the Presentation Tip.

HANDY TIP: Plain dental floss is a great way to slice goat cheese, especially when you need thin slices.

SUBSTITUTION: If serving on a hot day, consider serving the stacks cold, without the puff pastry, for a quick-and-easy starter.

Mesclun Greens with Chive Mustard Vinaigrette

SERVES 6 TO 8

Preparation Time: 10 min.

8 ounces mixed mesclun greens

DRESSING
2 tablespoons Champagne vinegar
1 teaspoon Dijon mustard
1 egg yolk, at room temperature

1 clove garlic, minced
2 teaspoons chopped fresh chives
1/2 teaspoon kosher salt
1/4 teaspoon freshly ground black pepper
1/3 cup extra-virgin olive oil

Rinse and spin dry the mixed greens. Place in a large bowl, cover with a damp towel and refrigerate until needed.

For the dressing: In a small bowl, whisk together the Champagne vinegar, Dijon mustard, egg yolk, garlic, chives, salt and pepper. While continuing to whisk, add the extra-virgin olive oil in a steady stream. Continue whisking until the dressing thickens and emulsifies. Set aside.

To serve family style, toss the mixed greens with enough dressing to coat. Serve immediately.

TO PREPARE AHEAD: Follow the directions above, stopping before you toss the mixed greens with the dressing. Cover and refrigerate the dressing.

TO FINISH: Whisk the dressing. Toss the mixed greens with enough dressing to coat and place on individual plates.

SUBSTITUTION: If you prefer, use 1 tablespoon mayonnaise in place of the raw egg yolk.

Orange Sorbet

SERVES 8

Preparation Time: 10 min.
Cooking Time: 5 min.
Ice Cream Maker: 20 min.
Total Time: 35 min. plus cooling time

1 1/2 cups sugar
1 1/2 cups water
Grated zest of 1 orange
1 cup good-quality orange juice

Juice of 1 lime
1 tablespoon vodka
Mint sprigs for garnish

In a medium saucepan, heat the sugar, water and orange zest until the sugar melts and the mixture starts to boil. Boil for 2 minutes.

Remove from the heat and stir in the orange juice and lime juice. Cool completely. Stir in the vodka. Pour into an ice cream maker and process according to the manufacturer's directions. When finished, pour into an airtight container and freeze until ready to serve.

TO FREEZE: Prepare the sorbet up to a month ahead, place in an airtight container, and freeze.

TO FINISH: Remove the sorbet 15 minutes before serving to allow it to soften slightly. When ready, scoop into bowls, garnish with the mint, and serve.

Salmon with Charmoula and Olives

CHARMOULA
2/3 cup chopped fresh cilantro
2/3 cup chopped fresh flat-leaf parsley
2 cloves garlic, minced
2 teaspoons ground cumin
2 teaspoons paprika
1 teaspoon ground cayenne pepper
Juice of 1 lemon

1/2 cup extra-virgin olive oil
1 teaspoon kosher salt

SALMON
1 (2 1/2-pound) skinless salmon fillet
3/4 cup coarsely chopped green olives
8 lemon slices, seeded

Preparation Time: 15 min.
Cooking Time: 15 to 20 min.
Total Time: 30 to 35 min. plus marinating time

The night before, or at least the morning before, your party, make up the Charmoula and assemble the dish so that it can marinate.

For the charmoula: In a small bowl, combine the cilantro, parsley, garlic, cumin, paprika, cayenne pepper, lemon juice, extra-virgin olive oil and salt.

For the salmon: Cut the salmon into 8 pieces. This makes serving the salmon much easier when it's done. Grease a 9×13-inch glass baking dish. Lay the salmon pieces in the dish, reassembling the pieces as best you can.

Cover the salmon with the Charmoula and then sprinkle with the chopped olives. Cover with aluminium foil and refrigerate for at least 6 hours or preferably overnight. Remove the salmon from the refrigerator about 1 hour before baking.

Preheat the oven to 350°F/180°C. Place the covered baking dish in the oven and bake the salmon for 15 to 20 minutes. Remove from the oven.

PRESENTATION TIP:
To serve, place a mound of Rice with Lemon and Parsley in the middle of each plate and top with a piece of salmon. Cut a lemon slice in half and place the 2 halves on top of the salmon. Place the Sugar Snap Peas and Peas in a ring around the outside of the Rice with Lemon and Parsley.

TO PREPARE AHEAD: You can make up the Charmoula and marinate the salmon, covered, overnight in the refrigerator. Cut the lemon slices, place in an airtight container, and refrigerate.

TO FINISH: Remove the salmon from the refrigerator an hour before baking. Bake as directed and serve according to the Presentation Tip.

SUBSTITUTION: If you can't find pitted green olives, you can always substitute pimento-stuffed olives instead.

Rice with Lemon and Parsley

SERVES 8

Preparation Time: 10 min.
Cooking Time: 20 min.
Total Time: 30 min.

2 1/2 cups long grain rice
1/3 cup finely chopped parsley
1/4 cup butter

Grated zest of 1 lemon
Kosher salt and freshly ground black pepper to taste

Cook the rice according to the package directions. When cooked, add the parsley, butter and lemon zest. Season with salt and pepper.

TO PREPARE AHEAD: You can make the rice up to a day ahead. Cool, cover, and refrigerate. Reheat in the microwave to serve.

Sugar Snap Peas and Peas

SERVES 8

Preparation Time: 10 min.
Cooking Time: 3 to 4 min.
Total Time: 13 to 14 min.

10 ounces sugar snap peas
1 teaspoon kosher salt
20 ounces frozen peas (about 4 cups)

2 tablespoons butter
Kosher salt to taste

Bring a large pot of water to a boil.

Rinse the sugar snap peas with water and drain. Peel the string at 1 end along the ridge of the pod. Peel the string at the other end along the other ridge.

Add 1 teaspoon salt to the boiling water. Add the frozen peas and return to a boil. After 2 minutes, add the sugar snap peas to the boiling water. Return to a boil. Boil for about 2 minutes longer, or until the sugar snap peas are tender-crisp. Drain and then add the butter. Season with salt to taste.

TO PREPARE AHEAD: You can make the Sugar Snap Peas and Peas up to a day ahead. Boil as directed above. Drain and plunge the drained sugar snap peas and peas into cold water to stop the cooking process. Drain and store the peas in a microwave-safe bowl, covered, in the refrigerator until ready to serve.

TO FINISH: Add the butter, reheat in the microwave, season with salt to taste, and serve.

Almond Tuiles

2	egg whites	$^1/_2$	teaspoon vanilla extract
$^1/_2$	cup sugar	$^1/_4$	cup butter, melted
$^1/_3$	cup flour	$^1/_2$	cup blanched flaked almonds

Preparation Time: 10 min.
Cooking Time: 6 to 8 min. per batch

Preheat the oven to 350°F/180°C. Line 2 cookie sheets with parchment paper.

In a small bowl, beat the egg whites and sugar until frothy. Stir in the flour and vanilla. Stir in the melted butter.

Drop the mixture by rounded teaspoonfuls onto the prepared cookie sheets. Sprinkle each with a few blanched flaked almonds. Bake for 6 to 8 minutes or until golden around the edges. Cool on the cookie sheets for 1 minute. If you want curled cookies, remove from the cookie sheets and wrap around a rolling pin greased with butter. Place on a wire rack to cool completely.

To Prepare Ahead: You can make the cookies up to a week ahead. You'll only need about 16 cookies for your dinner party. Freeze the extra cookie dough or bake the cookies and store in an airtight container.

To Finish: Place the cookies you need for your party on a small serving platter and cover securely with plastic wrap until ready to serve.

Chocolate Ganache Cake with Fresh Raspberries

SERVES 12

Preparation Time: 40 min.
Cooking Time: 75 min.
Total Time: 115 min.

PRESENTATION TIP:
Reheat the remaining Chocolate Topping in the microwave until melted. If using a plastic bag, cut a very small piece of plastic off 1 corner. Squeeze out the chocolate to produce a zigzag pattern on each plate. Place a slice of the cake on top. Garnish with the Whipped Cream and a few raspberries.

CHOCOLATE ALMOND CAKE

4	ounces dark chocolate
1/3	cup unsweetened cocoa powder
1/3	cup water
3/4	cup butter, melted
1 1/3	cups packed brown sugar
1	cup almond meal
4	egg yolks
4	egg whites

CHOCOLATE TOPPING AND ASSEMBLY

8	ounces dark chocolate, broken into pieces
2/3	cup whipping cream
18	ounces raspberries, divided

WHIPPED CREAM

1	cup whipping cream
2	tablespoons sugar

Preheat the oven to 325°F /160°C. Grease a 9-inch round cake pan. Line the base and side with parchment paper.

For the cake: Melt the chocolate by placing it in a bowl over a double boiler that has been removed from the heat. Let stand until melted, stirring occasionally, about 4 minutes. In a large bowl, blend the cocoa powder and water with an electric mixer until smooth. Blend in the melted chocolate, butter, brown sugar, almond meal and egg yolks.

In a small bowl, beat the egg whites with an electric mixer until soft peaks form. Fold a spoonful of the egg whites into the chocolate mixture to loosen. Then fold the remaining egg whites into the chocolate mixture in 2 batches. Pour the batter into the prepared pan. Bake for 75 minutes.

Let the cake stand for 15 minutes and then turn onto a wire rack. Peel off the parchment paper. Turn the cake top side up and cool completely.

For the topping: Place the chocolate and cream in a bowl over a double boiler that has been removed from the heat. Let sit for 4 minutes. Then stir a few times and let sit again until the chocolate has melted. Stir only until smooth.

To assemble: Spread a layer of the Chocolate Topping over the top of the cake. Rinse and pat dry the raspberries. Place the raspberries pointed end up over the top of the cake, reserving any extra for garnish. Drizzle some of the Chocolate Topping over the raspberries and around the edge, saving about 1/4 cup for garnishing the dessert plates. Place the reserved chocolate in a plastic squeeze bottle or sealable plastic bag and set aside. Let the cake stand until the chocolate sets.

For the whipped cream: Place the cream and sugar in a medium bowl. Beat with an electric mixer until firm peaks form, about 1 1/2 minutes.

TO PREPARE AHEAD CHOCOLATE CAKE: You can make and freeze the chocolate cake (without the topping) for up to 4 months. Before freezing, cool the cake completely, wrap tightly in plastic wrap, and place in a sealable plastic bag. Thaw the wrapped cake at room temperature for 2 to 3 hours. Remove the wrap, place on a cake plate, and let thaw completely.

TO FINISH: Make the Chocolate Topping and assemble as directed above. Place the raspberries for the garnish in a bowl and refrigerate. Make the Whipped Cream, cover, and refrigerate. Serve according to the Presentation Tip.

HANDY TIP: When melting the chocolate for the topping, beware! Chocolate can be very tricky. Don't let any water get into the chocolate, and don't let the chocolate get too hot, or it will separate and you'll have to start again.

Timeline

ONE WEEK BEFORE
(ABOUT 1 1/2 HOURS)

Buy groceries and create the ambience

Prepare ahead Chocolate Cake
for Chocolate Ganache Cake
with Fresh Raspberries

Prepare ahead Orange Sorbet

Prepare ahead Spinach Cheese Balls

TWO DAYS BEFORE
(ABOUT 1/4 HOUR)

Buy groceries and create the ambience

Put sparkling water, Champagne,
white wine, and dessert wine (if using)
in refrigerator

Put out red wine

ONE DAY BEFORE
(ABOUT 3/4 HOUR)

Prepare ahead Almond Tuiles

Prepare ahead Salmon with Charmoula
and Olives

DAY OF PARTY (ABOUT 3 HOURS)

Buy groceries and create the ambience

Remove Chocolate Cake from freezer and thaw

Prepare ahead Tomato and Goat Cheese Galettes with Raspberry Vinaigrette

Prepare ahead Eggplant Dip with Pita and Vegetables

Prepare ahead Mesclun Greens with Chive Mustard Vinaigrette

Prepare ahead Rice with Lemon and Parsley

Prepare ahead Sugar Snap Peas and Peas

Finish Chocolate Ganache Cake with Fresh Raspberries

5:00 PM
Shower and dress

6:30 PM
Prepare coffeemaker

Open wines, turn on music,
light candles

Put out starter plates, salad plates,
sorbet bowls, main course
plates, and dessert plates

Prepare sugar and milk for coffee

7:00 PM
Preheat oven to 350°F/180°C

Put butter pats and rolls on
butter plates

Put a cucumber slice in each
water glass

Prepare ahead Pomegranate
Champagne

Put out cashews

Serve Eggplant Dip according to
Presentation Tip

7:20 PM
Finish Spinach Balls

7:30 PM (Guests arrive)
Open and pour Champagne (have
water ready for those who
prefer water)

7:35 PM
Remove Spinach Balls from oven
and serve

Keep oven at 350°F/180°C

Remove salmon from refrigerator

7:55 PM
Finish Tomato and Goat Cheese
Galettes and put in oven

8:05 PM
Call people to table

Serve starter wine and water

8:10 PM
Serve Tomato and Goat Cheese
Galettes according to
Presentation Tip

Keep oven at 350°F/180°C

8:30 PM
Finish salad and serve

Take sorbet out of freezer

8:45 PM
Serve sorbet, garnished with mint

Put salmon, covered, in oven

9:00 PM
Reheat Rice with Lemon and Parsley
in microwave

Finish Sugar Snap Peas and Peas

Remove salmon from oven and serve
according to Presentation Tip

9:15 PM
Serve main course and wine

Turn on coffeemaker

9:45 PM
Serve Chocolate Ganache Cake with
Fresh Raspberries according to
Presentation Tip

Serve dessert wine (if using)

10:00 PM
Serve coffee, tea, and
after-dinner cookies

Grocery List

ONE WEEK BEFORE PARTY

Pantry Items

$1^1/2$ cups extra-virgin olive oil
3 tablespoons raspberry vinegar
2 tablespoons Champagne vinegar
Kosher salt
Freshly ground black pepper
$1/2$ teaspoon dried oregano
$1/4$ teaspoon ground nutmeg
2 teaspoons ground cumin
2 teaspoons paprika
1 teaspoon cayenne pepper
$2^3/8$ cups sugar
$1^1/3$ cups light brown sugar
$1/3$ cup flour
$1/2$ teaspoon vanilla extract
12 ounces dark chocolate
$1/3$ cup unsweetened cocoa powder
1 cup almond meal
$1/2$ cup blanched flaked almonds
2 tablespoons tahini
2 cups herbed stuffing mix or herb-seasoned bread crumbs
$1^1/3$ tablespoons Dijon mustard
$1/2$ cup walnuts
$3/4$ cup pitted green olives (plain or stuffed with pimento)
$2^1/2$ cups long grain white rice
1 (12-ounce) jar cashews
Decaffeinated and regular coffee
Regular and herbal tea bags

Alcohol and Drinks

2 bottles Champagne or sparkling wine
2 bottles white wine for starter (Oregon Pinot Gris)
2 bottles red wine for main (Rioja or Beaujolais-Villages)
1 bottle dessert wine, if using (Tawny Port)
4 bottles sparkling water
1 cup pomegranate juice
1 tablespoon vodka

Produce

1 medium onion
1 orange
1 lime

Dairy

12 eggs
$2^3/8$ cups butter
1 cup grated Parmesan cheese
1 cup good-quality orange juice

Freezer

20 ounces frozen chopped spinach
$1/2$ (17.3-ounce) package frozen puff pastry
20 ounces frozen peas

TWO DAYS BEFORE PARTY

Produce

5 lemons
18 ounces raspberries
1 bunch fresh curly parsley
1 tablespoon chopped fresh thyme
2 teaspoons chopped fresh chives
$2/3$ cup chopped fresh cilantro
1 cup chopped fresh flat-leaf parsley
1 bunch fresh mint for sorbet garnish
8 ounces mixed mesclun greens
1 large eggplant
7 cloves garlic
1 red bell pepper
$1/2$ pound carrots
8 medium vine-ripened tomatoes
10 ounces sugar snap peas
1 cucumber

Dairy

1 cup whole milk
$1/2$ cup full-fat yogurt
1 (11-ounce) log goat cheese
$1^2/3$ cups whipping cream

Meat, Fish and Deli

$2^1/2$ pounds skinless salmon

Bakery

3 pita bread rounds

DAY OF PARTY

Bakery

8 rolls

Pork with Dry Herb Rub and Orange Sauce

menu

SERVES 8

Cocktail & Hors d'Oeuvres

Cranberry Champagne

Spinach Phyllo Triangles

Thyme Dip with Gourmet Chips and Fresh Vegetables

Mixed Nuts

Starter

Butternut Squash Soup

Rolls and Butter

Viognier

Salad

Endive, Gorgonzola and Walnuts

Palate Cleanser

Cranberry Orange Sorbet

Main Course

Pork with Dry Herb Rub and Orange Sauce

Mushroom Risotto

Brussels Sprouts

Côtes du Rhône

Dessert

Apple Cranberry Crisp

Oatmeal Raisin Cookies

Sauternes

Coffee & Tea

Cranberry Champagne

2	tablespoons cranberry juice cocktail	1/2	cup plus 2 tablespoons Champagne or dry sparkling wine
1	teaspoon Cointreau		Cranberry for garnish

Preparation Time: 5 min.

Fill the bottom of a Champagne glass with the cranberry juice cocktail and Cointreau. Fill the glass with Champagne or dry sparkling wine. Garnish with a cranberry.

TO PREPARE AHEAD: Pour the cranberry juice cocktail and Cointreau into the bottom of each Champagne glass and place the glasses near where you are going to serve the apéritif. Have a few empty glasses available in case some guests prefer water.

TO FINISH: Pour the Champagne and serve.

HANDY TIP: One bottle of Champagne makes enough to serve 6.

SUBSTITUTIONS: If you can't find cranberry juice cocktail, you can substitute 2 tablespoons unsweetened cranberry juice and 1 teaspoon sugar. Place the sugar, cranberry juice, and Cointreau in the bottom of the Champagne glass, add the Champagne, and stir. If you don't have Cointreau, use Grand Marnier instead.

Spinach Phyllo Triangles

Preparation Time: 70 min.
Cooking Time: 20 to 25 min.
Total Time: 90 to 95 min.

1	(10-ounce) package frozen chopped spinach
8	ounces cream cheese, softened
6	ounces crumbled feta cheese
1/4	cup grated Parmesan cheese
1/2	cup minced green onions
1/4	cup chopped fresh flat-leaf parsley
2	tablespoons chopped fresh dill
1/8	teaspoon freshly ground black pepper
2	eggs, beaten
1	pound frozen phyllo sheets, thawed
3/4	cup butter, melted

Preheat the oven to 350°F/180°C.

Thaw the frozen spinach in the microwave. The easiest way is to put the spinach in a bowl, cover with plastic wrap, making a few slits with a knife, and microwave for about 3 minutes. Then let sit for a minute. If it's not yet thawed, microwave for another minute. When the spinach has thawed, squeeze out the excess liquid.

In a medium bowl, combine the spinach, cream cheese, feta cheese, Parmesan cheese, green onions, flat-leaf parsley, dill, pepper and eggs and mix with an electric mixer until well combined.

Lay 1 sheet of phyllo on a flat surface with the long side facing you. Brush well with melted butter. Lay another sheet of phyllo on top. Brush well with melted butter. Repeat with a third sheet of phyllo and brush well with butter. Cover the remaining phyllo sheets with a damp towel. Cut the buttered sheets into 6 strips, beginning from the long side.

For each appetizer, spoon about 1 teaspoon of filling about 1 inch from the end of each strip. Fold the right corner over the filling, creating a 45-degree angle. Continue folding as you would fold a flag to form a triangle that encloses the filling.

Repeat with the remaining phyllo sheets and the filling. Place the triangles on an ungreased baking sheet. Brush the tops of the phyllo triangles with melted butter.

Bake for 20 to 25 minutes or until golden brown. Remove from the oven and serve.

TO PREPARE AHEAD: You can make the Spinach Phyllo Triangles ahead, stopping before baking, and freeze them for up to 3 months. Place the unbaked triangles on an ungreased baking sheet and place in the freezer. When frozen, transfer the triangles to a sealable plastic bag.

TO FINISH: Just before your guests arrive, place the Spinach Phyllo Triangles on an ungreased baking sheet with the buttered side facing up. Bake as directed above.

HANDY TIP: I use the sharp tip of a knife to cut the phyllo sheets into strips. If you have used quite a bit of butter, they should cut fairly easily. Don't worry about rips and tears—you won't notice them after you've made the triangles.

Thyme Dip with Gourmet Chips and Fresh Vegetables

3/4 cup mayonnaise	1/2 pound sugar snap peas
1 cup sour cream	1 teaspoon kosher salt
Zest of 1 lemon	1/2 pound carrots, peeled and sliced
1 1/2 tablespoons lemon juice	1/2 pound celery, sliced
1 1/2 tablespoons chopped fresh thyme	8 ounces gourmet vegetable chips
Sprig of thyme for garnish	

Preparation Time: 15 min.
Cooking Time: 5 min.
Total Time: 20 min.

In a small bowl, combine the mayonnaise, sour cream, lemon zest, lemon juice and chopped thyme. Cover and refrigerate.

Bring a large pot of water to a boil. Rinse the sugar snap peas with water and drain. Peel the string at one end along the ridge of the pod. Peel the string at the other end along the other ridge.

Add the salt to the boiling water. Add the sugar snap peas and blanch for 2 minutes, or until the sugar snap peas are tender-crisp. Drain and plunge into cold water to stop the cooking process.

PRESENTATION TIP: Place the dip, garnished with a fresh sprig of thyme, in a bowl. Place the sugar snap peas, carrots, and celery in bowls or arrange on a platter with the dip. Place the gourmet vegetable chips in a basket or bowl.

TO PREPARE AHEAD: You can make the dip up to 2 days ahead. Cover and refrigerate. You can make up the vegetables a day ahead and store, covered, in the refrigerator.

TO FINISH: Serve according to the Presentation Tip.

HANDY TIP: Gourmet vegetable chips present well because of the different colors, but a good-quality potato chip will also taste great.

SUBSTITUTION: You can substitute 1 teaspoon dried thyme for the fresh thyme if necessary.

Butternut Squash Soup

Preparation Time: 20 min.
Cooking Time: 30 min.
Total Time: 50 min.

PRESENTATION TIP:
Ladle the soup into bowls. Garnish with a small dollop of sour cream and a pinch of freshly chopped chives.

2	carrots	Pinch of nutmeg	
1	celery stalk	Pinch of ginger	
1	onion	1 teaspoon brown sugar	
2	pounds butternut squash	Kosher salt and freshly ground	
2	large potatoes	black pepper to taste	
1	apple	1/4 cup sour cream for garnish	
2	tablespoons butter	2 tablespoons chopped chives	
5	cups chicken broth	for garnish	
1/2	teaspoon curry powder		

Peel and dice the carrots. Rinse and chop the celery. Peel and chop the onion. Set aside.

Peel, seed and dice the butternut squash. Peel and dice the potatoes. Peel, core and slice the apple.

Melt the butter in a large soup pot. Add the carrots, celery and onion. Sauté over medium heat until the onion is translucent, about 5 to 8 minutes.

Stir in the squash, potatoes, apple and chicken broth. Turn up the heat and bring to a boil.

Reduce the heat and simmer, partially covered, for 40 minutes. Add the curry powder, nutmeg and ginger. Purée in batches in a blender.

Return to the cleaned-out soup pot and add more broth, if needed, to thin. Add the brown sugar, salt and pepper to taste. Cook until heated through.

TO PREPARE AHEAD: You can make the Butternut Squash Soup ahead and freeze. Cool and freeze in an airtight container for up to 3 months. Thaw overnight in the refrigerator or in the microwave.

TO FINISH: Place in a large soup pot and reheat gently, whisking often. Serve according to the Presentation Tip.

Endive, Gorgonzola and Walnuts

SALAD
5 to 6 heads Belgian endive (about 1 pound)
1/4 cup coarsely chopped fresh flat-leaf parsley
3/4 cup coarsely chopped walnuts

DRESSING
2 tablespoons lemon juice
2 tablespoons honey
1/4 teaspoon kosher salt
1/8 teaspoon freshly ground black pepper
1/3 cup extra-virgin olive oil
6 ounces crumbled Gorgonzola cheese

Preparation Time: 10 min.
Cooking Time: 3 min.
Total Time: 13 min.

For the salad: Cut the ends off the heads of endive. Cut in half lengthwise and julienne the leaves into thin strips. Place in a large bowl and sprinkle with the chopped parsley. Cover with a damp towel and refrigerate until needed.

Place the walnuts in a small nonstick frying pan and toast over medium heat, stirring often, until the walnuts start to brown, about 3 minutes. Watch them carefully! Set aside.

For the dressing: In a small bowl, whisk together the lemon juice, honey, salt and pepper. While continuing to whisk, add the extra-virgin olive oil in a steady stream. Continue whisking until the dressing thickens and emulsifies. Set aside.

Toss the endive with enough dressing to coat. To serve family style, sprinkle with the toasted walnuts and the crumbled Gorgonzola.

TO PREPARE AHEAD: Follow the directions above, stopping before you toss the endive with the dressing. Cover and refrigerate the dressing. An hour before serving, remove the salad dressing from the refrigerator and return to room temperature.

TO FINISH: Whisk the dressing. Toss the endive with enough dressing to coat and place on individual plates. Top with the toasted walnuts and crumbled Gorgonzola cheese.

SUBSTITUTION: If you don't have Gorgonzola, feel free to substitute Roquefort or Stilton. Also, for a slightly different flavor, try adding a cored and diced apple just prior to serving.

Cranberry Orange Sorbet

Preparation Time: 10 min.
Cooking Time: 15 min.
Ice Cream Maker: 20 min.
Total Time: 45 min. plus cooling time

12	ounces fresh or frozen cranberries
1 1/2	cups sugar
2 1/2	cups water
1/2	cup orange juice

Juice of 1 lemon
2   tablespoons Cointreau
Mint sprigs for garnish

Rinse and remove any stems from the cranberries.

In a medium saucepan, heat the sugar and water until the sugar melts and the mixture starts to boil. Add the cranberries and orange juice. Return to a boil. Turn down the heat and simmer for 10 minutes.

Remove from the heat and cool slightly. Place the cranberry mixture in the bowl of a blender. Purée until as smooth as possible.

Pour the cranberry mixture through a fine sieve. Use the back of a spoon to push the mixture through the sieve. Stir in the lemon juice and Cointreau.

Refrigerate until completely cool. Pour into an ice cream maker and process according to the manufacturer's directions. When finished, pour into an airtight container and freeze until ready to serve.

To Freeze: Prepare the sorbet up to a month ahead, place in an airtight container, and freeze.

To Finish: Remove the sorbet 15 minutes before serving to allow it to soften slightly. When ready, scoop into bowls, garnish with the mint, and serve.

Substitution: If you don't have Cointreau, try Grand Marnier instead.

Pork with Dry Herb Rub and Orange Sauce

DRY HERB RUB

3 tablespoons dried thyme
1 tablespoon dried tarragon
1 tablespoon dried mustard
1 tablespoon kosher salt
1 tablespoon freshly ground
   black pepper

2$^1/_2$ pounds fillet of pork tenderloin,
   trimmed
3 tablespoons extra-virgin olive
   oil, divided

ORANGE SAUCE

$^1/_2$ cup orange marmalade
$^1/_4$ cup chicken broth

Orange spirals for garnish
Flat-leaf parsley for garnish

Preparation Time: 10 min.
Cooking Time: 20 to 25 min.
Total Time: 30 to 35 min. plus marinating time

PRESENTATION TIP:
To serve, slice the pork tenderloin into $^1/_2$-inch slices. Place a heaping spoonful of Mushroom Risotto on a plate, flatten slightly, and top with a few slices of Pork Tenderloin. Top with the Orange Sauce. Place the Brussels Sprouts on the plate and garnish with the orange spirals and flat-leaf parsley.

For the rub: In a medium bowl, mix together the thyme, tarragon, mustard, salt and pepper.

Rub the tenderloin with 1$^1/_2$ tablespoons of the extra-virgin olive oil and roll in the rub. Make sure to cover all exposed surfaces of the meat with the rub. Place in a sealable plastic bag and refrigerate overnight.

Preheat the oven to 400°F/200°C.

In a large skillet, heat the remaining 1$^1/_2$ tablespoons extra-virgin olive oil. Add the pork and sear for 5 to 8 minutes, turning to brown all sides.

Place the tenderloin on an ungreased rimmed baking sheet and roast in the oven for 10 to 15 minutes or until a meat thermometer reads 150°F to 160°F/66°C to 71°C. Remove from the oven and let rest, covered loosely with aluminum foil, for 5 minutes. While the pork is resting, make the Orange Sauce.

For the sauce: In a small saucepan, combine the marmalade and chicken broth. Heat over medium heat, stirring constantly until the mixture is heated through.

Serve according to the Presentation Tip.

TO PREPARE AHEAD: You can make the Dry Herb Rub and marinate the pork either overnight or during the day before your party.

TO SEAR: On the day of the party, sear the pork as directed above. Place on an ungreased baking sheet, let cool, cover, and refrigerate. Make the Orange Sauce, place in a microwave-safe bowl, and set aside. Prepare the orange slices and flat-leaf parsley garnish, cover, and refrigerate separately.

TO FINISH: Roast as directed above. Reheat the Orange Sauce in the microwave. Serve according to the Presentation Tip.

SUBSTITUTION: If you don't have tarragon, try rosemary instead.

Mushroom Risotto

Preparation Time: 10 min.
Cooking Time: 30 min.
Total Time: 40 min.

1	ounce dried mixed mushrooms	2	cups arborio rice
1	cup warm water	3/4	cup dry white wine
5	cups chicken broth	2	tablespoons butter
2	tablespoons extra-virgin olive oil	1/2	cup grated Parmesan cheese
2	tablespoons butter		Kosher salt and freshly ground black
1	medium onion, finely chopped		pepper to taste
1	clove garlic, minced		

Soak the mushrooms in the warm water for 30 minutes.

Drain the mushrooms, reserving the liquid. Strain the liquid. Rinse the mushrooms under cold water. Squeeze to remove any moisture.

Heat the chicken broth in a medium saucepan. Cover and keep warm.

Heat the extra-virgin olive oil and 2 tablespoons butter in a large deep skillet over medium-low heat. Add the onion and garlic. Sauté until translucent but not browned, about 5 minutes.

Add the rice and mix well for about 2 minutes, stirring constantly. Add the wine. Cook, stirring constantly, until the wine has been absorbed, about 2 minutes. Add the drained rehydrated mushrooms and reserved mushroom liquid. Stir until the liquid has been absorbed.

Add 1 cup of chicken broth at a time, cooking and stirring the rice until the liquid is absorbed. Continue until the rice is tender but firm to the bite, about 15 to 20 minutes. Stir in 2 tablespoons butter and the grated Parmesan cheese.

TO PREPARE AHEAD: Risotto is best served immediately. That said, you can partially cook it up to 2 days ahead. Follow the directions above, using 3 cups chicken broth instead of 5 cups. When the 3 cups of broth have been absorbed, place the rice in a shallow casserole dish, cool, cover, and refrigerate. About an hour before serving, remove the rice from the refrigerator and let sit at room temperature.

TO FINISH: When ready to serve, place the remaining 2 cups chicken broth in a large deep skillet and bring to a boil. Reduce the heat to medium-low and stir in the partially cooked rice. Stir until the liquid is absorbed and the rice is heated through, about 4 to 5 minutes. Add the remaining 2 tablespoons butter and the grated Parmesan cheese and serve immediately.

SUBSTITUTIONS: You can use 4 ounces fresh mushrooms instead of the dried mushrooms. Slice the mushrooms and sauté in 2 tablespoons butter until golden. Set aside. Make the risotto according to the directions above, using 1 cup additional chicken broth in place of the mushroom liquid. Instead of adding the mushrooms during cooking, add them with the butter and Parmesan cheese at the end.

Brussels Sprouts

2	pounds brussels sprouts		2	tablespoons butter
1	teaspoon kosher salt			Kosher salt to taste

Preparation Time: 10 min.
Cooking Time: 5 min.
Total Time: 15 min.

Bring a large pot of water to a boil.

If the brussels sprouts are not pre-prepared, remove any damaged leaves and trim the bases. Drop the sprouts into a bowl of warm water and swirl to remove any dirt. Drain.

When the water is boiling, add 1 teaspoon salt and the brussels sprouts. Small sprouts will cook in 4 to 5 minutes, medium sprouts will cook in 5 to 8 minutes and large sprouts will cook in 8 to 12 minutes; drain. Add the butter and season with salt to taste.

TO PREPARE AHEAD: On the day of the party, you can boil the brussels sprouts as directed above. Drain and plunge the brussels sprouts into cold water to stop the cooking process. Drain and store the brussels sprouts, covered, in a microwave-safe bowl in the refrigerator.

TO FINISH: Add the butter and reheat in the microwave until the butter is melted and the brussels sprouts are heated through. Season with salt and serve.

Apple Cranberry Crisp

4	pounds Granny Smith apples, peeled, cored and sliced (about 8 to 10)		1/4	teaspoon kosher salt
			2	tablespoons butter, melted
1	cup dried cranberries		1	cup packed light brown sugar
1/2	cup sugar		1	cup rolled oats
1/2	cup packed light brown sugar		1 1/2	cups flour
1 1/2	teaspoons cinnamon		3/4	cup butter, at room temperature
3	tablespoons flour		1	teaspoon vanilla extract
			1	quart vanilla ice cream

Preparation Time: 20 min.
Cooking Time: 50 to 60 min.
Total Time: 70 to 80 min.

PRESENTATION TIP: Serve the Apple Cranberry Crisp topped with a scoop of vanilla ice cream.

Preheat the oven to 350°F/180°C.

Butter a 9×13-inch baking pan. Combine the apples and cranberries in the buttered pan.

In a small bowl, combine the sugar, 1/2 cup light brown sugar, the cinnamon, 3 tablespoons flour and the salt. Sprinkle over the apple-cranberry mixture and toss until well coated. Drizzle the apple-cranberry mixture with 2 tablespoons melted butter.

In a medium bowl, combine 1 cup brown sugar, the oats, 1 1/2 cups flour, 3/4 cup butter and the vanilla. Rub together until crumbly. Sprinkle over the cranberry-apple mixture.

Bake, uncovered, for 50 to 60 minutes or until browned and bubbly.

TO PREPARE AHEAD: You can make the Apple Cranberry Crisp a day ahead. Cool and store, covered, in the refrigerator.

TO FINISH: To reheat, place the uncovered Apple Cranberry Crisp in a 350°F/180°C oven for 20 to 30 minutes or until heated through.

SUBSTITUTION: Substitute 1 cup raisins for the cranberries.

Oatmeal Raisin Cookies

1¹/₂ cups butter
1 cup packed light brown sugar
1¹/₄ cups sugar
2 eggs
1 tablespoon vanilla extract

2 cups flour
1¹/₂ teaspoons baking soda
1¹/₂ teaspoons cinnamon
3 cups rolled oats
1¹/₂ cups raisins

Preparation Time: 10 min.
Cooking Time: 8 to 10 min. per batch

Preheat the oven to 375°F/190°C. Grease 2 cookie sheets with butter.

In a medium bowl, cream together the butter, light brown sugar and sugar. Beat in the eggs and vanilla.

In a small bowl, mix together the flour, baking soda and cinnamon. Add to the egg mixture. Stir in the oats. Stir in the raisins.

Drop the dough by rounded heaping teaspoonfuls about 2 inches apart on the prepared cookie sheets. Bake for 8 to 10 minutes or until slightly browned around the edges.

Cool on the cookie sheet for a minute before removing to a wire rack.

TO PREPARE AHEAD: You can make the cookies up to a week ahead. You'll only need about 16 cookies for your dinner party. Freeze the extra cookie dough or bake the cookies and store in an airtight container.

TO FINISH: Place the cookies you need for your party on a small serving platter and cover securely with plastic wrap until ready to serve.

TO FREEZE: Refrigerate unbaked cookie dough until firm enough to handle, about 15 minutes. Place a piece of plastic wrap on your work surface. Separate the dough into 3 equal pieces (4 pieces, if you haven't baked a batch above). Shape each piece into a log with a 1¹/₂-inch diameter. Roll each log in plastic wrap, sealing the ends. Place the logs in a sealable plastic bag and freeze for up to 3 months. When ready to bake, thaw for 30 minutes at room temperature (or briefly in the microwave) and bake as directed above.

SUBSTITUTION: To make terrific Oatmeal Chocolate Chip Cookies, substitute a 12-ounce package of semisweet chocolate bits for the raisins.

Timeline

ONE WEEK BEFORE
(ABOUT 2 HOURS)

Buy groceries and create the ambience

Prepare ahead Cranberry Orange Sorbet

Prepare ahead Butternut Squash Soup

Prepare ahead Spinach Phyllo Triangles

TWO DAYS BEFORE
(ABOUT 1/4 HOUR)

Buy groceries and create the ambience

Put sparkling water, Champagne, white wine, and dessert wine (if using) in refrigerator

Put out red wine

ONE DAY BEFORE
(ABOUT 1 HOUR)

Prepare ahead Oatmeal Raisin Cookies

Prepare ahead Thyme Dip and Vegetables

Prepare ahead Pork with Dry Herb Rub

Thaw Butternut Squash Soup in refrigerator overnight

DAY OF PARTY (ABOUT 2 HOURS)

Buy groceries and create the ambience

Prepare ahead Apple Cranberry Crisp

Prepare ahead Mushroom Risotto

Prepare ahead Brussels Sprouts

Prepare ahead Endive, Gorgonzola and Walnuts

Sear Pork with Dry Herb Rub

5:00 PM
Shower and dress

6:30 PM
Prepare coffeemaker

Open wines, turn on music, light candles

Put out starter bowls, salad plates, sorbet bowls, main course plates, and dessert plates

Prepare sugar and milk for coffee

7:00 PM
Preheat oven to 350°F/180°C

Put butter pats and rolls on butter plates

Put a cucumber slice in each water glass

Prepare ahead Cranberry Champagne

Put out mixed nuts

7:15 PM
Finish Spinach Phyllo Triangles

Serve Thyme Dip with Gourmet Chips and Vegetables according to Presentation Tip

Remove salad dressing from refrigerator

7:30 PM (GUESTS ARRIVE)
Open and pour Champagne (have water ready for those who prefer water)

7:35 PM
Remove Spinach Phyllo Triangles from oven and serve

Turn up oven to 400°F/200°C

Start to reheat soup over medium-low heat; whisk and check occasionally

8:00 PM
Check soup is hot

Remove Mushroom Risotto from refrigerator

8:05 PM
Call people to table

Serve starter wine and water

8:10 PM
Serve soup according to Presentation Tip

8:30 PM
Finish salad and serve

Take sorbet out of freezer

8:45 PM
Serve sorbet, garnished with mint

Put Pork with Dry Herb Rub in oven

9:00 PM
Remove Pork with Dry Herb Rub from oven and let rest, covered loosely with aluminum foil

Turn down oven to 350°F/180°C

Finish Mushroom Risotto

Reheat Brussels Sprouts in microwave

Plate Pork with Dry Herb Rub according to Presentation Tip

9:10 PM
Serve main course and wine

Put Apple Cranberry Crisp, uncovered, in oven to warm

Turn on coffeemaker

9:45 PM
Remove Apple Cranberry Crisp from oven

Serve Apple Cranberry Crisp according to Presentation Tip

Serve dessert wine (if using)

10:00 PM
Serve coffee, tea, and after-dinner cookies

Grocery List

PANTRY ITEMS

$2/3$ cup extra-virgin olive oil
Kosher salt
Freshly ground black pepper
3 teaspoons cinnamon
$1/2$ teaspoon curry powder
Pinch of nutmeg
Pinch of ginger
3 tablespoons dried thyme
1 tablespoon dried tarragon
1 tablespoon dried mustard
$3^1/2$ cups sugar
$2^1/2$ cups light brown sugar
4 cups flour
$1^1/2$ teaspoons baking soda
4 cups rolled oats
4 teaspoons vanilla extract
$3/4$ cup coarsely chopped walnuts
$1/3$ cup mayonnaise
$10^1/4$ cups chicken broth
2 tablespoons honey
$1/2$ cup orange marmalade
2 cups arborio rice
1 ounce dried mixed mushrooms
1 cup dried cranberries
$1^1/2$ cups raisins
8 ounces gourmet vegetable chips
1 (12-ounce) jar mixed nuts
Decaffeinated and regular coffee
Regular and herbal tea bags

ALCOHOL AND DRINKS

2 bottles Champagne or sparkling wine
2 bottles white wine for starter (Viognier)

2 bottles red wine for main
  (Côtes du Rhône)
1 bottle dessert wine, if using (Sauternes)
4 bottles sparkling water
5 tablespoons Cointreau
1 cup cranberry juice cocktail
$3/4$ cup dry white wine

PRODUCE

3 lemons
1 apple
12 ounces cranberries, fresh or frozen
$1/4$ cup chopped flat-leaf parsley
2 tablespoons chopped fresh dill
1 pound carrots
$3/4$ pound celery
2 onions
$1/2$ cup minced green onions
2 pounds butternut squash
2 large potatoes

DAIRY

$4^1/8$ cups butter
4 eggs
8 ounces cream cheese
6 ounces crumbled feta cheese
$1/4$ cup grated Parmesan cheese
6 ounces crumbled Gorgonzola cheese
$1/2$ cup orange juice

FREEZER

1 (1-pound) package frozen phyllo sheets
10 ounces frozen chopped spinach
1 quart vanilla ice cream

TWO DAYS BEFORE PARTY

PRODUCE

1 orange for main garnish
4 pounds Granny Smith apples
  (8 to 10 apples)
1 bunch fresh thyme
2 tablespoons fresh chopped chives
1 bunch fresh mint for sorbet garnish
$1/4$ cup fresh chopped flat-leaf parsley
1 bunch fresh flat-leaf parsley for
  main garnish
5 or 6 heads Belgian endive
  (about 1 pound)
$1/2$ pound sugar snap peas

2 pounds brussels sprouts
  (fresh or frozen)
1 clove garlic
1 cucumber

DAIRY

1 cup whole milk
1 cup sour cream
$1/2$ cup grated Parmesan cheese

MEAT, FISH AND DELI

$2^1/2$ pounds fillet of pork tenderloin

DAY OF PARTY

BAKERY

8 rolls

Thanksgiving Turkey
menu

SERVES 10

Cocktail & Hors d'Oeuvres

Champagne

Dill Dip and Vegetables

Cashews

Main Course

Roast Turkey with Pork and Herb Stuffing

Cranberry Chutney

Mashed Potato Casserole

Candied Yams

Green Beans with Almonds

Corn Bread Pudding

Banana Bread

Fruity Zinfandel, Beaujolais, or Rosé

Dessert

Pumpkin Cake

Chocolate-Covered Peanut Butter Balls

Chewy Molasses Cookies

Lake Harvest Riesling

Coffee & Tea

Dill Dip and Vegetables

1 cup sour cream
1 cup mayonnaise
1 1/2 tablespoons minced onion
2 teaspoons dried dill
1 1/2 teaspoons dried parsley
1 1/2 teaspoons Beau Monde seasoning

1/2 pound carrots, peeled and sliced
1/2 pound celery, sliced
1 red bell pepper, cored, seeded and sliced
1/2 pound broccoli florets, broken into bite-size pieces

Preparation Time: 20 min.

PRESENTATION TIP: Place the Dill Dip in a serving bowl in the middle of a platter surrounded by the vegetables.

In a small bowl, mix together the sour cream and mayonnaise. Add the minced onion and stir. Add the dill, parsley and Beau Monde seasoning. Cover and refrigerate.

TO PREPARE AHEAD: Prepare the Dill Dip up to 2 days ahead, cover, and refrigerate. Cut up the vegetables the day before the party and store in sealable plastic bags until you are ready to assemble the platter.

TO FINISH: On the day of the party, prepare the appetizer platter, cover, and refrigerate until ready to serve.

Cranberry Chutney

1 (12-ounce) can pineapple tidbits (in own juice)
12 ounces fresh or frozen cranberries
3/4 cup sugar
1 cup golden raisins

1/2 teaspoon cinnamon
1/2 teaspoon ground ginger
1/4 teaspoon allspice
3/4 cup chopped walnuts

Preparation Time: 10 min.
Cooking Time: 20 to 25 min.
Total Time: 30 to 35 min.

Drain the pineapple tidbits, reserving the juice.

In a medium saucepan, combine the cranberries, sugar, raisins, cinnamon, ginger, allspice and pineapple juice. Bring to a boil over medium heat. Turn down the heat to low and simmer for 20 to 25 minutes or until tender.

While the cranberries are simmering, place the walnuts in a small nonstick frying pan. Heat over medium heat, tossing occasionally, until the walnuts start to turn brown, about 3 minutes. Set aside. Remove the cranberry mixture from the heat. Stir in the pineapple tidbits and walnuts.

Cool, cover and refrigerate.

TO PREPARE AHEAD: You can make the Cranberry Chutney up to a week ahead. Store, covered, in the refrigerator until ready to serve.

TO FREEZE: Freeze the cooled chutney in an airtight container for up to 3 months.

HANDY TIP: Try the Cranberry Chutney on top of a wheel of Brie. Preheat the oven to 325°F/160°C. Place a round of Brie on a parchment-lined baking sheet. Top with about 1/2 cup Cranberry Chutney for a 1-pound wheel of Brie and 1/4 cup Cranberry Chutney for an 8-ounce wheel of Brie. Bake for about 10 minutes or until warm. Serve with French baguette slices.

Roast Turkey

Preparation Time: 15 min.
Cooking Time: 4 1/2 hours
Total Time: 4 3/4 hours
plus resting time

PRESENTATION TIP:
Cut through the skin
between the thigh
and breast. Move the
drumstick to locate the
thigh joint and then cut
through the joint to
separate the drumstick.
Remove the other
drumstick and the wings
in the same manner.
You can either serve the
drumstick whole or slice
off the meat parallel to
the bone. To carve the
breast, make a horizontal
cut just above the thigh
and wing joints, cutting
deep toward the bone.
This will help the breast
pieces come away easily.
Starting near the
breastbone, slice the
turkey vertically in thin
slices, ending at the
horizontal cut you have
made. Place the wings,
drumsticks, and breast
slices on a serving
platter. Place the warm
gravy in a gravy boat
and serve immediately.

HERB RUB AND TURKEY

1	(20-pound) turkey, thawed if frozen
1 1/2	tablespoons dried parsley
1 1/2	teaspoons dried rosemary
1 1/2	teaspoons dried thyme
2	teaspoons kosher salt
1	tablespoon freshly ground black pepper
2	tablespoons extra-virgin olive oil
1/2	cup butter, melted

GRAVY

3	cups chicken broth
1/4	cup dry white wine
1/4	cup water
1/4	cup flour

Kosher salt and freshly ground
black pepper to taste
Curly parsley for garnish

Remove the turkey from the refrigerator 1 hour before roasting and let rest at room temperature. Move the oven rack to the lower third of the oven and preheat the oven to 325°F/160°C. Set aside an 11×17-inch roasting pan with a wire roasting rack.

In a small bowl, mix together the dried parsley, rosemary, thyme, salt and pepper.

Remove the neck and giblets from the cavity of the turkey. Rinse the turkey inside and out with cold running water. Pat dry with paper towels. If stuffing the turkey, spoon the stuffing into the cavity. If not stuffing the turkey, spoon a tablespoon of the herb rub in the cavity.

Place the turkey breast side up on the wire rack in the roasting pan. Tie the legs together and tuck the wings underneath. Brush the outside of the turkey with the extra-virgin olive oil and then rub on the herb rub. Drizzle with half the melted butter.

Place the turkey in the oven. Baste the turkey every 30 minutes with a large spoon or a bulb baster, pouring the juices over the turkey. If there aren't any juices initially, use the leftover melted butter.

After 3 1/2 hours, begin checking the temperature of the turkey meat with a meat thermometer. The turkey is done when a meat thermometer reaches 165°F/74°C when inserted into the thickest part of the breast but not touching the bone, or when it reaches 180°F/82°C when inserted in the thigh. A 20-pound unstuffed turkey should take about 4 1/2 hours to roast, while a 20-pound stuffed turkey should take about 4 3/4 hours.

When the turkey is done, remove it from the oven and transfer to a carving board. Cover loosely with aluminium foil and let rest for 20 minutes. While the turkey is resting, make the gravy.

For the gravy: Place the chicken broth in a medium saucepan and heat over medium heat until simmering. Pour off the liquid from the roasting pan into a heatproof bowl. Skim off the fat and set aside 1/4 cup of the remaining pan juices. Add the wine and water to the roasting pan and heat over medium heat, scraping up the brown bits on the bottom. Boil for 2 minutes. Strain the mixture into a bowl. In a medium saucepan, bring the reserved pan juices to a boil. Add the flour and stir until combined. Add the strained wine mixture and 2 1/2 cups of the chicken broth. Cook until thickened, stirring constantly. Add the remaining 1/2 cup broth as needed to reach the right consistency. Season with salt and pepper.

HANDY TIP: When you take the turkey out of the oven to rest, turn up the temperature to 350°F/180°C. While the turkey is resting, reheat the Pork and Herb Stuffing, Mashed Potato Casserole, Candied Yams, and Corn Bread Pudding. By the time you finish the gravy and slice the turkey, all the side dishes should be heated through.

Pork and Herb Stuffing

SERVES 10 TO 12

Preparation Time: 10 min.
Cooking Time: 20 min.
Total Time: 30 min.

1	pound ground pork sausage		2	teaspoons dried sage
1/2	cup butter		1/2	teaspoon kosher salt
1	cup chopped onion		1/2	teaspoon freshly ground
1	cup chopped celery			black pepper
2	cups sliced mushrooms		1	(14-ounce) package sage and
2 1/2	cups chicken broth			onion stuffing
1	tablespoon dried parsley			

Preheat the oven to 350°F/180°C. In a large deep skillet, cook the sausage over medium heat until browned. Remove the sausage to a bowl.

In the same skillet, melt the butter over medium heat. Add the chopped onion and celery and cook until tender, about 5 to 8 minutes. Add the mushrooms and cook until browned.

Add the chicken broth, parsley, sage, salt and pepper. Turn up the heat and bring to a boil. Once boiling, remove from the heat and add the stuffing and sausage.

Toss with a fork. Serve immediately.

TO PREPARE AHEAD: Pour into a buttered 3-quart baking dish. Cool, cover, and refrigerate until needed.

TO FINISH: Preheat the oven to 350°F/180°C and bake until heated through, about 20 to 30 minutes. An easy rule of thumb is to return the Stuffing to the oven when the turkey comes out.

SUBSTITUTION: You can substitute ground pork for the ground pork sausage.

Mashed Potato Casserole

SERVES 10 TO 12

Preparation Time: 15 min.
Cooking Time: 45 to 55 min.
Total Time: 60 to 70 min.

5	pounds Yukon Gold potatoes		1/4	teaspoon freshly ground
8	ounces cream cheese			black pepper
8	ounces sour cream		1/2	to 1 cup whole milk
1/2	cup butter		1/2	cup grated white Cheddar cheese
1	teaspoon kosher salt			

Preheat the oven to 350°F/180°C.

Peel the potatoes and cut into quarters. Place in a large pot of water and bring to a boil. Turn down the heat and simmer until tender, about 15 minutes; drain. Using a ricer, mash the potatoes. Add the cream cheese, sour cream, butter, salt and pepper. Stir in enough of the milk to reach the desired consistency.

Pour into a buttered 3-quart baking dish. Sprinkle the grated Cheddar cheese over the top and bake, uncovered, for 30 to 40 minutes or until heated through.

TO PREPARE AHEAD: Assemble the Mashed Potato Casserole, stopping before baking. Cool, cover, and refrigerate up to 2 days. When ready to serve, bake as directed above.

Candied Yams

6	yams (about 4 pounds)		1/2	cup sugar
1/4	cup butter, melted		1/4	cup packed light brown sugar

Preparation Time: 10 min.
Cooking Time: 65 to 75 min.
Total Time: 75 to 85 min.

Grease a 9×13-inch baking dish with butter.

Place the yams in a large pot and add enough water to cover. Bring the water to a boil. Turn down the heat to low and simmer the yams for 35 to 45 minutes or until tender. Drain and let cool enough to handle easily.

Preheat the oven to 350°F/180°C.

Peel the yams and cut into 1/2-inch slices. Layer the slices in the buttered dish.

In a small bowl, mix together the melted butter, sugar and light brown sugar. Spoon the butter mixture over the yam slices. Cover with aluminum foil and bake for 30 minutes or until heated through.

TO PREPARE AHEAD: You can prepare the Candied Yams up to 2 days ahead, stopping before baking. Cover with aluminum foil and store in the refrigerator. When ready to serve, bake as directed above.

Green Beans with Almonds

2	pounds fresh green beans		2	tablespoons butter
2	teaspoons kosher salt			Kosher salt to taste
1/2	cup sliced almonds			

Preparation Time: 10 min.
Cooking Time: 5 min.
Total Time: 15 min.

Put a large pot of water on to boil. Meanwhile, snap off the ends of the beans and rinse the beans well with water.

Add 2 teaspoons salt to the boiling water and then add the beans. Return to a boil. Boil thicker beans for 4 to 5 minutes and thinner beans for just about 3 minutes.

While the beans are cooking, place the almonds in a small nonstick frying pan. Heat over medium heat, tossing occasionally, until the almonds start to turn golden brown, about 3 minutes. Watch them closely. Remove from the heat and set aside.

When the green beans are cooked, drain. Add the butter, season with salt to taste and sprinkle with the toasted sliced almonds.

TO PREPARE AHEAD: You can make Green Beans with Almonds up to a day ahead. Cook the green beans as directed above. Drain and plunge into cold water to stop the cooking process. Place in a microwave-safe bowl, cover, and refrigerate. Toast the almonds, cool, cover, and place in an airtight container.

TO FINISH: When ready to serve, add the butter and reheat in the microwave. Season with salt to taste and sprinkle with the toasted almonds.

Corn Bread Pudding

Preparation Time: 10 min.
Cooking Time: 40 min.
Total Time: 50 min.

2	eggs		1 1/4	cups flour
1/2	cup butter, melted		3/4	cup cornmeal
1	(14 1/2-ounce) can corn		1/4	cup sugar
1	(14 1/2-ounce) can corn, drained		2	teaspoons baking powder
1	(14 1/2-ounce) can cream-style corn		1/2	teaspoon kosher salt
8	ounces sour cream			

Preheat the oven to 350°F/180°C.

Grease a 9×13-inch baking pan.

In a large bowl, beat the eggs. Add the melted butter, undrained corn, drained corn, cream-style corn and sour cream.

In a separate bowl, sift together the flour, cornmeal, sugar, baking powder and salt. Add the flour mixture to the corn mixture and stir until combined. Pour into the prepared pan and bake for 40 minutes.

TO PREPARE AHEAD: You can make the Corn Bread Pudding ahead on the day. Cool, cover, and let rest at room temperature. To reheat, place the uncovered Corn Bread Pudding in a 350°F/180°C oven for 20 to 30 minutes or until heated through.

Banana Bread

1	cup butter, softened	2	teaspoons baking soda
3	cups sugar	1/4	teaspoon kosher salt
4	eggs	1/2	cup buttermilk
2	teaspoons vanilla extract	6	small ripe bananas
3 1/2	cups flour		

Preparation Time: 20 min.
Cooking Time: 60 min.
Total Time: 80 min.

Preheat the oven to 350°F/180°C. Grease two 5×9-inch loaf pans.

In a large bowl, cream together the butter and sugar with an electric mixer. Add the eggs 1 at a time, beating after each addition. Blend in the vanilla.

In a separate bowl, mix together the flour, baking soda and salt. Add the flour mixture alternately with the buttermilk to the egg mixture, beating until blended.

In a medium bowl, mash the bananas. Mix into the batter. Pour into the prepared pans and bake for 60 minutes or until a wooden pick inserted in the center comes out clean.

Remove from the oven. Let cool in the pans for 5 minutes. Then remove the loaves from the pans and let cool completely on a wire rack

TO PREPARE AHEAD: Make the Banana Bread as directed above. Cool completely. Wrap the cooled loaves in plastic wrap and then place them in a sealable plastic bag. Freeze for up to 3 months. Remove from the freezer and let thaw at room temperature for several hours or overnight.

HANDY TIP #1: If you don't have buttermilk, use 1/2 cup milk mixed with 1 1/2 teaspoons white vinegar.

HANDY TIP #2: At the holidays, I sometimes like to make the Banana Bread in a greased angel food cake pan. Follow the directions above but increase the cooking time to 1 1/2 to 1 3/4 hours, or until a wooden pick inserted in the middle comes out clean.

SUBSTITUTION: If you like nuts, feel free to add 1 cup chopped pecans to the batter when you mix in the mashed bananas.

Pumpkin Cake

Preparation Time: 20 min.
Cooking Time: 20 to 25 min.
Total Time: 40 to 45 min.

CAKE

1	cup vegetable oil
2	cups sugar
1	(15-ounce) can pumpkin
4	eggs
2	cups flour
1	teaspoon baking soda
2	teaspoons baking powder
2	teaspoons cinnamon
1/2	teaspoon kosher salt

CREAM CHEESE FROSTING

8	ounces cream cheese, at room temperature
1/2	cup butter, at room temperature
2	teaspoons vanilla extract
4	cups confectioners' sugar

Preheat the oven to 350°F/180°C. Grease and flour two 9-inch round cake pans.

For the cake: In a large bowl, combine the oil, sugar and pumpkin. Blend with an electric mixer until combined. Add the eggs 1 at a time, beating after each addition.

In a medium bowl, mix together the flour, baking soda, baking powder, cinnamon and salt. Add to the egg mixture and blend until combined. Pour into the prepared pans. Bake for 20 to 25 minutes or until wooden picks inserted in the centers come out clean. Cool in the pans for 15 minutes and then turn out onto a wire rack. Cool completely.

For the frosting: In a medium bowl, blend together the cream cheese, butter and vanilla with an electric mixer until smooth. Add the confectioners' sugar and blend on Low speed until combined. Spread the frosting between the cooled cake layers and over the top and side of the cake.

TO PREPARE AHEAD: You can prepare the Pumpkin Cake up to 2 days ahead. Store, covered, in the refrigerator. Before serving, let rest at room temperature for 30 to 60 minutes.

Chocolate-Covered Peanut Butter Balls

1   (16-ounce) jar creamy peanut butter
1   pound confectioners' sugar
     (about 3 1/2 to 4 cups)

1/2   cup butter, at room temperature
20   ounces cocoa candy melts or
       chocolate almond bark

Preparation Time: 60 min.
Cooking Time: 5 min.
Total Time: 65 min. plus
freezing time

Line 2 baking sheets with wax paper.

In a large bowl, mix together the peanut butter, confectioners' sugar and butter. Blend with an electric mixer until smooth.

Form the peanut butter mixture into 1-inch balls and place on the prepared baking sheets. Freeze for 30 minutes.

Melt the chocolate in a bowl in the microwave. Do not overcook. Microwave for 1 minute and then stir the chocolate. Then microwave for 20 seconds and check. It should be nearly melted. Stir until smooth.

Using a wooden pick, dip the peanut butter balls in the chocolate until completely covered. Place on the wax paper-lined baking sheets. Drag the wooden pick over the hole to cover with chocolate.

Refrigerate the Chocolate-Covered Peanut Butter Balls until set. Store in an airtight container in the refrigerator, separating the layers with wax paper.

To Prepare Ahead: You can make the Chocolate-Covered Peanut Butter Balls up to a week ahead. Store in an airtight container in the refrigerator.

Chewy Molasses Cookies

Preparation Time: 20 min.
Cooking Time: 9 to
10 min. per batch

1	cup butter, softened	2 1/4	teaspoons baking soda
1 1/2	cups sugar	2 1/2	teaspoons ground ginger
1/2	cup dark molasses	1 1/2	teaspoons ground cloves
2	eggs	1 1/2	teaspoons ground cinnamon
4	cups flour	1/2	cup sugar for rolling
1/2	teaspoon kosher salt		

Preheat the oven to 350°F/180°C. Grease 2 cookie sheets with butter.

In a large bowl, cream the butter and 1 1/2 cups sugar together with an electric mixer until light and fluffy. Add the molasses and eggs and beat until smooth.

In a medium bowl, mix together the flour, salt, baking soda, ginger, cloves and cinnamon.

Add the flour mixture to the molasses mixture. Stir to combine well. The dough will be quite thick.

Roll the dough into 1 1/2-inch balls. Roll each ball in 1/2 cup sugar until completely coated. Place the balls 2 inches apart on the prepared cookie sheets. Bake for 9 to 10 minutes. Remove to a wire rack to cool completely.

TO PREPARE AHEAD: You can make the cookies up to a week ahead. Place the cooled cookies on a serving platter and cover securely with plastic wrap.

TO FREEZE: Place the unbaked sugar-coated dough balls on a cookie sheet and freeze. Once frozen, transfer the dough balls to a sealable plastic bag. You can freeze the unbaked balls for up to 3 months. Bake as directed above, but increase the baking time to 11 to 13 minutes.

Timeline

ONE WEEK BEFORE (ABOUT 1 1/2 HOURS)

Buy groceries and create the ambience

Prepare ahead Banana Bread and freeze

Prepare ahead Chocolate-Covered Peanut Butter Balls

Order fresh turkey or plan to thaw frozen

TWO DAYS BEFORE (ABOUT 1 HOUR)

Buy groceries and create the ambience

Put sparkling water, Champagne, and dessert wine (if using) in refrigerator

Put out red wine

Prepare ahead Cranberry Chutney

Prepare ahead Chewy Molasses Cookies

ONE DAY BEFORE (ABOUT 2 HOURS)

Prepare ahead Pumpkin Cake

Prepare ahead Mashed Potato Casserole

Prepare ahead Candied Yams

Prepare ahead Dill Dip and Vegetables

Remove Banana Bread from freezer and thaw overnight

DAY OF PARTY

Create the ambience

9:45 AM
Remove the turkey from the refrigerator

Prepare ahead Corn Bread Pudding

Prepare ahead Pork and Herb Stuffing

Prepare ahead Green Beans with Almonds

10:45 AM
Preheat oven to 325°F/160°F

Prepare Roast Turkey

11:00 AM
Put the turkey in the oven, remember to baste every 30 minutes

2:00 PM
Prepare coffeemaker

Open wine, turn on music, and light candles

Put out Champagne glasses, main course plates, and dessert plates

Prepare sugar and milk for coffee

Refrigerate butter pats on a small serving plate

2:45 PM
Put out Dill Dip and Vegetables according to Presentation Tip

Put out cashews

3:00 PM (GUESTS ARRIVE)
Open and pour Champagne (have water ready for those who prefer water)

3:30 PM
Remove turkey from oven (if done) and cover loosely with aluminum foil

Turn up oven to 350°F/180°F

Put Pork and Herb Stuffing (covered), Mashed Potato Casserole (uncovered), Candied Yams (covered), and Corn Bread Pudding (uncovered) in the oven to reheat

Make gravy for turkey

3:50 PM
Put out butter pats

Put out Banana Bread on a board with a knife

Slice turkey and arrange on a platter

4:00 PM
Finish Green Beans

Remove side dishes from oven and put out

Remove Pumpkin Cake from refrigerator

Call people to buffet

Serve wine and water

5:00 PM
Put out Pumpkin Cake, Chocolate-Covered Peanut Butter Balls and Chewy Molasses Cookies

Serve dessert wine (if using)

Serve coffee and tea

Grocery List

PANTRY ITEMS

$1/8$ cup extra-virgin olive oil
1 cup vegetable oil
1 cup mayonnaise
Kosher salt
Freshly ground black pepper
2 teaspoons dried dill
3 tablespoons dried parsley
$1^1/2$ teaspoons dried rosemary
$1^1/2$ teaspoons dried thyme
2 teaspoons dried sage
$1^1/2$ teaspoons Beau Monde seasoning
4 teaspoons cinnamon
3 teaspoons ground ginger
$1^1/2$ teaspoons ground cloves
$1/4$ teaspoon allspice
$8^1/2$ cups sugar
$1/4$ cup light brown sugar
2 pounds confectioners' sugar
11 cups flour
$3/4$ cup yellow cornmeal
$6^1/4$ teaspoons baking powder
3 teaspoons baking soda
4 teaspoons vanilla extract
$1/2$ cup dark molasses
20 ounces cocoa candy melts or chocolate almond bark
$3/4$ cup chopped walnuts
$1/2$ cup sliced almonds
1 cup golden raisins

$5^1/2$ cups chicken broth
2 ($14^1/2$-ounce) cans corn
1 ($14^1/2$-ounce) can cream-style corn
1 (15-ounce) can pumpkin
1 (12-ounce) can pineapple tidbits in own juice
1 (14-ounce) package sage and onion stuffing
1 (16-ounce) jar creamy peanut butter
1 (12-ounce) jar cashews
Decaffeinated and regular coffee
Regular and herbal tea bags

ALCOHOL AND DRINKS

2 bottles Champagne
2 bottles wine for main course (fruity Zinfandel, Beaujolais, or rosé)
1 bottle dessert wine, if using (Late Harvest Riesling)
4 bottles sparkling water
$1/4$ cup dry white wine (for gravy)

PRODUCE

6 small ripe bananas

DAIRY

$1/2$ cup buttermilk (or substitute milk and white vinegar)
12 eggs
$5^7/8$ cups butter

PRODUCE

12 ounces cranberries (fresh or frozen)
1 bunch curly parsley for garnish
$1^1/4$ onions
$1/2$ pound carrots
$3/4$ pound celery
1 red bell pepper
$1/2$ pound broccoli florets
2 cups sliced mushrooms
5 pounds Yukon Gold potatoes
4 pounds yams (about 6)
2 pounds green beans

DAIRY

2 cups whole milk
3 cups sour cream
16 ounces cream cheese
$1/2$ cup grated white Cheddar cheese

MEAT, FISH AND DELI

1 (20-pound) turkey (fresh or frozen— thaw if frozen)
1 pound ground pork sausage

Winter

Christmas Prime Rib

SERVES 10

Brie with Cranberries, Almonds and Raisins • Prime Rib • Creamed Spinach • Wild Rice Casserole • Buttered Corn • Popovers • Pumpkin Bread • Maple Apple Cake • Pecan Turtle Candies • Chocolate-Dipped Strawberries

Rustic Seafood Bake

SERVES 8

Pear Champagne • Spinach Artichoke Dip • Garden Pea Soup • Corn Bread • Mixed Greens with Tarragon Vinaigrette • Lime Sorbet • Rustic Seafood Bake • Broccoli Florets • Carrot Cake • Sugared Pecans • Butterscotch Chocolate Chip Cookies

Filet of Beef with Balsamic Onions and Asparagus

SERVES 8

Kir Royale • Pear and Roquefort Crostini • Cheese Straws • Cream of Mushroom Soup • Herb Salad with Sugared Almonds • Lemon Sorbet • Filet of Beef with Balsamic Onions and Asparagus • Creamy Mashed Potatoes • Individual Baked Alaska • Lace Cookies

Mushroom Lasagna

SERVES 8

Grand Marnier and Champagne • Asparagus Puffs • Assortment of Cheese and Crackers • Spinach Coconut Soup • Roasted Vegetables in Phyllo with Balsamic Vinaigrette • Strawberry Sorbet • Mushroom Lasagna • Frozen Chocolate Mousse Cake with Raspberry Coulis • Pecan Crisps

Christmas Prime Rib

menu

SERVES 10

Cocktail & Hors d'Oeuvres

Champagne

Brie with Cranberries, Almonds and Raisins

Cashews and Party Mix

Main Course

Prime Rib

Creamed Spinach

Wild Rice Casserole

Buttered Corn

Popovers

Pumpkin Bread

 Cabernet Sauvignon

Dessert

Maple Apple Cake

Pecan Turtle Candies

Chocolate-Dipped Strawberries

 Sauternes

Coffee & Tea

Brie with Cranberries, Almonds and Raisins

1/4	cup slivered almonds	1/3	cup golden raisins
1	(1-pound) wheel Brie cheese	2	apples, cored and sliced
2	tablespoons Cointreau	2	pears, cored and sliced
1/3	cup dried cranberries	1	package flatbread

Preheat the oven to 325°F/160°C. Line a baking sheet with parchment paper.

Place the almonds in a small nonstick frying pan and toast over medium heat, stirring often, until the almonds start to brown, about 3 to 5 minutes. Set aside.

Place the cheese on the prepared baking sheet and prick the top with a fork in about a dozen places. Drizzle 1/2 tablespoon of the Cointreau over the top.

In a small bowl, mix together the remaining 1 1/2 tablespoons Cointreau, the cranberries, raisins and toasted almonds. Spoon the mixture over the top of the cheese. Bake for 10 minutes or until the cheese warms and softens slightly. Using a spatula (or even 2 spatulas), transfer the cheese to a cutting board.

Preparation Time: 15 min.
Cooking Time: 10 min.
Total Time: 25 min.

PRESENTATION TIP: Arrange the apples and pears around the cheese and place the flatbread in a basket.

TO PREPARE AHEAD: You can make the Brie early on the day of the party, stopping before heating. Store, covered, in the refrigerator until ready to heat.

TO FINISH: Heat as directed above. Slice the apples and pears. Serve according to the Presentation Tip.

HANDY TIP: Brie topped with Cranberry Chutney is also delightful. If you happen to have some frozen leftover Cranberry Chutney (page 149) from Thanksgiving, thaw it and place on top of the Brie. Heat as directed above and serve with the fruit and flatbread.

Prime Rib

Preparation Time: 15 min.
Cooking Time: 2¹/₂ to
3 hours
Total Time: 2³/₄ to
3¹/₄ hours plus
resting time

PRESENTATION TIP:
Remove the bone from
the prime rib and cut into
¹/₂-inch slices. Place the
slices of prime rib on a
platter and garnish with
the curly parsley. Serve
with the strained juices
and Horseradish Cream.

1	(9- to 10-pound) prime rib or standing rib roast, bone removed and tied back on (about 5 ribs)
¹/₂	cup beef broth
	Kosher salt and freshly ground black pepper to taste

HORSERADISH CREAM

1	cup sour cream
¹/₄	cup horseradish
1	tablespoon lemon juice
¹/₂	teaspoon kosher salt
	Curly parsley for garnish

Remove the prime rib from the refrigerator. Place the prime rib fat side up in a roasting pan. Cover loosely with aluminum foil and let stand at room temperature for 2 hours prior to roasting. Preheat the oven to 450°F/230°C. Place the oven rack in the bottom third of the oven.

Roast the prime rib for 30 minutes. Turn the oven down to 325°F/160°C and roast until done, about 2 to 2¹/₂ hours. Using a meat thermometer, start checking the internal temperature an hour after you turn the temperature down to 325°F/160°C. Make sure that you stick the thermometer into the thickest part of the meat but away from the bone.

When the prime rib has reached your desired temperature (125°F to 130°F/52°C to 54°C for medium-rare and 130°F to 140°F/54°C to 60°C for medium), remove from the oven and transfer to a carving board. Cover loosely with aluminum foil and let rest for 15 to 20 minutes before carving.

Meanwhile, pour off the fat from the roasting pan, leaving the juices in the pan. Add ¹/₂ cup beef broth and heat over medium heat, scraping up the brown bits on the bottom. Boil for 2 minutes and then strain into a bowl. Season with salt and pepper.

For the cream: In a small bowl, combine the sour cream, horseradish, lemon juice and salt. Stir until combined. Cover and refrigerate until needed.

HANDY TIP: Prime rib is the most expensive and best cut you can buy. As a result, I often use a standing rib roast instead. It's more reasonably priced, and it will still taste great. Also, I like to have the butcher remove the bone and tie it back on. That way, all I have to do is to cut the strings, remove the bone, and carve.

Creamed Spinach

4	(10-ounce) packages frozen chopped spinach	1/2	cup whipping cream
3	tablespoons butter	2	cups milk
1	large onion, chopped	2/3	cup grated Parmesan cheese, divided
2	cloves garlic, minced	1/2	teaspoon kosher salt
3	tablespoons flour	1/2	teaspoon freshly ground black pepper
1/4	teaspoon nutmeg		

Preparation Time: 25 min.
Cooking Time: 20 to 30 min.
Total Time: 45 to 50 min.

Preheat the oven to 350°F/180°C. Grease a 1 1/2-quart baking dish.

Thaw the spinach in the microwave. The easiest way is to put the spinach in a bowl, cover with plastic wrap, make a few slits with a knife and microwave until thawed. Once thawed, squeeze out the excess water.

Melt the butter in a large deep skillet. Add the chopped onion and garlic and cook over medium heat, stirring occasionally, until tender, about 10 minutes.

Add the flour and nutmeg. Cook, stirring constantly, for about 2 minutes. Add the cream and milk. Stir until combined. Cook until thickened and bubbling, about 5 minutes.

Stir in the spinach. Stir in 1/3 cup of the grated Parmesan cheese. Add the salt and pepper. Pour into the prepared baking dish and sprinkle with the remaining 1/3 cup Parmesan cheese. Bake for 20 to 30 minutes, or until heated through.

To Prepare Ahead: You can prepare the Creamed Spinach up to 2 days ahead, stopping before reheating. Cover and refrigerate.

To Finish: When ready to serve, bake, uncovered, in a 350°F/180°C oven for 30 minutes or until heated through.

Wild Rice Casserole

¹/₂	cup butter		1	cup chopped pecans
1	onion, chopped		1	cup wild rice
¹/₄	cup chopped green bell pepper		3	cups chicken broth
1	clove garlic, minced			Kosher salt and freshly ground black
8	ounces sliced mushrooms			pepper to taste
	(about 3 cups)			

Preheat the oven to 350°F/180°C. Grease a 2-quart baking dish with a lid.

Melt the butter in a large frying pan. Add the onion, green pepper and garlic. Cook over medium heat, stirring often, for 5 minutes or until the onion is translucent. Add the mushrooms and sauté until they lose their liquid. Add the pecans and sauté for 1 minute.

Place the mixture in the baking dish. Stir in the rice and broth. Season with salt and pepper. Cover and bake for 60 minutes. Remove from the oven and let rest for 10 minutes.

To Prepare Ahead: You can make the Wild Rice Casserole up to 2 days ahead. Bake the casserole for an hour. Remove from the oven. Cool, cover, and store in the refrigerator.

To Finish: When you are ready to serve, return the Wild Rice Casserole, covered, to the oven for 30 minutes at 350°F/180°C.

Substitution: I really like this Wild Rice Casserole, but if you feel strongly about serving potatoes with your Prime Rib, you could always substitute the Mashed Potato Casserole (page 152) from the Thanksgiving menu for the Wild Rice Casserole.

Popovers

3	large eggs, at room temperature	1½	tablespoons butter, melted
1½	cups whole milk, at room temperature	1½	cups flour
		¾	teaspoon kosher salt

Preheat the oven to 425°F/210°C. Using butter, grease a 12-cup muffin pan or popover pan. Whisk the eggs until beaten. Whisk in the milk and the melted butter. Add the flour and salt and whisk until smooth.

Place the muffin pan or popover pan in the oven to preheat for about 2 minutes. Fill the muffin or popover cups less than half full. Bake for 30 minutes. Remove from the oven and pierce each popover with a knife to let out steam. Serve with butter.

TO PREPARE AHEAD: Believe it or not, you can make the Popovers ahead on the day and reheat before serving. They're not exactly the same, but it sure takes any last-minute stress out of the process. Bake as directed above. When the Popovers are done, pierce with a knife and remove to a wire rack to cool.

TO FINISH: Just before serving, place on a cookie sheet and reheat at 425°F/210°C for 2 to 3 minutes.

HANDY TIP: If your eggs aren't at room temperature, place them in a bowl of warm water and let them sit for about 5 minutes. Bring your milk to room temperature in the microwave.

Pumpkin Bread

3¹/₂ cups flour
2 teaspoons baking soda
1 teaspoon kosher salt
1 teaspoon nutmeg
1 teaspoon cinnamon
¹/₈ teaspoon ground cloves

4 eggs
1 cup vegetable oil
²/₃ cup water
1 (15-ounce) can pumpkin
3 cups sugar

Preparation Time: 15 min.
Cooking Time: 60 min.
Total Time: 75 min.

Preheat the oven to 350°F/180°C. Grease two 5×9-inch loaf pans.

In a medium bowl, mix together the flour, baking soda, salt, nutmeg, cinnamon and cloves. In a separate bowl, beat the eggs lightly. Add the oil, water, pumpkin and sugar and mix until combined.

Add the flour mixture to the pumpkin mixture, mixing until well blended. Pour into the prepared pans. Bake for 60 minutes or until wooden picks inserted in the centers come out clean. Let cool in the pans for 5 minutes. Remove the loaves from the pans and cool completely on a wire rack.

TO PREPARE AHEAD: Make the Pumpkin Bread as directed above. After the loaves have cooled completely, wrap them in plastic wrap and place them in a sealable plastic bag. Freeze for up to 3 months. Remove from the freezer and let thaw at room temperature for several hours or overnight.

SUBSTITUTION: If you like nuts, feel free to add 1 cup chopped pecans to the batter after you stir in the flour mixture.

Maple Apple Cake

Preparation Time: 30 min.
Cooking Time: 45 to 55 min.
Total Time: 75 to 85 min.

APPLE CAKE

2	cups sugar
3/4	cup vegetable oil
1/4	cup cold coffee
3	eggs
1	teaspoon vanilla extract
1	teaspoon maple flavoring
2 1/2	cups flour
1	teaspoon cinnamon
2	teaspoons baking powder
1	teaspoon baking soda
1	teaspoon kosher salt
3	cups finely chopped peeled cored apples
3/4	cup chopped pecans

FROSTING

1	cup packed light brown sugar
1/2	cup sugar
1/4	cup butter
1/3	cup milk
1	tablespoon corn syrup
1/4	teaspoon kosher salt
1	teaspoon vanilla extract

If you don't have any cold coffee, make the coffee! Preheat the oven to 350°F/180°C. Grease and flour a 9×13-inch cake pan.

For the cake: In a large bowl, beat together the sugar, oil, coffee, eggs, vanilla and maple flavoring. In a medium bowl, combine the flour, cinnamon, baking powder, baking soda and salt. Add the flour mixture to the egg batter and blend until combined. The batter will be very thick. Stir in the apples and the pecans.

Pour into the prepared pan. Bake 45 to 55 minutes or until a wooden pick inserted in the center comes out clean. Remove the cake from the oven. Cool in the pan for 5 minutes and then invert onto a wire rack to cool, ending with the top facing up. Once cool, place on a rectangular serving platter.

For the frosting: In a medium saucepan, combine the light brown sugar, sugar, butter, milk, corn syrup and salt. Heat over medium heat, stirring constantly, until the mixture melts and comes to a boil. Boil for 1 minute. Remove from the heat and cool to lukewarm. Stir in the vanilla and beat until the frosting reaches a spreadable consistency. Frost the cooled cake. If the frosting becomes too hard to spread, you can reheat briefly until it reaches the desired consistency.

TO PREPARE AHEAD: You can make the Maple Apple Cake up to 2 days ahead. Store, covered, at room temperature. Frankly, I think this cake tastes better after it has had a chance to sit at least overnight.

Pecan Turtle Candies

1	(14-ounce) package caramels, unwrapped	10	ounces pecan halves
2	tablespoons butter	20	ounces cocoa candy melts or chocolate almond bark
2	tablespoons water		

Preparation Time: 30 min.
Cooking Time: 20 min.
Total Time: 50 min. plus cooling time

Grease 2 baking sheets with butter.

Place the caramels, butter and water in the top of a double boiler. Heat, stirring often, until the caramels melt and the mixture becomes smooth.

Remove from the heat. Stir in the pecans. Drop by heaping teaspoonfuls onto the prepared baking sheets. Cool. If you need to rearrange the shape, do so after the caramel has had a chance to firm up slightly. Refrigerate until set.

Melt the chocolate in a bowl in the microwave. Do not overcook. Microwave for 1 minute and then stir the chocolate. Then microwave for 20 seconds and check. It should be nearly melted. Stir until smooth.

Dip the caramel-coated pecans in the chocolate using tongs. Make sure to cover all of the caramel with chocolate. Place each candy back on the baking sheet. Let cool until the chocolate sets.

TO PREPARE AHEAD: You can make the Pecan Turtle Candies up to a week ahead. Store the candies in an airtight container, separating each layer with wax paper.

SUBSTITUTION: If you can't find caramels, you can make your own. In a large saucepan, combine 1 1/3 cups whipping cream, 1/3 cup milk, 1 cup sugar, 1/2 cup light corn syrup, and 1/4 cup butter. Heat, stirring constantly, until the sugar dissolves. Bring to a boil, clip a candy thermometer on the side, and heat, stirring constantly, until the temperature reaches 234°F/112°C. Remove from the heat and stir in the vanilla. Immediately stir in the pecans and then continue as directed above.

Chocolate-Dipped Strawberries

Preparation Time: 15 min.
plus 60 min. resting time

1	pound fresh strawberries, with stems attached	12	ounces semisweet chocolate bits
		3	ounces white chocolate bits

Rinse and pat dry the strawberries. Line a baking sheet with wax paper.

Melt the chocolate in a bowl in the microwave. Do not overcook. Microwave for 1 minute and then stir the chocolate. Then microwave for 20 seconds and check. It should be nearly melted. Stir until smooth.

Take each strawberry by the top and dip into the chocolate. Coat with the chocolate about ¾ of the way up the strawberry. Gently place the strawberry on the prepared baking sheet. Repeat with the rest of the strawberries.

Melt the white chocolate in a small bowl in the microwave. Place the white chocolate in a small plastic bag. Cut off a very small part of the corner and squeeze in a zigzag pattern over the strawberry. Let the strawberries set at room temperature for 60 minutes before serving.

TO PREPARE AHEAD: These are really best the day they are made. You can make them early in the day and refrigerate.

TO FINISH: Remove from the refrigerator an hour before serving and return to room temperature.

Timeline

ONE WEEK BEFORE
(ABOUT 1 1/2 HOURS)

Buy groceries and create the ambience

Prepare ahead Pumpkin Bread and freeze

Prepare ahead Pecan Turtle Candies

Order Prime Rib to pick up two days before Christmas

TWO DAYS BEFORE
(ABOUT 1 1/2 HOURS)

Buy groceries and create the ambience

Put sparkling water, Champagne, and dessert wine (if using) in refrigerator

Put out red wine

Prepare ahead Maple Apple Cake

ONE DAY BEFORE
(ABOUT 1 1/2 HOURS)

Prepare ahead Wild Rice Casserole

Prepare ahead Creamed Spinach

Remove Pumpkin Bread from freezer and thaw overnight

DAY OF PARTY

Create the ambience

11:30 AM
Remove the Prime Rib from refrigerator, place in roasting pan, cover loosely, and let sit

Prepare ahead Popovers

Prepare ahead Horseradish Cream (in Prime Rib recipe)

Prepare ahead Chocolate-Dipped Strawberries

12:45 PM
Preheat oven to 450°F/230°C

1:00 PM
Put Prime Rib in oven

1:30 PM
Turn down the oven to 325°F/160°C

2:00 PM
Prepare coffeemaker

Open wine, turn on music, light candles

Put out Champagne glasses, main course plates, and dessert plates

Prepare sugar and milk for coffee

Refrigerate butter pats on a small serving plate

2:30 PM
Put out cashews and party mix

Prepare Brie with Cranberries, Almonds and Raisins

2:45 PM
Put Brie in oven with the Prime Rib at 325°F

2:55 PM
Put out Brie with Cranberries, Almonds and Raisins according to Presentation Tip

3:00 PM (GUESTS ARRIVE)
Open and pour Champagne (have water ready for those who prefer water)

3:30–4:00 PM
Take Prime Rib out of oven, transfer to a cutting board, and cover loosely with aluminum foil

Turn up oven to 350°F/180°C

Put Wild Rice Casserole (covered) and Creamed Spinach (uncovered) in oven to warm

Make au jus for Prime Rib according to recipe

3:50–4:20 PM
Put out butter pats

Put out Pumpkin Bread on a board with a knife

Prepare corn according to the package directions. Place in serving dish and add butter and salt.

Slice Prime Rib and arrange on a platter

Remove Wild Rice Casserole and Creamed Spinach from oven

Turn up oven to 425°F/220°C

Put Popovers in oven to warm for 2 to 3 minutes

Remove Popovers from oven and put in a basket

4:00–4:30 PM
Remove Chocolate-Dipped Strawberries from refrigerator

Call people to buffet

Serve wine and water

Turn on coffeemaker

5:00 PM
Put out Maple Apple Cake, Pecan Turtle Candies, and Chocolate-Dipped Strawberries

Serve dessert wine (if using)

Serve coffee and tea

Grocery List

PANTRY ITEMS

1³/₄ cups vegetable oil
Kosher salt
Freshly ground black pepper
1¹/₄ teaspoons ground nutmeg
2 teaspoons ground cinnamon
¹/₈ teaspoon ground cloves
2 teaspoons vanilla extract
1 teaspoon maple flavoring
5¹/₂ cups sugar
1 cup light brown sugar
7³/₄ cups flour
2 teaspoons baking powder
3 teaspoons baking soda
1 (12-ounce) package semisweet
chocolate bits
20 ounces cocoa candy melts or chocolate
almond bark
3 ounces white chocolate bits
1 (14-ounce) package caramels
1 tablespoon light corn syrup
10 ounces pecan halves
2¹/₄ cups pecan halves
¹/₄ cup slivered almonds
¹/₃ cup dried cranberries
¹/₃ cup golden raisins
¹/₂ cup beef broth

3 cups chicken broth
¹/₄ cup horseradish
1 cup wild rice
1 (15-ounce) can pumpkin
1 package flatbread or other crackers
1 (12-ounce) jar cashews
1 (8.75-ounce) package party mix
Decaffeinated and regular coffee
Regular and herbal tea bags

ALCOHOL AND DRINKS

2 bottles Champagne
2 bottles red wine for main
(Cabernet Sauvignon)
1 bottle dessert wine, if using (Sauternes)
5 bottles sparkling water
2 tablespoons Cointreau

DAIRY

4¹/₂ cups whole milk
2 cups butter
10 eggs
¹/₂ cup whipping cream

FREEZER

40 ounces frozen chopped spinach
32 ounces frozen corn

PRODUCE

1 lemon
6 apples
2 pears
1 pound large strawberries with stems
attached
1 bunch curly parsley for main garnish
2 onions
¹/₄ green bell pepper
3 cloves garlic
8 ounces fresh sliced mushrooms

DAIRY

5 cups whole milk
1 (1-pound) wheel of brie
1 cup sour cream
²/₃ cup grated Parmesan cheese

MEAT, FISH AND DELI

1 (9- to 10-pound) prime rib or standing
rib roast, bone removed and tied back
on (about 5 ribs)

Rustic Seafood Bake

menu

SERVES 8

Cocktail & Hors d'Oeuvres

Pear Champagne

Spinach Artichoke Dip

Mixed Nuts

Starter

Garden Pea Soup

Corn Bread

Sauvignon Blanc

Salad

Mixed Greens with Tarragon Vinaigrette

Palate Cleanser

Lime Sorbet

Main Course

Rustic Seafood Bake

Broccoli Florets

Unoaked Chardonnay

Dessert

Carrot Cake

Sugared Pecans

Butterscotch Chocolate Chip Cookies

Late Harvest Riesling

Coffee & Tea

Pear Champagne

PEAR SYRUP FOR 8
1/2 cup sugar
1/2 cup French pear brandy

FOR EACH COCKTAIL
1 1/2 tablespoons Pear Syrup
1/2 cup plus 2 tablespoons Champagne or dry sparkling wine

Preparation Time: 10 min.
Cooking Time: 5 min.
Total Time: 15 min. plus cooling time

In a small saucepan, heat the sugar and French pear brandy over medium heat until the sugar has dissolved. Remove from the heat and cool completely. Cover and refrigerate until needed.

Pour 1 1/2 tablespoons cooled Pear Syrup into the bottom of a Champagne glass. Fill the glass with Champagne or dry sparkling wine. Use a stirrer to mix the syrup and the Champagne together.

TO PREPARE AHEAD THE PEAR SYRUP: Make the Pear Syrup up to 2 days ahead according to the directions above. Cool, cover, and refrigerate until needed.

TO PREPARE AHEAD: Pour the Pear Syrup into the bottom of each Champagne glass and place the glasses near where you are going to serve the apéritif. Have a few empty glasses available in case some guests prefer water. Pour the Champagne and serve.

HANDY TIP: One bottle of Champagne makes enough to serve 6.

Spinach Artichoke Dip

1 (10-ounce) package frozen chopped spinach
16 ounces cream cheese, softened
1/2 cup mayonnaise
1 (14-ounce) can artichoke hearts, drained and chopped

1 clove garlic, minced
1/2 cup grated Parmesan cheese
1 teaspoon Tabasco sauce
1 French baguette, sliced thinly

Preparation Time: 15 min.
Cooking Time: 20 to 25 min.
Total Time: 35 to 40 min.

Preheat the oven to 350°F/180°C.

Thaw the frozen spinach in the microwave. The easiest way is to put the spinach in a bowl, cover with plastic wrap, making a few slits with a knife, and microwave for about 3 minutes. Then, let sit for a minute. If it's not yet thawed, microwave for another minute. When the spinach has thawed, squeeze out the excess liquid.

In a medium bowl, beat the cream cheese and mayonnaise until well blended. Add the artichokes, garlic, Parmesan cheese and Tabasco sauce and mix well. Spoon into an ovenproof bowl.

Bake for 20 to 25 minutes or until lightly browned and heated through. Serve with French baguette slices.

TO PREPARE AHEAD: Make the dip up to 2 days ahead, stopping before baking. Cover and refrigerate.

TO FINISH: Bake as directed above. Just before serving, slice the baguette into slices and arrange on a platter with the dip. Don't forget to put out a knife!

SERVES 8

Garden Pea Soup

Preparation Time: 15 min.
plus refrigeration

PRESENTATION TIP:
Ladle the soup into
bowls. Garnish with
a teaspoonful of sour
cream and top with
the fresh dill.

32	ounces frozen peas, thawed	3/4	teaspoon white pepper
1½	cups chicken broth	1½	cups half-and-half
3	tablespoons chopped fresh dill	1/4	cup sour cream for garnish
1½	teaspoons kosher salt		Fresh dill sprigs for garnish

Place the peas, chicken broth, chopped dill, salt and white pepper in a blender. Purée until smooth. Add the half-and-half.

If serving cold, cover and refrigerate for at least 2 hours.

If serving warm, pour into a large pot and heat over medium heat, stirring constantly.

TO PREPARE AHEAD: You can make the Garden Pea Soup up to 2 days ahead. Cover and refrigerate.

TO FINISH: If serving hot, reheat gently, stirring often. Serve according to the Presentation Tip.

HANDY TIP: This is another soup you can serve either hot or cold. You choose!

SERVES 9

Corn Bread

Preparation Time: 10 min.
Cooking Time: 15 to
20 min.
Total Time: 30 to 35 min.

1	cup flour	3/4	teaspoon kosher salt
1	cup cornmeal	2	eggs
1/4	cup sugar	1	cup milk
1	tablespoon baking powder	1/4	cup vegetable oil

Preheat the oven to 400°F/200°C. Grease a 9×9-inch baking pan or a 12-cup muffin pan.

In a large bowl, stir together the flour, cornmeal, sugar, baking powder and salt. In a small bowl, beat the eggs and milk with an electric mixer. Beat in the vegetable oil. Add the egg mixture to the dry ingredients and stir just until moistened and combined.

Pour the batter into the prepared pan. Bake for 15 to 20 minutes or until light golden brown. Serve immediately.

TO PREPARE AHEAD: Corn Bread muffins tend to dry out fairly quickly. As a result, if you want to make the Corn Bread ahead, I would recommend that you make it ahead on the day of your party and use a 9×9-inch baking pan. When the Corn Bread has finished baking, remove from the oven and let sit for about 5 minutes. Remove from the pan, cool, cover, and store at room temperature. You can serve the Corn Bread either warm or at room temperature.

TO FINISH: To serve warm, preheat the oven to 375°F/190°C and place the Corn Bread on an ungreased baking sheet. Bake until heated through, about 5 to 8 minutes. Cut into squares and serve immediately.

Mixed Greens with Tarragon Vinaigrette

Preparation Time: 10 min.
Cooking Time: 3 to 5 min.
Total Time: 13 to 15 min.

SALAD
8 ounces mixed baby greens
1/2 cup chopped hazelnuts

DRESSING
3 tablespoons minced shallots
2 tablespoons tarragon vinegar
1 tablespoon chopped fresh tarragon
1 teaspoon Dijon mustard
1/4 teaspoon kosher salt
1/8 teaspoon freshly ground black pepper
1/3 cup hazelnut oil

For the salad: Rinse and spin dry the mixed greens, place in a large bowl, cover with a damp towel and refrigerate until needed.

Place the hazelnuts in a small nonstick frying pan and roast over medium heat, stirring often, until browned, about 3 to 5 minutes. Remove from the heat and from the frying pan. Set aside.

For the dressing: In a small bowl, combine the shallots, tarragon vinegar, chopped tarragon, Dijon mustard, salt and pepper. While continuing to whisk, add the hazelnut oil in a steady stream. Continue whisking until the dressing thickens and emulsifies. Set aside.

To serve family style, toss the mixed greens with enough dressing to coat. Sprinkle with the toasted hazelnuts.

TO PREPARE AHEAD: Follow the directions above, stopping before you toss the mixed greens with dressing. Cover and refrigerate the dressing. An hour before serving, remove the salad dressing from the refrigerator and return to room temperature.

TO FINISH: Toss the mixed greens with enough dressing to coat and place on individual plates. Sprinkle with the toasted hazelnuts.

SUBSTITUTION: I prefer to use fresh herbs, especially in salad dressing, but if you must, you can substitute 1 teaspoon dried tarragon for the fresh.

Lime Sorbet

1½ cups sugar	1	cup fresh lime juice
1½ cups water		(about 6 or 7 limes)
Zest of 3 limes	1	tablespoon vodka
		Mint sprigs for garnish

Preparation Time: 10 min.
Cooking Time: 5 min.
Ice Cream Maker: 20 min.
Total Time: 35 min. plus cooling time

In a medium saucepan over medium heat, combine the sugar, water and lime zest. Heat until the mixture comes to a boil. Boil for 2 minutes. Add the lime juice and stir well.

Remove from the heat and cool completely. Stir in the vodka. Pour into an ice cream maker and process according to the manufacturer's directions. When finished, pour into an airtight container and freeze until ready to serve.

TO PREPARE AHEAD: Prepare the sorbet up to a month ahead, place in an airtight container, and freeze.

TO FINISH: Remove the sorbet 15 minutes before serving to allow it to soften slightly. When ready, scoop into bowls, garnish with the mint, and serve.

HANDY TIP: The average lime contains approximately 2 to 3 tablespoons of juice and 1 to 2 teaspoons of zest.

Rustic Seafood Bake

Preparation Time: 25 min.
Cooking Time: 45 min.
Total Time: 70 min.

PRESENTATION TIP:
Serve the rice, topped with a generous portion of the Rustic Seafood Bake. Garnish with flat-leaf parsley. Accompany with the steamed Broccoli Florets.

2	medium onions, finely chopped
1/2	cup butter
1	pound fresh shrimp, peeled and deveined
1	pound fresh scallops
2	cloves garlic, minced
1 1/2	pounds crab meat or crab meat substitute
3/4	cup sherry
6	tablespoons butter
2/3	cup flour

3	cups milk
1/2	cup sherry
1	teaspoon kosher salt
1/2	teaspoon freshly ground black pepper
3	slices country-style bread
2	tablespoons butter
1/2	cup grated Parmesan cheese
2	cups brown rice

Flat-leaf parsley for garnish

Preheat the oven to 400°F/200°C.

In a large deep skillet, sauté the onions in 1/2 cup butter until translucent, about 5 to 8 minutes. Add the shrimp, scallops and garlic. Sauté until cooked, about 3 minutes. Stir in the crab meat. Sprinkle the seafood mixture with 3/4 cup sherry. Set aside.

In a large saucepan, melt 6 tablespoons butter over medium heat. Add the flour and cook, stirring constantly, for 1 minute. Slowly stir in the milk and 1/2 cup sherry. Stir until smooth. Season with the salt and pepper.

Combine the sherry cream sauce and the seafood mixture and spoon into a 9×13-inch baking pan. Cut the crusts off the bread slices and cut the slices into 1/2-inch cubes. Melt 2 tablespoons butter in a large frying pan, add the bread cubes and toss. Place the bread cubes over the top of the seafood mixture and sprinkle with the grated Parmesan cheese.

Bake for 30 to 35 minutes. While the Rustic Seafood Bake is in the oven, make the brown rice according to the package directions.

TO PREPARE AHEAD: You can make the Rustic Seafood Bake early in the day, stopping before topping with the bread cubes and grated Parmesan cheese. Cover and refrigerate. Cook the brown rice, place in a microwave-safe bowl, cool, cover, and refrigerate.

TO FINISH: Top the Rustic Seafood Bake with the bread cubes and grated Parmesan cheese and bake according to the directions above. Reheat the brown rice in the microwave until heated through. Serve according to the Presentation Tip.

Broccoli Florets

2	pounds broccoli		Kosher salt and freshly ground black
2	tablespoons butter		pepper to taste

Preparation Time: 5 min.
Cooking Time: 5 to 7 min.
Total Time: 10 to 12 min.

Trim the stems from the broccoli and set aside. Cut the top of the bunch into equal size florets.

In a large pot, bring 1 inch water to a boil. Fill a steamer basket with the broccoli and place over the boiling water. Cover and steam until tender, about 5 to 7 minutes.

Remove the steamed florets and place in a bowl. Dot with the butter and season with salt and pepper to taste. Serve immediately.

To Prepare Ahead: You can steam the florets up to a day ahead. Drain and plunge into cold water to stop the cooking process. Place the drained florets in a microwave-safe bowl, cover, and refrigerate.

To Finish: Add the butter and reheat in the microwave. Season with salt and pepper and serve.

Sugared Pecans

SERVES 12

1/2	cup sugar	1 1/2	teaspoons water
3/4	teaspoon cinnamon	1/2	teaspoon vanilla extract
1/2	teaspoon kosher salt	8	ounces pecan halves (about 2 cups)
1	egg white		

Preparation Time: 10 min.
Cooking Time: 30 min.
Total Time: 40 min.

Preheat the oven to 300°F/140°C. Line a 10×15-inch baking sheet with aluminum foil.

In a sealable plastic bag, combine the sugar, cinnamon and salt. Shake well to mix. In a small bowl, beat together the egg white, water and vanilla until foamy. Stir in the pecans, making sure to coat them well.

Remove the pecans with a slotted spoon and add to the plastic bag. Shake until well coated. Spread the pecans out over the foil-lined baking sheet, separating the nuts into a single layer. Bake for 30 minutes, stirring after 15 minutes. Cool and store in an airtight container.

To Prepare Ahead: You can make the Sugared Pecans up to a week ahead and store in an airtight container.

To Freeze: After the Sugared Pecans have cooled completely, place in a sealable plastic bag and freeze for up to 2 months. Return to room temperature before serving.

Carrot Cake

CARROT CAKE

2	cups flour
2	teaspoons baking powder
1½	teaspoons baking soda
2	teaspoons cinnamon
1	teaspoon kosher salt
4	large eggs
2	cups sugar
1½	cups vegetable oil
2	cups finely grated peeled carrots (1 pound)

1	(8-ounce) can crushed pineapple in its own juice
¾	cup chopped pecans

CREAM CHEESE FROSTING

½	cup chopped pecans
12	ounces cream cheese, softened
¾	cup butter, softened
1	tablespoon vanilla extract
6	cups confectioners' sugar

Preheat the oven to 325°F/160°C. Grease three 9-inch round cake pans and line the bottoms with parchment paper.

In a medium bowl, mix together the flour, baking powder, baking soda, cinnamon and salt.

In a large bowl, beat the eggs with an electric mixer. Beat in the sugar and then the oil. Stir in the carrots, the pineapple and juice and pecans. Add the flour mixture and stir until well combined.

Pour into the prepared pans. Bake for 40 to 45 minutes, or until wooden picks inserted in the centers come out clean. Remove the cakes from the oven and cool in the pans for 10 minutes before inverting onto wire racks. Cool the cakes completely and then remove the parchment paper from the bottom of the cakes.

For the frosting: While the cakes are cooling, toast the chopped pecans. Place the pecans in a small nonstick frying pan and toast over medium heat, stirring often, until browned, about 3 to 5 minutes. Remove from the heat and set aside to cool.

In a medium bowl, blend together the cream cheese, butter and vanilla with an electric mixer until smooth. Add the confectioners' sugar and blend on Low speed until combined.

To assemble: Place 1 of the cake layers on a serving platter and spread with ⅓ of the frosting. Top with another layer and spread with another ⅓ of the frosting. Place the last layer on top, bottom side up, and frost the top and side of the cake with the remaining frosting. Sprinkle the toasted pecans on the top of the cake.

TO PREPARE AHEAD: You can make the Carrot Cake up to 2 days ahead. Cover and refrigerate.

TO FINISH: Remove from the refrigerator 30 to 60 minutes before serving.

HANDY TIP: To make 2 cups of grated carrots, I use a 1-pound bag of carrots. I peel them, cut off the ends, and process them in the bowl of a food processor until finely grated.

SUBSTITUTION: For a slightly different flavor, try adding 1 cup coconut when you stir in the chopped pecans.

Butterscotch Chocolate Chip Cookies

1 1/2   cups butter
3/4   cup packed light brown sugar
1 1/2   cups sugar
2   eggs
1   tablespoon vanilla extract
2 1/4   cups flour
1 1/2   teaspoons baking soda
1 1/2   teaspoons cinnamon

2 1/4   cups rolled oats
1   (12-ounce) package semisweet
    chocolate bits
1   (12-ounce) package
    butterscotch bits
1/2   (8-ounce) package Heath Bar Bits

Preparation Time: 10 min.
Cooking Time: 8 to
10 min. per batch

Preheat the oven to 375°F/190°C. Grease 2 cookie sheets with butter.

Cream together the butter, light brown sugar and sugar. Beat in the eggs and vanilla.

In a small bowl, mix together the flour, baking soda and cinnamon. Add to the egg mixture. Stir in the chocolate bits, butterscotch bits and Heath Bar Bits.

Drop the dough by rounded heaping teaspoonfuls about 2 inches apart on the prepared sheets. Bake for 8 to 10 minutes per batch or until slightly browned around the edges. Cool on the cookie sheet for a minute before removing to a wire rack.

TO PREPARE AHEAD: You can make the cookies up to a week ahead. You'll only need about 16 cookies for your dinner party. Place the cooled cookies you need for your party on a small serving platter and cover securely with plastic wrap. Freeze the extra cookie dough or bake the cookies and store in an airtight container.

TO FREEZE: Refrigerate unbaked cookie dough until firm enough to handle, about 15 minutes. Place a piece of plastic wrap on your work surface. Separate the dough into 3 equal pieces (4 pieces if you haven't baked a batch above). Shape each piece into a log with a 1 1/2-inch diameter. Roll each log in plastic wrap, sealing the ends. Place the logs in a sealable plastic bag and freeze for up to 3 months. When ready to bake, thaw for 30 minutes at room temperature (or briefly in the microwave) and bake as directed above.

SUBSTITUTION: If you can't find Heath Bar Bits, you can always use toffee bits instead.

Timeline

<table>
<tr>
<td valign="top">

ONE WEEK BEFORE
(ABOUT 1 1/2 HOURS)

Buy groceries and create the ambience

Prepare ahead Lime Sorbet

Prepare ahead Sugared Pecans

</td>
<td valign="top">

TWO DAYS BEFORE
(ABOUT 3/4 HOUR)

Buy groceries and create the ambience

Put sparkling water, Champagne, white wines, and dessert wine (if using) in refrigerator

Prepare ahead Butterscotch Chocolate Chip Cookies

</td>
<td valign="top">

ONE DAY BEFORE
(ABOUT 1 1/2 HOURS)

Prepare ahead Carrot Cake

Prepare ahead Spinach Artichoke Dip

Prepare ahead Pear Syrup for the Pear Champagne

</td>
</tr>
</table>

DAY OF PARTY (ABOUT 1 1/2 HOURS)

Buy groceries and create the ambience

Prepare ahead Garden Pea Soup

Prepare ahead Corn Bread

Prepare ahead Mixed Greens with Tarragon Vinaigrette

Prepare ahead Rustic Seafood Bake

Prepare ahead Broccoli Florets

5:00 PM
Shower and dress

6:30 PM
Prepare coffeemaker

Open wines, turn on music, light candles

Put out starter bowls, salad plates, sorbet bowls, main course plates, and dessert plates

Prepare sugar and milk for coffee

7:00 PM
Preheat oven to 350°F/180°C

Put butter pats on butter plates

Put a cucumber slice in each water glass

Prepare ahead Pear Champagne

Put out mixed nuts

7:10 PM
Put Spinach Artichoke Dip in oven

Remove salad dressing from refrigerator

7:30 PM (GUESTS ARRIVE)
Open and pour Champagne (have water ready for those who prefer water)

7:35 PM
Remove Spinach Artichoke Dip from oven and serve

If serving soup hot, start to reheat soup over medium-low heat; stir and check occasionally

8:00 PM
If serving soup hot, check soup is hot

Put Corn Bread on butter plates

Turn up oven to 400°F/200°C

8:05 PM
Call people to table

Serve starter wine and water

8:10 PM
Serve Garden Pea Soup, hot or cold, according to Presentation Tip

8:30 PM
Finish salad and serve

Put Rustic Seafood Bake, uncovered, in oven

Take sorbet out of freezer

8:45 PM
Serve sorbet, garnished with mint

Remove Carrot Cake from refrigerator

9:00 PM
Reheat brown rice in microwave

Remove Rustic Seafood Bake from oven and plate according to Presentation Tip

9:15 PM
Serve main course and wine

Turn on coffeemaker

9:45 PM
Serve Carrot Cake, garnished with Sugared Pecans

Serve dessert wine (if using)

10:00 PM
Serve coffee, tea, Sugared Pecans, and after-dinner cookies

Grocery List

ONE WEEK BEFORE PARTY

PANTRY ITEMS
1³/₄ cups vegetable oil
¹/₃ cup hazelnut oil
2 tablespoons tarragon vinegar
¹/₂ cup mayonnaise
Kosher salt
Freshly ground black pepper
³/₄ teaspoon white pepper
4¹/₄ teaspoons cinnamon
6¹/₄ cups sugar
³/₄ cup light brown sugar
6 cups confectioners' sugar
6 cups flour
1 cup yellow cornmeal
2¹/₄ cups rolled oats
5 teaspoons baking powder
3 teaspoons baking soda
2¹/₃ tablespoons vanilla extract
1 (12-ounce) package semisweet chocolate bits
1 (12-ounce) package butterscotch bits
¹/₂ (8-ounce) package Heath Bar Bits or toffee bits
¹/₂ cup chopped hazelnuts
1¹/₄ cups chopped pecans
8 ounces pecan halves
1¹/₂ cups chicken broth
1 (14-ounce) can artichoke hearts
1 (8-ounce) can crushed pineapple in its own juice
2 cups brown rice

1 teaspoon Tabasco sauce
1 teaspoon Dijon mustard
1¹/₄ cups cooking sherry
1 (12-ounce) jar mixed nuts
Decaffeinated and regular coffee
Regular and herbal tea bags

ALCOHOL AND DRINKS
2 bottles Champagne or sparkling wine
2 bottles white wine for starter (Sauvignon Blanc)
2 bottles white wine for main (Unoaked Chardonnay)
1 bottle dessert wine, if using (Late Harvest Riesling)
4 bottles sparkling water
¹/₂ cup French pear brandy
1 tablespoon vodka

PRODUCE
7 limes

DAIRY
4¹/₄ cups butter
9 eggs

FREEZER
10 ounces frozen chopped spinach
32 ounces frozen peas

TWO DAYS BEFORE PARTY

PRODUCE
1 bunch fresh dill
1 bunch fresh mint for sorbet garnish
1 tablespoon chopped fresh tarragon
1 bunch flat-leaf parsley for main garnish
8 ounces mixed baby greens
3 cloves garlic
3 tablespoons minced shallots
2 medium onions
2 pounds broccoli
1 pound carrots
1 cucumber

DAIRY
5 cups whole milk
28 ounces cream cheese
1¹/₂ cups half-and-half
¹/₄ cup sour cream
1 cup grated Parmesan cheese

MEAT, FISH AND DELI
1 pound raw fresh shrimp, peeled and deveined
1 pound fresh scallops
1¹/₂ pounds crab meat or crab meat substitute

BAKERY
3 slices country-style bread

DAY OF PARTY

BAKERY
1 French baguette

Filet of Beef with Balsamic Onions and Asparagus

menu

SERVES 8

Cocktail & Hors d'Oeuvres

Kir Royale

Pear and Roquefort Crostini

Cheese Straws

Cashews

Starter

Cream of Mushroom Soup

Rolls and Butter

White Burgundy, Unoaked Chardonnay, or Pinot Noir

Salad

Herb Salad with Sugared Almonds

Palate Cleanser

Lemon Sorbet

Main Course

Filet of Beef with Balsamic Onions and Asparagus

Creamy Mashed Potatoes

Malbec

Dessert

Individual Baked Alaska

Lace Cookies

Chenin Blanc Dessert Wine

Coffee & Tea

Kir Royale

1½ tablespoons crème de cassis

½ cup plus 2 tablespoons Champagne or dry sparkling wine

Preparation Time: 5 min.

Fill the bottom of a Champagne glass with the crème de cassis. Fill the glass with Champagne or dry sparkling wine.

TO PREPARE AHEAD: Pour the crème de cassis into the bottom of each Champagne glass and place the glasses near where you are going to serve the apéritif. Have a few empty glasses available in case some guests prefer water.

TO FINISH: Pour the Champagne and serve.

HANDY TIP: One bottle of Champagne makes enough to serve 6.

Pear and Roquefort Crostini

CROSTINI
1   French baguette
2   tablespoons extra-virgin olive oil

ASSEMBLY
4   ounces creamy Roquefort cheese
1   pear, cored and thinly sliced
2   tablespoons honey

Preparation Time: 10 min.
Cooking Time: 20 min.
Total Time: 30 min.

For the crostini: Preheat the oven to 350°F/180°C. Cut the baguette into ⅜-inch slices. Brush both sides of each slice with extra-virgin olive oil and place on an ungreased baking sheet. Bake for 10 minutes, turn the slices over and bake for 10 minutes more, or until lightly toasted. Remove to a wire rack to cool completely.

To assemble: Preheat the broiler. Top each crostini with some of the Roquefort cheese and place on an ungreased baking sheet. Place in the oven and broil for about 30 seconds or until the cheese starts to melt. Remove from the oven.

Place the crostini on a serving platter, top with a pear slice and drizzle with a little honey.

TO PREPARE AHEAD: You can toast the crostini up to 2 days ahead. When cool, store the crostini in a sealable plastic bag at room temperature.

TO FINISH: Just before serving, assemble as directed above, place on a platter, and serve.

Cheese Straws

Preparation Time: 15 min.
Cooking Time: 15 min.
Total Time: 30 min.

PRESENTATION TIP:
Place the Cheese Straws, wrapped in a colorful napkin, in a decorative vase.

1   (17.3-ounce) package frozen puff pastry, thawed
1   egg
1   tablespoon water
1   cup grated sharp white Cheddar cheese
1/2   cup grated Parmesan cheese
1   teaspoon minced fresh rosemary or other herb
1   teaspoon kosher salt
Freshly ground black pepper to taste

Preheat the oven to 400°F/200°C. Grease 2 baking sheets and line with parchment paper.

Spread 1 sheet of puff pastry on a floured work surface. Roll out until the pastry is about 10×12 inches. Beat the egg and water together. Brush over the pastry.

Combine the Cheddar cheese and Parmesan cheese in a bowl and sprinkle half over the pastry. Sprinkle with half of the minced rosemary, half of the salt and freshly ground black pepper to taste. Cover with a sheet of plastic wrap and roll until the cheeses are pressed into the pastry. Remove the plastic wrap.

Cut the pastry in half starting from the middle of the long side. Then cut the pastry along the original short side into strips roughly 3/8 × 6 inches.

Twist the strips and place on the prepared baking sheets. Repeat with the remaining ingredients. Bake for 10 to 12 minutes. When lightly browned, flip the straws over and bake for another few minutes. Cool on a wire rack and serve.

TO PREPARE AHEAD: Follow the recipe above. Once the Cheese Straws have cooled, place in sealable plastic bag and freeze for up to 3 months.

TO FINISH: Prior to serving, preheat the oven to 400°F/200°C. Place the frozen Cheese Straws on an ungreased baking sheet and bake for about 3 minutes or until crisp and warm. Cool on a wire rack and serve.

SUBSTITUTION: I like to make up lots of Cheese Straws in advance and freeze them. Be creative! Make up 1 sheet of puff pastry with rosemary and another with chives. Or, try using a different cheese.

Cream of Mushroom Soup

1/4	cup butter		1/4	teaspoon dried thyme
1 1/2	cups chopped onions		1	teaspoon kosher salt
1	pound russet or Idaho potatoes, peeled and diced (about 3 small potatoes)		2	cups milk
			1	cup whipping cream
			1/4	cup dry sherry
1	stalk celery, diced			Freshly ground black pepper to taste
1 1/2	pounds sliced mushrooms		1/3	cup whipping cream for garnish
2	cups vegetable broth			Freshly chopped chives for garnish
1	cup water			

Preparation Time: 10 min.
Cooking Time: 35 min.
Total Time: 45 min.

PRESENTATION TIP:
Ladle the soup into bowls. Place a small amount of cream in the middle of each bowl and top with a pinch of chives.

Melt the butter in a large soup pot and sauté the onions over medium heat until translucent, about 5 minutes. Add the diced potatoes and celery. Cook over low heat for about 3 minutes, stirring often.

Add the mushrooms, vegetable broth, water, thyme and salt. Turn up the heat and bring to a boil. Cover and cook over low heat for 15 minutes or until the potatoes and celery are tender.

Remove from the heat and cool to lukewarm. Purée in a blender until smooth. The mixture will be very thick. Return the mushroom mixture to the cleaned-out soup pot.

Over low heat, whisk in the milk, then 1 cup whipping cream, the sherry and pepper. Heat, stirring constantly, until the soup is hot but not boiling.

TO PREPARE AHEAD: You can make the soup a day ahead, stopping before reheating. Cool, cover, and refrigerate.

TO FINISH: Reheat the soup gently, stirring often, and serve according to the Presentation Tip.

HANDY TIP: In a hurry? Buy cleaned and sliced mushrooms. Button mushrooms work fine, but feel free to substitute other mushrooms or a combination of mushrooms.

SUBSTITUTION: Don't have vegetable broth on hand? Substitute bouillon cubes and hot water.

Herb Salad with Sugared Almonds

SALAD

8	ounces mixed baby greens
3	tablespoons chopped fresh chives
3	tablespoons chopped fresh dill
1/3	cup chopped flat-leaf parsley
1	small zucchini, quartered and sliced
5	green onions, sliced
8	ounces cherry tomatoes, halved
1/3	cup blanched flaked almonds
1	tablespoon sugar

DRESSING

2	tablespoons balsamic vinegar
1/4	teaspoon kosher salt
1/8	teaspoon freshly ground black pepper
1/3	cup extra-virgin olive oil

For the salad: Rinse and spin dry the mixed greens. Place in a large bowl. Add the chives, dill and parsley. Add the zucchini, green onions and cherry tomatoes. Cover with a damp towel and refrigerate until needed.

Place the flaked almonds and sugar in a small nonstick frying pan. Cook over medium heat until the sugar is melted. Cool on parchment paper and break into pieces. Set aside.

For the dressing: In a small bowl, whisk together the balsamic vinegar, salt and pepper. While continuing to whisk, add the extra-virgin olive oil in a steady stream until the dressing thickens and emulsifies.

To serve family style, toss the mixed greens with enough dressing to coat and sprinkle with the sugared almonds.

TO PREPARE AHEAD: Follow the directions above, stopping before you toss the mixed greens with the dressing. Cover and refrigerate the dressing. An hour before serving, remove the salad dressing from the refrigerator and return to room temperature.

TO FINISH: Whisk the dressing. Toss the mixed greens with enough dressing to coat and place on individual plates. Spinkle with the sugared almonds.

Lemon Sorbet

1 1/2 cups sugar
1 1/2 cups water
Grated zest of 2 lemons
1   cup fresh lemon juice
     (about 4 or 5 lemons)

1   tablespoon vodka
Mint sprigs for garnish

Preparation Time: 10 min.
Cooking Time: 5 min.
Ice Cream Maker: 20 min.
Total Time: 35 min. plus
cooling time

In a medium saucepan over medium heat, combine the sugar, water and lemon zest. Heat until the mixture comes to a boil. Boil for 2 minutes. Add the lemon juice and stir well.

Remove from the heat and cool completely. Stir in the vodka. Pour into an ice cream maker and process according to the manufacturer's directions. When finished, pour into an airtight container and freeze until ready to serve.

TO PREPARE AHEAD: Prepare the sorbet up to a month ahead, place in an airtight container, and freeze.

TO FINISH: Remove the sorbet 15 minutes before serving to allow it to soften slightly. When ready, scoop into bowls, garnish with the mint, and serve.

HANDY TIP: The average lemon contains approximately 3 to 4 tablespoons of juice and 1 tablespoon of zest.

Filet of Beef with Balsamic Onions and Asparagus

Preparation Time: 15 min.
Cooking Time: 60 min.
Total Time: 75 min.

PRESENTATION TIP:
Place a filet on each plate.
Top with a spoonful of
Balsamic Onions and
3 asparagus spears.
Serve with Creamy
Mashed Potatoes.

BALSAMIC ONIONS
3   large Spanish onions, thickly sliced
1/4 cup balsamic vinegar
1/4 cup extra-virgin olive oil
2   teaspoons sugar
1   teaspoon kosher salt
1/2 teaspoon freshly ground black
     pepper

FILETS
2   tablespoons extra-virgin olive
     oil, divided
8   (6-ounce) filets mignons

Kosher salt and freshly ground black
     pepper to taste
1   tablespoon balsamic vinegar
     to finish

ASPARAGUS
1   teaspoon kosher salt
24   pencil thin asparagus spears,
     trimmed (about 1 pound)
1   tablespoon butter
Kosher salt to taste

For the onions and filets: Preheat the oven to 375°F/190°C. Place the thickly sliced onions on a baking sheet. Add 1/4 cup balsamic vinegar, the extra-virgin olive oil, sugar, salt and pepper. Toss until well coated. Bake for 60 minutes or until tender. While the onions are roasting, heat 1 tablespoon olive oil in a large frying pan. Sprinkle the filets liberally with salt and pepper.

Add 4 filets to the pan and sear for 5 minutes, turning once after 2¹/₂ minutes. Remove the filets to an ungreased baking sheet. Add the remaining 1 tablespoon extra-virgin olive oil to the frying pan and repeat with the remaining filets. Place the filets in the oven with the onions after the onions have been baking for 40 minutes. Roast the filets for 15 to 20 minutes or until a meat thermometer reaches your desired temperature (125°F to 130°F/ 52°C to 54°C for medium-rare and 130°F to 140°F/54°C to 60°C for medium). Remove the filets from the oven and let rest for 5 minutes, covered loosely with aluminum foil. Place the onions in a bowl and stir in 1 tablespoon balsamic vinegar. Cover to keep warm.

For the asparagus: While the filets are roasting, bring a large pot of water to a boil. After you remove the filets from the oven to rest, add the salt to the boiling water and then the asparagus. Simmer until tender-crisp, about 1¹/₂ to 2 minutes if the spears are pencil thin or 3 to 4 minutes if the spears are thick. Remove from the heat, add the butter and season with salt to taste.

Serve according to the Presentation Tip.

TO PREPARE AHEAD: You can make the Balsamic Onions up to 2 days ahead. Store in a microwave-safe bowl, covered, in the refrigerator. You can cook the asparagus ahead on the day. Drain and plunge into cold water to stop the cooking process. Pat dry and place in a microwave-safe bowl. Cover and refrigerate until needed. You can sear the filets ahead on the day. Sear as directed above and place on an ungreased baking sheet. Cool, cover, and refrigerate.

TO FINISH: Preheat the oven to 375°F/190°C and bake the filets, uncovered, for 20 to 25 minutes or until a meat thermometer reaches your desired temperature. Let rest for 5 minutes before serving.

SUBSTITUTION: You can substitute a 3-pound filet of beef tenderloin, tied if necessary, for the filets. An hour before cooking, remove the beef tenderloin from the refrigerator. Preheat the oven to 400°F/200°C. Pat dry the filet and place it on a roasting rack over a roasting pan. If you don't have a roasting rack, just place the filet in a roasting pan. Put the filet in the oven and roast for 20 minutes. Turn down the temperature to 325°F/160°C. Roast the filet for an additional 20 minutes or until a meat thermometer reaches 125°F to 130°F/ 52°C to 54°C (for medium-rare) or 130°F to 140°F/54°C to 60°C (for medium). Remove from the oven and let rest for 5 minutes, covered loosely with aluminum foil. To serve, slice the tenderloin thickly. Place 2 slices of tenderloin on each plate. Top with the Balsamic Onions and 3 asparagus spears.

Creamy Mashed Potatoes

Preparation Time: 15 min.
Cooking Time: 20 min.
Total Time: 35 min.

5	pounds Yukon Gold potatoes, peeled and chopped into 1 1/2-inch cubes
1	teaspoon kosher salt
1/2	cup butter

2/3	to 1 cup whole milk
	Kosher salt and freshly ground black pepper to taste
2	tablespoons chopped fresh chives for garnish

Place the potatoes in a large pot and add enough water to cover. Add 1 teaspoon salt. Place over high heat, partially covered, and bring to a boil. Simmer for 15 minutes or until tender. Using a ricer, mash the potatoes.

Add the butter. Stir in the milk a little at a time until you reach the desired consistency. Season with salt and freshly ground pepper to taste. Garnish with fresh chopped chives.

TO PREPARE AHEAD: Although mashed potatoes are best served right away, you can prepare them ahead and reheat, which is what I do for a dinner party. Prepare the Creamy Mashed Potatoes as directed above, place in a microwave-safe bowl, cool, cover, and refrigerate.

TO FINISH: When ready to serve, reheat in the microwave until heated through, about 5 minutes. Serve garnished with fresh chopped chives.

Lace Cookies

2¼	cups rolled oats	1	cup butter, melted
2¼	cups packed light brown sugar	1	egg
3	tablespoons flour	1	teaspoon vanilla extract
1	teaspoon kosher salt		

Preheat the oven to 375°F/190°C. Grease 2 airbake cookie sheets and line with parchment paper.

In a large bowl, stir together the oats, brown sugar, flour and salt. With an electric mixer, blend in the melted butter. Add the egg and vanilla. Blend until combined.

Drop the dough by ½ teaspoonfuls 2 inches apart onto the cookie sheets. Bake for about 5 minutes or until the tops are bubbly. Let cool until firm enough to easily transfer to a wire rack.

TO PREPARE AHEAD: You can make the cookies up to a week ahead. You'll only need about 16 cookies for your dinner party. Place the cooled cookies you need on a small serving platter and cover securely with plastic wrap. Freeze the extra cookie dough or bake the cookies and store in an airtight container.

TO FREEZE: Refrigerate the unbaked cookie dough until firm enough to handle, about 15 minutes. Place a piece of plastic wrap on your work surface. Separate the dough into 3 equal pieces (4 pieces if you haven't baked a batch above). Shape each piece into a log with a 1½-inch diameter. Roll each log in plastic wrap, sealing the ends. Place the logs in a sealable plastic bag and freeze for up to 3 months. When ready to bake, thaw for 30 minutes at room temperature (or briefly in the microwave) and bake as directed above.

SUBSTITUTION: If you don't have an airbake cookie sheet, use a regular cookie sheet lined with parchment paper, and then go out and buy an airbake cookie sheet the next time you have a chance! They are great for baking cookies.

Individual Baked Alaska

Preparation Time: 25 min.
Cooking Time: 25 to 30 min.
Total Time: 50 to 55 min. plus freezing time

BROWNIE BASE
3	squares unsweetened chocolate
1/2	cup butter
1 1/2	cups sugar
2	eggs
3/4	teaspoon vanilla extract
3/4	cup flour

ICE CREAM FILLING
1 1/2	quarts chocolate ice cream, slightly softened
1 1/2	quarts vanilla ice cream, slightly softened

TOPPING
9	large egg whites, at room temperature
1/2	teaspoon cream of tartar
1 1/2	cups sugar

Preheat the oven to 350°F/180°C. Grease a 9×13-inch baking pan and line the bottom and sides with parchment paper.

For the base: In a large microwave-safe bowl, microwave the chocolate and butter on high for 2 minutes or until the butter is melted. Stir until the chocolate is completely melted. Stir in the sugar. Blend in the eggs and vanilla. Stir in the flour and mix until combined.

Spread in the prepared pan. Bake for 20 to 25 minutes or until a wooden pick inserted in the center comes out with crumbs. Remove from the oven and cool on a wire rack.

When cool, invert onto a wire rack and then invert again so that the top is facing upward.

Using a 3-inch pastry cutter, cut out 8 rounds. If you don't have a pastry cutter, an empty clean 6-ounce tuna can will do. Place the brownie rounds on parchment paper, wrap in foil and freeze.

For the filling: While the brownies are baking, prepare the ice cream filling. Place a standard muffin pan on your work surface.

Carefully fill 8 of the muffin cups half full with the chocolate ice cream. Fill to the top with the vanilla ice cream. Skim a knife across the top to create a flat surface. Cover with plastic wrap and place in the freezer until firm, about an hour.

To assemble: Grease 2 baking sheets and line with parchment paper. Make sure the baking sheets will fit in your freezer and in your oven. Place 4 of the brownie rounds on each baking sheet, leaving plenty of space between each one. Remove the ice cream from the freezer. Dip the bottom of the muffin pan briefly in some warm water to loosen the ice cream. Use a fork to help twist out the ice cream. Place the ice cream on top of a brownie, with the vanilla side down. Repeat with the rest of the ice cream. Return the brownies topped with the ice cream to the freezer.

Preheat the oven to 500°F/240°C. Place the egg whites and the cream of tartar in a large bowl. Beat until the egg whites form soft peaks. Beat in the sugar 1 tablespoon at a time. The egg mixture should be glossy and form stiff peaks. Remove the ice cream/brownie stacks from the freezer. Completely cover each stack with the egg white mixture. Use the back of a spoon to pull the egg white into decorative peaks. At this point, you can bake the dessert or return it to the freezer for later use.

To bake, place the 2 baking sheets in the oven. Bake for 3 to 5 minutes, watching carefully. Remove from the oven when the peaks start to brown. Transfer with a spatula to individual dessert dishes and serve immediately.

TO PREPARE AHEAD: Follow the directions above, stopping after you have frozen the brownies and the ice cream filling.

TO ASSEMBLE: You can assemble the baked Alaska up to 2 days before your party. After you have covered the ice cream/brownie stacks with the egg white mixture and pulled the egg whites into peaks, as directed above, return the Individual Baked Alaska to the freezer.

TO FINISH: When ready to serve, bake as directed above.

HANDY TIP: If you want to save some time, you can always make up a single Baked Alaska. Take a 4- to 6-cup bowl (or saucepan), invert it onto the cooled brownie, and cut out a circle of brownie around the opening of the bowl. Wrap and freeze the brownie circle. Line the bowl with plastic wrap, leaving extra wrap overhanging the edges. As above, fill the bottom half of the bowl with softened chocolate ice cream and then return to the freezer to harden. When hardened, fill the remaining half with vanilla ice cream, smoothing the top with a knife. Return to the freezer. Follow directions as above but for 1 large mold. When the mold comes out of the oven, let it rest for 3 to 5 minutes before serving, as the ice cream in the middle will still be very hard.

SUBSTITUTION: In a hurry? Feel free to use a brownie mix to save some time.

Timeline

ONE WEEK BEFORE
(ABOUT 1¹/₂ HOURS)

Buy groceries and create the ambience

Prepare ahead Lemon Sorbet

Prepare ahead Individual Baked Alaska

Prepare ahead Cheese Straws

TWO DAYS BEFORE
(ABOUT ¹/₄ HOUR)

Buy groceries and create the ambience

Put sparkling water, Champagne, white wine (if using), and dessert wine (if using) in refrigerator

Put out red wine

ONE DAY BEFORE
(ABOUT 1 HOUR)

Assemble Individual Baked Alaska

Prepare ahead Lace Cookies

DAY OF PARTY (ABOUT 2¹/₂ HOURS)

Buy groceries and create the ambience

Remove Cheese Straws from freezer

Prepare ahead Pear and Roquefort Crostini

Prepare ahead Cream of Mushroom Soup

Prepare ahead Herb Salad with Sugared Almonds

Prepare ahead Filet of Beef with Balsamic Onions and Asparagus

Prepare ahead Creamy Mashed Potatoes

5:00 PM
Shower and dress

6:30 PM
Preheat oven to 400°F/200°C

Prepare coffeemaker

Open wines, turn on music, light candles

Put out starter bowls, salad plates, sorbet bowls, main course plates, and dessert plates

Prepare sugar and milk for coffee

Finish Cheese Straws and set out according to Presentation Tip

7:00 PM
Preheat the broiler

Put butter pats and rolls on butter plates

Put a cucumber slice in each water glass

Prepare ahead Kir Royale

Put out cashews

7:25 PM
Finish Pear and Roquefort Crostini

7:30 PM (GUESTS ARRIVE)
Open and pour Champagne (have water ready for those who prefer water)

Remove salad dressing from refrigerator

7:35 PM
Start to reheat soup over medium-low heat; stir and check occasionally

Serve Pear and Roquefort Crostini

8:00 PM
Check soup is hot

Preheat oven to 375°F/190°C

8:05 PM
Call people to table

Serve starter wine and water

8:10 PM
Serve Cream of Mushroom Soup according to Presentation Tip

8:30 PM
Finish salad and serve

Take sorbet out of freezer

8:45 PM
Put filets, uncovered, in oven

Start reheating Creamy Mashed Potatoes in microwave

Serve sorbet, garnished with mint

9:00 PM
Remove filets from oven, cover loosely with aluminum foil and let rest for 5 minutes

Finish reheating Creamy Mashed Potatoes in microwave

Add butter and reheat Asparagus in microwave; season with salt

Plate Filet according to Presentation Tip

Turn up oven to 500°F/260°C

9:10 PM
Serve main course and wine

Turn on coffeemaker

9:45 PM
Finish Individual Baked Alaska and serve

Serve dessert wine (if using)

10:00 PM
Serve coffee, tea, and after-dinner cookies

Grocery List

PANTRY ITEMS

1   cup extra-virgin olive oil
1/2 cup balsamic vinegar
Kosher salt
Freshly ground black pepper
1/4 teaspoon dried thyme
4 5/8 cups sugar
2 1/4 cups light brown sugar
1   cup flour
1/2 teaspoon cream of tartar
1 3/4 teaspoons vanilla extract
2 1/4 cups rolled oats
3   ounces unsweetened chocolate
1/3 cup blanched flaked almonds
2   cups vegetable broth
2   tablespoons honey
1   (12-ounce) jar cashews
Decaffeinated and regular coffee
Regular and herbal tea bags

ALCOHOL AND DRINKS

2   bottles Champagne or sparkling wine
2   bottles wine for starter (White Burgundy, Unoaked Chardonnay, or Pinot Noir)
2   bottles red wine for main (Malbec)
1   bottle dessert wine, if using (Chenin Blanc dessert wine)
4   bottles sparkling water
3/4 cup crème de cassis
1/4 cup dry sherry
1   tablespoon vodka

PRODUCE

1   teaspoon minced fresh rosemary
5   lemons

DAIRY

3   cups butter
13   eggs
1   cup grated sharp white Cheddar cheese
1/2 cup grated Parmesan cheese

FREEZER

1   (17.3-ounce) package frozen puff pastry
1 1/2 quarts chocolate ice cream
1 1/2 quarts vanilla ice cream

PRODUCE

1   pear
7   tablespoons chopped fresh chives
3   tablespoons chopped fresh dill
1/3 cup fresh chopped flat-leaf parsley
1   bunch fresh mint for sorbet garnish
8   ounces mixed baby greens
2   onions
3   large Spanish onions
1   stalk celery
1 1/2 pounds sliced mushrooms
1   small zucchini
5   green onions
8   ounces cherry tomatoes
24   asparagus spears (pencil thin if possible)
5   pounds Yukon Gold potatoes
1   pound russet or Idaho potatoes
1   cucumber

DAIRY

4   cups whole milk
4   ounces creamy Roquefort cheese
1 1/3 cups whipping cream

MEAT, FISH AND DELI

8   (6-ounce) filets mignons

BAKERY

8   rolls
1   French baguette

Mushroom Lasagna

menu

SERVES 8

Cocktail & Hors d'Oeuvres

Grand Marnier and Champagne

Asparagus Puffs

Assortment of Cheese and Crackers

Roasted Almonds

Starter

Spinach Coconut Soup

Rolls and Butter

 Chenin Blanc

Salad

Roasted Vegetables in Phyllo with Balsamic Vinaigrette

Palate Cleanser

Strawberry Sorbet

Main Course

Mushroom Lasagna

 White Burgundy

Dessert

Frozen Chocolate Mousse Cake with Raspberry Coulis

Pecan Crisps

 Tawny Port or Banyuls

Coffee & Tea

Grand Marnier and Champagne

1	teaspoon Grand Marnier	1/2	cup plus 2 tablespoons Champagne
1	teaspoon curaçao		or dry sparkling wine
1	teaspoon crème de cassis		

Fill the bottom of a Champagne glass with the Grand Marnier, curaçao and crème de cassis. Fill the glass with Champagne or dry sparkling wine.

TO PREPARE AHEAD: Pour the Grand Marnier, curaçao, and crème de cassis into the bottom of each Champagne glass and place the glasses near where you are going to serve the apéritif. Have a few empty glasses available in case some guests prefer water. Pour the Champagne and serve.

HANDY TIP: One bottle of Champagne makes enough to serve 6.

Asparagus Puffs

1	teaspoon kosher salt	1	egg
20	thin asparagus spears	1	teaspoon water
1	sheet frozen puff pastry, thawed	1/2	cup grated Parmesan cheese
1/3	cup grated Gruyere cheese		

Preheat the oven to 400°F/200°C.

Bring a large saucepan of water to a boil. Add the salt. Trim the asparagus spears to 3 1/2 inches. Add the asparagus and boil until tender-crisp, about 2 to 3 minutes. Drain, plunge into cold water to stop the cooking process and set aside.

Roll out the puff pastry on a floured work surface to measure 10×12 inches. With a knife, cut the pastry into 20 squares (4 down and 5 across). Sprinkle a little grated Gruyere cheese in the middle of each square. Top with an asparagus spear placed on the diagonal.

Fold the corners of each puff pastry square over the asparagus, sealing with a little water. Place the Asparagus Puffs 2 inches apart on an ungreased baking sheet.

Beat the egg with 1 teaspoon water. Brush the tops of the puffs with the egg mixture and sprinkle with the Parmesan cheese. Bake for 12 to 15 minutes or until puffed and golden brown. Remove from the oven. Place on a platter and serve immediately.

TO PREPARE AHEAD: You can make up the Asparagus Puffs as directed above, stopping before baking. Place the Asparagus Puffs in the freezer on the ungreased baking sheet. When frozen, transfer to a sealable plastic bag and freeze for up to 3 months.

TO FINISH: Place the Asparagus Puffs on an ungreased baking sheet and bake as directed above.

HANDY TIP: I like to freeze batches of Asparagus Puffs, Phyllo Cheese Bites (page 53), and Spinach Phyllo Triangles (page 136). That way, just before a party, I can bake a few of each and serve on a platter. Because you only need a few per person, you will still have plenty in the freezer for later use.

Assortment of Cheese and Crackers

FIRM CHEESES
Cheddar, Gruyère, Manchego, Gouda,
    Fontina, Pecorino Toscano

SEMI-SOFT CHEESES
Muenster, Havarti, Vacherin, St. Nectaire,
    Pere Joseph, Chimay

SOFT CHEESES
Brie, Camembert, St. Andre, Taleggio,
    Fromager d'Affinois

BLUE-VEINED CHEESES
Roquefort, Gorgonzola, Danish Blue,
    Shropshire

GOAT AND SHEEP'S MILK CHEESES
Soft—Couturier, Montchevre, Montrachet
Hard—Chevagne, Goat Gouda,
    Midnight Moon

Assorted crackers
1   pound seedless red grapes
1   pound seedless green grapes
Bay leaves for garnish

Preparation Time: 10 min.

PRESENTATION TIP:
Decorate the cheeseboard with bay leaves and small bunches of grapes. Place the crackers in a basket. Make sure to put out cheese knives.

Select 3 to 5 cheeses. Remove the cheeses from the refrigerator 1 hour before serving. Unwrap and place the cheeses on a cheeseboard. If you don't have one large enough to hold all the cheeses, use two. Cover the cheeses with a bowl (or bowls) and let come to room temperature. Rinse the grapes and pat dry.

TO PREPARE AHEAD: An hour before serving, remove the cheeses from the refrigerator and unwrap. Place on a cheeseboard and cover with a bowl (or bowls).

TO FINISH: Serve according to the Presentation Tip.

Spinach Coconut Soup

Preparation Time: 20 min.
Cooking Time: 30 min.
Total Time: 50 min.

PRESENTATION TIP:
Ladle the soup into
bowls and serve. If
you are feeling more
adventurous, you can
garnish with a dollop of
coconut milk, if you have
an extra can available.

2	tablespoons butter
1½	cups chopped onions
1	pound potatoes, peeled and diced (about 3 small potatoes)
3	cups vegetable broth
1½	cups water

3	(10-ounce) packages frozen chopped spinach
1	(14-ounce) can coconut milk
	Kosher salt and freshly ground black pepper to taste

Melt the butter in a large soup pot with a lid. Add the onions and sauté, stirring often, over medium heat until translucent, about 5 minutes. Add the potatoes and cook for about 2 minutes, or until the potatoes are well coated in butter. Stir to prevent sticking.

Add the vegetable broth and water. Turn up the heat and bring to a boil. Turn down the heat to low. Cover and simmer until the potatoes are tender, about 10 minutes.

Add the frozen spinach and cook until the spinach has thawed. Do not overcook, as the spinach will lose its color.

Purée the soup in batches in a blender until smooth. If the soup is very hot, make sure you hold down the top of the blender with a towel. Return the soup to the cleaned-out soup pot and add the can of coconut milk.

Reheat gently, stirring often to prevent sticking. Season with salt and freshly pepper.

TO PREPARE AHEAD: You can prepare the soup up to 2 days ahead, stopping before reheating, and store, covered, in the refrigerator. If making the soup further in advance, stop before reheating, cool the soup, place in an airtight container, and freeze for up to 3 months. Thaw overnight in the refrigerator or in the microwave.

TO FINISH: Reheat the soup gently, stirring often.

HANDY TIP: This is a very thick and hearty soup. If you prefer a thinner consistency, add some water a little at a time.

Roasted Vegetables in Phyllo with Balsamic Vinaigrette

SERVES 8

ROASTED VEGETABLES IN PHYLLO
2 carrots, peeled and julienned
1 shallot, sliced
1 red bell pepper, cored and julienned
1½ cups mushrooms, sliced
6 asparagus spears, sliced thinly lengthwise
¼ cup extra-virgin olive oil
½ teaspoon kosher salt
¼ teaspoon freshly ground black pepper
¼ teaspoon marjoram
¼ teaspoon oregano
¼ teaspoon thyme
1 cup grated Gruyère cheese
½ pound frozen phyllo dough, thawed
½ cup butter, melted

SALAD AND DRESSING
5 ounces mixed baby greens
1½ tablespoons balsamic vinegar
¼ teaspoon kosher salt
⅛ teaspoon freshly ground black pepper
¼ cup extra-virgin olive oil

Preparation Time: 30 min.
Cooking Time: 25 min.
Total Time: 55 min.

PRESENTATION TIP:
Place a small mound of the dressed mixed greens on each plate. Make a diagonal cut through each phyllo roll. Prop the 2 halves on each plate and serve immediately.

For the vegetables: Preheat the oven to 375°F/190°C. Place the sliced vegetables in a large bowl. Add the extra-virgin olive oil and spices. Toss until well combined. Spread the vegetable mixture in a single layer on an ungreased baking sheet and roast for 10 minutes. Remove from the oven and cool completely. When cool, combine the vegetables and the Gruyère cheese in a large bowl.

Line a baking sheet with parchment paper.

Place the thawed phyllo dough on your work surface and cover with a damp towel. Remove 1 sheet of phyllo dough and place on the work surface with the short end facing you. Brush with the melted butter. Place another sheet of phyllo dough on top. Brush with melted butter. Place a third sheet of phyllo dough on top and brush with melted butter. Cover the remaining phyllo sheets with a damp towel to prevent them from drying out. Cut the buttered phyllo in half, beginning in the middle of the long side, creating 2 rectangles.

Using a ½ cup measuring cup, place a mound of the vegetable mixture along the long side of 1 of the rectangles, leaving at least a 1-inch border on each side. Start to roll up from the long side with the vegetable mixture. Stop when you are halfway and fold in the 2 side edges. Continue to roll up, making an enclosed parcel.

Place the parcel on the parchment-lined baking sheet. Brush with melted butter. Repeat the process with the other rectangle of buttered phyllo. Once you have finished with the 2 parcels, begin again, repeating the whole process until you have 8 parcels. Bake the parcels in the oven for 12 to 15 minutes, or until crisp and golden. Remove from the oven and let sit for a few minutes.

For the salad: Rinse and spin dry the mixed greens and place in a large bowl. In a small bowl, whisk together the balsamic vinegar, salt, pepper and extra-virgin olive oil. Toss the mixed greens with enough dressing to coat.

TO PREPARE AHEAD THE ROASTED VEGETABLES IN PHYLLO: You can make up the phyllo parcels, stopping just before baking, and store, covered, in the refrigerator for up to 2 days.

TO PREPARE AHEAD THE SALAD AND DRESSING: Early on the day of the party, rinse and spin dry the mixed greens. Place in a large bowl, cover with a damp towel, and refrigerate until needed. Make the salad dressing and store, covered, in the refrigerator. An hour before serving, remove the salad dressing from the refrigerator and return to room temperature.

TO FINISH: Bake the phyllo parcels as directed above. Whisk the dressing and toss the mixed greens with enough dressing to coat. Serve according to the Presentation Tip.

Strawberry Sorbet

1	cup sugar	Juice of 2 lemons
1	cup water	1 tablespoon vodka
16	ounces fresh strawberries	Mint sprigs for garnish

In a medium saucepan, heat the sugar and water until the sugar melts and the mixture starts to boil. Boil for 2 minutes. Remove from the heat and cool completely.

Rinse, pat dry and hull the strawberries. Place the strawberries, sugar syrup, lemon juice and vodka in the bowl of a blender. Purée until smooth.

Pour into an ice cream maker and process according to the manufacturer's directions.

When finished, pour into an airtight container and freeze until ready to serve.

TO PREPARE AHEAD: Prepare the sorbet up to a month ahead, place in an airtight container, and freeze.

TO FINISH: Remove the sorbet 15 minutes before serving to allow it to soften slightly. When ready, scoop into bowls, garnish with the mint, and serve.

HANDY TIP: If you don't have vodka, you can substitute Grand Marnier or Cointreau, which will add a slight orange flavor to the sorbet.

Mushroom Lasagna

Preparation Time: 20 min.
Cooking Time: 95 min.
Total Time: 115 min.

PRESENTATION TIP:
Cut the lasagna into squares and serve, garnished with the flat-leaf parsley.

BÉCHAMEL SAUCE

6	cups milk
1/2	cup butter
6	tablespoons flour
2	teaspoons kosher salt
1	teaspoon nutmeg

MUSHROOMS

1/3	cup butter
1 1/2	pounds mushrooms, sliced
2	cloves garlic, minced

Juice of 1/2 lemon

TOMATOES AND ASSEMBLY

2	tablespoons extra-virgin olive oil
1	medium onion, chopped
1	(28-ounce) can diced tomatoes

Kosher salt and freshly ground black pepper to taste

8	ounces lasagna noodles
1 1/3	cups grated Parmesan cheese
2	tablespoons butter

Flat-leaf parsley sprigs for garnish

Preheat the oven to 350°F/180°C. Grease a 9×13-inch pan with butter. Bring a large pot of water to a boil.

For the béchamel sauce: Pour the milk into a microwave-safe bowl and heat in the microwave until hot but not boiling.

In a large saucepan, melt the butter over medium heat. Add the flour and stir. Cook for 1 minute. Add the hot milk to the flour mixture, whisking constantly. Bring to a boil and cook for about 10 minutes, stirring constantly. Remove from the heat and add the salt and nutmeg.

For the mushrooms: In a large frying pan, melt the butter. Add the mushrooms and cook until the mushrooms start to give off their juices. Add the garlic and lemon juice. Cook until almost all of the liquid has evaporated.

For the tomatoes: In a medium frying pan, heat the extra-virgin olive oil. Sauté the onion over medium heat until translucent, about 5 minutes. Add the diced tomatoes and cook until most of the liquid has evaporated, a few minutes. Season with salt and pepper.

Cook the lasagna noodles according to the package directions. Drain and lay the noodles side by side on parchment paper.

To assemble: Put about 1 cup of béchamel sauce in the bottom of the buttered pan. Place a layer of pasta on top. Cover the pasta with half of the mushrooms. Then, top the mushrooms with béchamel sauce. Sprinkle with 1/3 cup of the grated Parmesan cheese.

Place another layer of pasta on top. Cover the pasta with half of the tomato mixture. Then, top the tomato mixture with béchamel sauce. Sprinkle with 1/3 cup of the grated Parmesan cheese. Repeat the mushroom and tomato layers. Dot with the butter.

Bake for 50 to 60 minutes or until heated through. Remove from the oven, cover loosely with aluminum foil and let the lasagna sit for 5 to 10 minutes before serving.

TO PREPARE AHEAD: You can assemble the Mushroom Lasagna up to 2 days ahead, stopping before baking. Cover with plastic wrap and refrigerate.

TO FINISH: Bake, uncovered, as directed above and serve according to the Presentation Tip.

SUBSTITUTION: If you want to save on preparation and cooking time, use 8 ounces oven-ready lasagna noodles. Assemble as directed above. Bake the lasagna, covered wih aluminum foil, at 350°F/180°C for 30 minutes. Uncover and bake for an additional 20 minutes. Remove from the oven, cover loosely with foil, and let sit for 5 to 10 minutes before serving.

Frozen Chocolate Mousse Cake with Raspberry Coulis

CRUST
24   Oreo cookies
1/4   cup butter, melted

FILLING
16   ounces semisweet chocolate bits
2   whole eggs
4   egg yolks
2   cups whipping cream
1/4   cup sugar
4   egg whites

RASPBERRY COULIS (OPTIONAL)
1   cup fresh raspberries
2   tablespoons sugar
1/2   teaspoon fresh lemon juice

WHIPPED CREAM
1   cup whipping cream
2   tablespoons sugar
1   cup fresh raspberries for garnish

Preparation Time: 40 min.
plus freezing time

PRESENTATION TIP:
Remove the Mousse Cake from the freezer 15 minutes before serving. Drizzle the Raspberry Coulis over the bottom of each plate in a zigzag pattern. Top with a slice of the Mousse Cake and garnish with the Whipped Cream and fresh raspberries. If serving with a Pecan Crisp, stand the Pecan Crisp in the Whipped Cream.

For the crust: Place the Oreo cookies in the bowl of a food processor and process until you have fine crumbs. Add the melted butter through the feed tube, processing until combined. Press over the bottom of a 9- or 10-inch springform pan and refrigerate until ready to use.

For the filling: Place the semisweet chocolate bits in a large microwave-safe bowl and microwave on high for 2 minutes; stir. If the bits haven't melted, microwave a little longer; cool.

Add the whole eggs and egg yolks to the melted chocolate and blend with an electric mixer until well combined.

In a separate bowl, beat the whipping cream and sugar until stiff peaks form. Set aside.

In another bowl, beat the egg whites until stiff.

Fold a little whipped cream into the chocolate mixture to loosen. Then alternate folding in the rest of the whipped cream and the egg whites.

Pour over the crust, cover and freeze for at least 2 hours and preferably overnight.

For the coulis: Rinse the raspberries and pat dry. Purée the raspberries, sugar and lemon juice in a blender. Strain the mixture through a fine sieve into a bowl, using the back of a spoon to push the mixture through.

For the whipped cream: In a medium bowl, beat the whipping cream and sugar until stiff peaks form.

TO PREPARE AHEAD THE FROZEN CHOCOLATE MOUSSE CAKE: You can make the Frozen Chocolate Mousse Cake up to 2 weeks ahead and store, covered, in the freezer.

TO PREPARE AHEAD THE RASPBERRY COULIS AND WHIPPED CREAM: On the day of the party, make up the Raspberry Coulis and the Whipped Cream. Cover and refrigerate until needed.

HANDY TIP: If you have leftover Raspberry Coulis, you can freeze it for up to a month. Thaw overnight or in the microwave before using.

HANDY TIP #2: I use a plastic squeeze bottle to drizzle the Coulis. It's an easy way to store the Coulis and to drizzle it nicely. If you don't have one, try putting the Coulis in a sealable plastic bag and cutting a very small hole in 1 corner. Remember, if you're pressed for time, you can always skip the coulis altogether. The Frozen Chocolate Mousse Cake tastes great all on its own.

SUBSTITUTION: If you prefer, you can use pasteurized eggs for the mousse.

Pecan Crisps

Preparation Time: 10 min.
plus refrigeration
Cooking Time: 25 min.
per batch

1	cup butter		1/2	teaspoon kosher salt
1/3	cup packed light brown sugar		1	cup finely chopped pecans
1/3	cup sugar		1/2	cup sugar for dipping
1 3/4	cups all-purpose flour			

In a large bowl, cream the butter, brown sugar and 1/3 cup sugar with an electric mixer until light and fluffy. Add the flour, salt and pecans and mix until fully combined.

Spread a piece of wax paper on your work surface. With floured fingers, shape the dough into 2 logs, each with a 1-inch diameter. Wrap each in plastic wrap, twisting the ends to seal. Refrigerate for an hour.

Remove the logs from the refrigerator and gently roll back and forth to smooth any imperfections. Put back in the refrigerator and chill for another hour.

Preheat the oven to 300°F/140°C.

Cut the logs into 3/8-inch-thick slices. Dip 1 side of each slice in 1/2 cup sugar and place sugar side up on 2 ungreased cookie sheets. Bake the slices until they are slightly golden, about 25 minutes. Remove to a wire rack and cool completely.

TO PREPARE AHEAD: Make the Pecan Crisp dough as directed above. Once you have shaped the dough into logs, wrap them in plastic wrap and place in a sealable plastic bag. Freeze for up to 3 months.

TO FINISH: When ready to bake, thaw as many logs as you'll need for 30 minutes (or briefly in the microwave). Cut the logs into 3/8-inch-thick slices. Dip 1 side of each slice in the sugar and place sugar side up on an ungreased cookie sheet. Bake as directed above. When cool, place on a small serving platter and cover securely with plastic wrap.

Timeline

ONE WEEK BEFORE (ABOUT 1 3/4 HOURS)

Buy groceries and create the ambience

Prepare ahead Strawberry Sorbet

Prepare ahead Asparagus Puffs

Prepare ahead Pecan Crisps

TWO DAYS BEFORE (ABOUT 1 HOUR)

Buy groceries and create the ambience

Put sparkling water, Champagne, and white wine in refrigerator

Put out dessert wine (if using)

Prepare ahead Spinach Coconut Soup

Remove phyllo dough from freezer and thaw overnight in refrigerator

ONE DAY BEFORE (ABOUT 1 1/2 HOURS)

Prepare ahead Frozen Chocolate Mousse Cake

Prepare ahead Roasted Vegetables in Phyllo

DAY OF PARTY (ABOUT 1 1/2 HOURS)

Buy groceries and create the ambience

Prepare ahead Mushroom Lasagna

Prepare ahead Salad and Dressing for Roasted Vegetables in Phyllo

Prepare ahead Raspberry Coulis and Whipped Cream for Frozen Chocolate Mousse Cake

---

5:00 PM
Shower and dress

6:30 PM
Prepare coffeemaker

Open wines, turn on music, light candles

Put out starter bowls, salad plates, sorbet bowls, main course plates, and dessert plates

Prepare sugar and milk for coffee

Prepare ahead Assortment of Cheese and Crackers

7:00 PM
Preheat oven to 400°F/200°C

Put butter pats and rolls on butter plates

Put a cucumber slice in each water glass

Prepare ahead Grand Marnier and Champagne

Put out roasted almonds

7:20 PM
Finish Asparagus Puffs

Remove salad dressing from refrigerator

7:30 PM (GUESTS ARRIVE)
Open and pour Champagne (have water ready for those who prefer water)

7:35 PM
Remove Asparagus Puffs from oven and serve

Turn down oven to 375°F/190°C

Start to reheat soup over medium-low heat; stir and check occasionally

8:00 PM
Check soup is hot

8:05 PM
Call people to table

Serve starter wine and water

Put Mushroom Lasagna, uncovered, in oven

8:10 PM
Serve Spinach Coconut Soup

Bake Roasted Vegetables in Phyllo

8:30 PM
Finish salad and serve according to Presentation Tip

Take sorbet out of freezer

8:45 PM
Serve sorbet, garnished with mint

9:00 PM
Remove Frozen Chocolate Mousse from freezer and put in refrigerator

Remove Mushroom Lasagna from oven and plate according to Presentation Tip

9:10 PM
Serve main course and wine

Turn on coffeemaker

9:45 PM
Serve Frozen Chocolate Mousse according to Presentation Tip

Serve dessert wine (if using)

10:00 PM
Serve coffee, tea, and after-dinner cookies

Grocery List

PANTRY ITEMS

5/8 cup extra-virgin olive oil
1 1/2 tablespoons good-quality
  balsamic vinegar
Kosher salt
Freshly ground black pepper
1/4 teaspoons dried marjoram
1/4 teaspoon dried oregano
1/4 teaspoon dried thyme
1 teaspoon ground nutmeg
1 3/4 cups sugar
1/3 cup light brown sugar
2 1/3 cups flour
3 cups vegetable broth
1 (14-ounce) can coconut milk
1 (28-ounce) can diced tomatoes
8 ounces lasagna noodles
24 Oreo cookies
16 ounces semisweet chocolate bits
1 cup finely chopped pecans
Assorted crackers for cheese platter
1 (12-ounce) jar roasted almonds
Decaffeinated and regular coffee
Regular and herbal tea bags

ALCOHOL AND DRINKS

2 bottles Champagne or sparkling wine
2 bottles white wine for starter
  (Chenin Blanc)

2 bottles white wine for main
  (White Burgundy)
1 bottle dessert wine, if using
  (Tawny Port or Banyuls)
4 bottles sparkling water
2 2/3 tablespoons Grand Marnier
2 2/3 tablespoons curaçao
2 2/3 tablespoon crème de cassis
1 tablespoon vodka

PRODUCE

20 thin asparagus spears
3 onions
1 pound potatoes
16 ounces strawberries
3 lemons

DAIRY

3 1/3 cups butter
7 eggs
1 1/3 cups grated Gruyère cheese
2 cups grated Parmesan cheese

FREEZER

1/2 (17.3-ounce) package frozen puff pastry
1/2 (16-ounce) package frozen phyllo sheets
30 ounces frozen chopped spinach

PRODUCE

2 cups raspberries
1 pound green grapes
1 pound red grapes
1 package fresh bay leaves for
  cheese garnish
1 bunch flat-leaf parsley for main garnish
1 bunch fresh mint for sorbet garnish
5 ounces mixed baby greens
2 carrots
1 shallot
1 red bell pepper
32 ounces sliced mushrooms

6 asparagus spears
2 cloves garlic
1 cucumber

DAIRY

7 cups whole milk
1/2 pound firm cheese for appetizer
1/2 pound semi-soft or soft cheese for
  appetizer
1/2 pound blue-veined or goat or sheep's
  milk cheese for appetizer
3 cups whipping cream

BAKERY

8 rolls

Title Index

Index

To order additional copies of

FAST TRACK

TO *Fine Dining*

or for more information, contact

Linda Mutschler
Box 135
4230 N. Oakland Avenue
Shorewood, WI 53211-2042

www.fasttracktofinedining.com